"Anderson's book is a worthwhile excursion for students of journalism who want some idea of how to rake muck in Washington, or for students of history who want a better insight into the manner in which the Anderson column and its scoops have—in their own way—helped to shape history."

—Detroit *Free Press*

"Strong evidence of why Jack Anderson is a valuable national resource."

—*New Times*

"Gives a fascinating insight into the limitations of investigative reporting . . . *The Anderson Papers* constitute a do-it-yourself manual for anyone wanting to go into stolen-documents journalism."

—Chicago *Tribune*

THE ANDERSON PAPERS

By
Jack Anderson

with George Clifford

BALLANTINE BOOKS • NEW YORK

Library of Congress Catalog Card Number: 72-11407

SBN 345-23951-2-175

This edition published by arrangement with
    Random House, Inc.

First Printing: May, 1974

Printed in the United States of America

BALLANTINE BOOKS
A Division of Random House, Inc.
201 East 50th Street, New York, N.Y. 10022

Contents

A COMMUNICATION FROM
INSIDE THE WHITE HOUSE

MEMORANDUM

THE WHITE HOUSE
Washington
February 11, 1971

CONFIDENTIAL
MEMORANDUM FOR H. R. HALDEMAN
FROM: JACK CAULFIELD
SUBJECT: *ANDERSON LEAKS AND ALLEGED AC-
CESS TO PRESIDENTIAL MEMORANDA*

During his recent appearance on the Dick Cavett Show, Jack Anderson made the following comments:

"I have access to intelligence digests because people show them to us."

"—some of the President's private memos, some of the transcripts of confidential minutes."

"Two thirds of the State of the Union Message two or three days before it was delivered."

"I can assure you that if the President knew who was leaking these memos, he would be fired tomorrow."

Writer has analyzed the Anderson column for the three month period preceding the State of the Union leak, as well as discreetly conferring with selected White House staff members. Resultingly, the following observations are offered:

A) Anderson does, indeed, have access to intelligence digests, and he proves it on a daily basis. It also appears his reference to private Presidential memoranda is valid, but most likely when such material leaves the White House and is circulated on an agency level. On more than one occasion, examination of a Presidential quote in context indicates strongly that the leak came not from within the White House, but from the agency concerned with the subject matter.

B) Anderson's comment regarding "some of the transcripts of confidential minutes" possibly refers to verbatim quotes of comments made at White House leadership meetings.

Two of the White House Staff members interviewed independently expressed the view that Senator Hugh Scott or a member of Scott's staff are suspect. If you were not aware of this possibility and wish the names of the staff members, they will be furnished to Larry Higby upon request.

Examination of the Anderson columns of January 21, 22 and 23, all of which are concerned with the reorganization of the federal government, apparently refers to his State of the Union comment indicated above.

In this connection, it has been determined that *all of the above information* contained in those three articles appeared in our black bound, working looseleaf booklet. Further, that twelve late copies of such booklet were prepared and forwarded to the Office of Management and Budget from the Domestic Council under strict security conditions in advance of the Anderson leak.

An examination of the subject document, along with a studied review of the subject Anderson columns indicates that the book was made available to Anderson, most likely in its entirety.

Domestic Council members interviewed make a valid case for the leak to be pinned on OMB, Bureau Resources Section. I, personally, wish to reserve judgment until more evidence is at hand. It has been brought to my attention that George Shultz has been apprised of these suspicions, and has taken the position that a "smoking out" type investigation would be inadvisable.

Resultingly, I do not feel it proper to proceed with this aspect of the inquiry, unless or until you so advise.

Having looked at this matter with all its serious implications for the future I feel it advisable to immediately suggest that all of the section chiefs on the White House staff be briefed by your office with a view towards a minimization of leaked material and comment. I also suggest that an overt firing of a person directly connected with a leak would go a long way towards making the ability of the Andersons of the world to gain White House information both difficult and hazardous.

Please advise.

THE
ANDERSON
PAPERS

PROLOGUE

A Word about Power and the Press

Presidents and policy-makers, like other people, can be what they choose to be. They can serve the nation or they can serve themselves. For many men in public life the mere possession of power is an end in itself. For them the struggle to the top is expensive, both in dollars and a more precious currency—human integrity. The values of even the most honorable are under constant assault, like boulders on an ocean beach. Erosion seems inevitable.

Power is Washington's main marketable product. Those who come to the capital to serve the government, and those who come to manipulate the servants, strive for power to accomplish their goals. Power is the driving force that brings together people of different philosophies and varying interests in the constantly evolving battle for control. Alliances are conveniently arranged and are seldom permanent, shifting with the pressures of the times and the advantages of the moment.

Honest men will lie and decent men will cheat for power. Few reach the political pinnacles without selling what they do not own and promising what is not theirs to give. In the great and grueling quest for power it is easy to forget that power belongs not to those who possess it for the moment but to the nation and its people.

While power need not be corrupting, it is impossible to deny that the American political system invites corruption. Men must accumulate funds to campaign for office. Those who finance the campaigns expect a return on their investment. Those who are elected must listen to the special interests while they preach about the pub-

3

lic interest. To lead they often must follow men whose motives are self-serving.

To keep the White House, Richard Nixon raised more campaign cash than it cost him originally to gain the White House. His agents systematically contacted the nation's great corporations and gave them campaign quotas for their executives to raise. Some paid their allotments hoping it would keep the government off their backs. Others, like International Telephone and Telegraph, sought to make a deal in return for a campaign commitment. Only a few, like American Motors, refused to ante up. Staggering sums were raised to·reelect the President. The cost to the people of the United States, and to the free enterprise system, is still being paid in installments.

Only a few men can survive the crawl to the top with their values unimpaired. These values can become even more tarnished by the heady, rarefied atmosphere on the mountaintop. The dazzling heights separate and estrange the President from the citizens below, until the mighty voice of the nation becomes stilled to a whisper.

The powerful everywhere are surrounded by fawning servants, obedient aides, and the symbols of success. In the most powerful nation, those who reach the mountaintop are so pampered and so insulated by the trappings of power they can easily forget they are servants, not masters, of the nation.

High fences, patrolled by armed men and sophisticated electronic devices, keep the President remote from reality. Bulletproof limousines move him over the highways. Helicopters are always ready to lift him above the traffic snarls, which irritate most of us, above the stink of the cities and the heads of the people who live in the squalor. On short notice, specialists can assemble hordes of sycophants to render homage, while other specialists keep critics at a distance. Every public gesture and every public utterance is reported in print and on television as though it all carried some genuine importance. At his whim, the President can command the nation's communications and project his image and his words into every American home, or to any spot on earth, or —in the historic moments of discovery—to the moon.

The homage and the emoluments could turn the head of a saint, and few men who occupy the White House are saints. It is little wonder that the President, elected to serve the people, does not always feel like a servant. On the contrary, he often feels that the people should serve him. In Washington, with its adulation of power, few like to acknowledge that power rightfully belongs to the people.

The experience of ascending the pinnacle of power changes the men who must exercise power. Some men can grow and be strengthened by the process. Most are diminished. When Lyndon Johnson was President, it was possible sometimes to glimpse the gangling adolescent from the Texas dirt farm. And somewhere under the brittle shell of Richard Nixon lurks the quiet, studious youngster in Whittier who wanted to be a railroad engineer. But in the White House, they no longer were the men they once had been. The aging process for all human beings tends to replace idealism with cynicism; for the powerful the change is often more pervasive.

The men of the press seldom remind the leaders of their obligations, nor the citizens that they are the true owners of power. All too many who write about government have been seduced by those who govern. The press, like the powerful, often forgets its obligations to the public. Too many Washington reporters consider it their function to court the high and mighty rather than condemn them; to extol public officials rather than expose them.

It is far more pleasant to write puffery about the powerful, of course, than it is to probe their perfidy. Public officeholders are usually likable; that is why they got elected. Many reporters are taken in by this personal charm, are awed by the majesty of office; and they become publicists rather than critics of the men who occupy the offices.

The political pundits and big by-liners consider themselves journalists, not reporters. The powerful men of the press develop close and cordial relationships with the powerful men in government. They converse together; they dine together; they party together. The experience is enough to convince some reporters that they are architects rather than chroniclers of policy. Yet those who hobnob with the great learn little more than the lesser reporters who take notes at press conferences and rewrite press releases.

Those taken in adopt the attitudes of the people they cover. They become the lap dogs of government instead of the watchdogs over government. They wag their tails and seek approval instead of growling at the abuses of power. The reporters who go along with the powerful, and act as explainers and apologists for those who violate the public trust, must be considered accessories to the pillage. Like the politicians and the special seekers, these men sell a little of themselves each day; and the chumminess between the power structure and the press apparatus robs the reporters of integrity.

The need for the press to occupy an adversary role was clear to America's founding fathers. That is why they made freedom of the press the first guarantee of the Bill of Rights. Without press freedom, they knew, the other freedoms would fall. For government, by its nature, tends to oppress. And government, without a watchdog, would soon oppress the people it was created to serve.

Thomas Jefferson understood that the press, as the watchdog, must be free to criticize and condemn, to expose and oppose. "Were it left to me to decide whether we should have a government without newspapers, or newspapers without a government, I should not hesitate a moment to prefer the latter," he wrote. Nor did he retract this statement after he, as President, had been abused by irresponsible newspapers. Rather, as he neared the end of his first term, he wrote to a friend: "No experiment can be more interesting than that we are now trying, and which we trust will end in establishing the fact, that men may be governed by reason and truth. Our first object should therefore be, to leave open to him all the avenues of truth. The most effective hitherto found, is the freedom of the press. It is, therefore, the first shut up by those who fear the investigation of their actions."

We have tried, in our own way, to become a watchdog of Washington, to be numbered among the few investigative reporters who seek to discover what is really happening in the nation's capital. It is seldom what the press spokesmen and the public relations experts say is happening. There are no press secretaries to brief those who search after concealed facts, no hucksters to package the suppressed details in attractive press kits. We have never known a government official to call a press conference to confess his wrong-doing, nor a government agency to issue a press release citing its mistakes.

Men in power, and men seeking power, do not relish having their cozy relationships exposed, their sources of money bared, and their blunders brought to light. Rather than cooperate, they obstruct investigative reporters. Doors are closed; files are locked; phones are slammed back into receivers. The last thing people at the top of government want to see are stories about government wrongs. For they know that exposure can bring an end to power.

Investigative reporters grate against the political conviviality and easy friendships of official Washington. They avoid the social entanglements that inhibit straightforward reporting about the high and mighty. They are not impressed with the Henry Kissingers and William Rogerses and Elliot Richardsons whom the establishment reporters cultivate. The pashas of the press consider good journalism to be an appointment once a week with Henry Kissinger. But investigative reporters know that Henry Kissinger is never going to tell them anything the President doesn't want them to know.

At the time President Nixon was secretly supporting Pakistan, for instance, Kissinger and Rogers deliberately misled the reporters they saw. They swore the Nixon

Administration was neutral in the India-Pakistan conflict. They denied the Administration was secretly shipping weapons to Pakistan. They pretended that a naval task force was not dispatched to bring military pressure upon India. These were all lies. They lied because the President wanted them to lie.

The top officials and the authorized sources will always say what the President wants them to say. They will not disclose the real policy that is often hidden behind the stated policy, nor will they reveal the backroom deals that promote and protect the privileged. Investigative reporters, therefore, must rely more on unauthorized than on authorized sources.

The most reliable sources are the professional, nonpolitical public servants whom the public never sees. Their first loyalty is to the citizens who pay them, not to their political superiors. The professionals know what the intelligence reports really show and what the Administration's policies really are. These career people implement the policies and therefore know the truth about them. Some are willing to tell the truth, at considerable risk to themselves. The information they possess, and the documents they produce to back it up, are often exactly the opposite of the kind of news that is officially leaked or passed out at press conferences or printed in press releases.

Unquestionably, the way an investigative reporter is compelled to operate is an imperfect system of newsgathering. Sometimes the sources do not have all the details. Sometimes the jigsaw pieces of information do not form a complete picture and the missing pieces are buried too deeply. Investigative reporters must work without the power of subpoena. They lack the money and manpower that the government can marshal to counter their efforts. The authority to classify embarrassing facts, the ability to shut off channels of information, the power to intimidate sources who could tell the truth—all these are on the side of the government.

It is not altogether surprising, therefore, that investigative reporters do not always get all the facts. They can uncover enough hidden scraps, however, to cast light on a blunder or an embarrassment or a scandal that the people in power had conspired to conceal. If our society was as free and open as it should be, and if government officials fully subscribed to their oaths to protect the public interest, there would be little difficulty in quickly establishing the truth. But officials all too often cover up the facts and then lie to the public.

Investigative reporters must work harder, dig deeper, and verify their facts more carefully than establishment reporters. Preposterous lies can be told to make the powerful look good; grievous blunders can be committed by officials in the name of the government; the public can be cheated by men sworn to uphold the public trust. But let an investigative reporter make a mistake and there will be howls of outrage. There can be a good word for a Lyndon Johnson who sent boys to die in a senseless war, or a General Motors which releases unsafe cars upon the highways, or a Richard Nixon who condones lawlessness while preaching law and order. But there is no good word for an investigative reporter who wrongly condemns someone in authority.

We have made our share of errors, despite our pains to avoid them. Most of them could have been avoided if we had been willing to report only the news that is produced at press conferences or printed in press releases or whispered to chosen reporters by officials. We believe it is better to err on the side of freedom, however, than to submit to such censorship.

Time and again, meanwhile, our leaders have used the stamp of official secrecy to protect themselves. This is censorship at the source. There are relatively few documents that must be kept secret in the interest of national security. The number does not even begin to approach the twenty million documents and papers the government hides from the people.

There is nothing sacred about the secrecy stamp. The President does not hesitate to release classified information if it will win support for his policies or help him squeeze money out of Congress. Often secret papers are shown to reporters by the same officials who prosecute others for leaking those papers which reflect unfavorably on themselves. Like dictators, our leaders stay in power by barring the public's access to unfavorable facts. We are free to select our leaders, but this freedom is constantly abridged by leaders who seek to curtail our knowledge of their activities.

The question of how much truth government spokesmen should give out—and how much the people are entitled to—may never be precisely defined. Most people would probably agree that the government, for the protection of its citizens, need not always tell every last detail about every situation. On the other hand, it should not lie or mislead lest it lose the trust of the very persons it is seeking to protect. In a democracy, when the government cannot tell the whole truth, it should stand by its privilege to be silent.

The reporters, for their part, should never accept as final the government's refusal to comment. And those who publish official, selective facts as the whole truth do themselves and their nation a disservice. Newsmen are out of their element when they share with the governors the view from the mountaintop upon the governed below. A reporter should keep on the same footing with the people he is supposed to inform. And he should always look with skepticism upon the politicians.

Meanwhile, the pressures for conformity and the domination of the government over the news have combined to suppress controversy. It has become the fashion for writers to be high-minded and carefully objective, presenting every view but taking stands only on safe subjects. Radio and television producers shy away from controversy as if it were unpatriotic. They hire motivational researchers, statisticians, sociologists, psychologists, and, of course, pollsters to make sure they don't offend the mass mind.

There is menace in too much conformity, in the government's Uncle-knows-best attitude, in the willingness of the press to accept the government's version of the news. The democratic machinery should never run so smoothly and so silently that the rumble of opposition becomes muffled. Let there be a few cogs, at least, that grate against the massive wheels of Big Government.

THE SEEDS OF
IMPEACHMENT

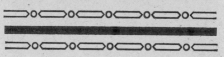

A Hate Affair

One day historians will trace the origins and gradual growth of the hate affair between President Nixon and elements of the press—which by the 1970s had led the press to the conviction that no presidential secret was worthy of being respected, and Nixon to the conclusion that the traditional function of the press must be abolished even if it took extralegal and illegal means.

The beginnings probably go all the way back to the summer of 1946, when young Richard Nixon was making his first campaign against Congressman Jerry Voorhis. And into the equation must be thrown considerations that had little to do with Nixon's relationship with newsmen when he assumed office in 1969—the guilt feeling among reporters over being so easily deceived by the Johnson Administration regarding the Vietnam War; the widespread feeling that government secrecy was merely a device for covering up crimes, blunders, and deceptions; the general decline in tolerance and civility throughout our society.

I attempt no such ambitious historical project here, but I do wish to recount some of the highlights of the escalation of hostilities between the working press and Nixon as President. These may help to explain why Nixon, who seemed so certain of reelection in 1972, presided over a campaign so defensive and secretive. He was a man haunted by dark secrets which he feared might leak out and drive him from public office. In seeking to contain the press and to shut off the leaks, the Nixon presidency committed first the blunders and then the crimes that produced the greatest political scandal in American history—Watergate.

If in this recounting I give more weight than is warranted to my own part, it is because I know that part best. I joined Drew Pearson in 1947, when he was at the zenith of his fantastic career. He was an irrepressible idealist at the height of his influence, which he sometimes used to manipulate events. From the start, I was caught up in Drew's many crusades and vendettas.

Contrary to popular theology, there is nothing that produces as much exhilaration, zest for living, and all-round gratification as a protracted, ugly, bitter-end vendetta that rages for years and comes close to ruining both sides. One of the secrets of Drew's resilience and buoyancy to the end of his life was his involvement in several of these mortal feuds.

Drew developed a special hostility for Richard Nixon. Scarcely had the young Whig from Whittier made his first misrepresentation than Drew cast the evil eye on him. Of all the anti-Nixon stories Drew wrote and all the investigations we conducted together, the most damaging exposed the strange relationship of Richard and his brother Donald with the phantom billionaire, Howard Hughes.

F. Donald Nixon is an overweight, overly talkative wheeler-dealer whose loud boasts and voracious appetites are in excessive contrast with Richard's obsession with secrecy and sublimation. Donald not only has embraced the free-enterprise system but has exploited it. More than a few of his machinations would fit into what Richard, attacking other men in other administrations, quite accurately labeled influence peddling.

A few weeks after Richard won reelection as Vice President in 1956, Donald tapped Howard Hughes for a $205,000 loan. Noah Dietrich, then in charge of Hughes' far-flung interests, flew to Washington and urged the Vice President to keep his brother from taking the money. Dietrich warned that too many people knew of the deal and, therefore, the word was sure to leak out. Richard Nixon refused to listen. "My family comes first," he said, according to Dietrich, who related the conversation to us.

Donald supposedly wanted the cash for a small drive-in restaurant chain. He saw himself as a West Coast Ronald MacDonald, with a product far more exciting than the Big Mac. Donald called it the Nixonburger. But unhappily, he went through Hughes' $205,000 in less than two months, without even paying off major creditors.

It took a little longer than Noah Dietrich had thought for the word to leak out. Not until 1960 did Drew and I reveal the strange circumstances of the Hughes loan—how the money passed from the Hughes Tool Company to an attorney, then from the lawyer to Nixon's mother, Hannah, who delivered the money to Donald. Even more peculiar was the collateral on the loan, a family lot in Whittier, California, a gas station site valued at $13,000. Hughes was so embarrassed over the foreclosure that he put the property in the name of one of his accountants. But meanwhile—indeed, just eight days after the loan was negotiated—Trans World Airlines, the airline Hughes then controlled, began benefitting from what can only be called favored status with the government.

After John Kennedy beat out Richard Nixon by fewer than 120,000 votes in the 1960 election, the disappointed Nixon blamed our stories about the Hughes loan as one of the reasons for his defeat. The loan was an even bigger issue in his inglorious defeat for the California governorship two years later. "I am an honest man," he assured the voters of California. Their verdict indicated they may have had some doubt about this.

Through the early years of the Pearson-Nixon acrimony, I managed to get along quite affably with Nixon. I have never been able to develop enough enthusiasm for Democrats to resent Republicans the way Drew did, and I suffer from some phlegmatism of spirit that inhibits bitter personal animosities.

After Nixon ascended to the presidency, I espoused the spirit of Herb Block who gave Nixon a free shave and made him look more presentable in the *Washington Post* cartoons. I, too, tried to humanize this dogged, dauntless President with the unfortunate sloping nose, the marionette hand gestures, and the robot-like personality.

I knew Nixon to be a deeply private person, a warm, shy, sensitive man, who sometimes woke up wondering whether he was President. "I would have a feeling," he told a friend, "that I had something to tell the President. Then I would suddenly shake myself awake and realize I am the President."

I tried to look beneath the psychological scar tissue he had accumulated as he drove himself into one bruising battle after another, slashing his way to the top, suffering inwardly from the political shellfire. I tried to understand this lonely, suspicious President who fought so hard for public approval and was rebuffed so often.

I must have betrayed enough sympathy to raise hopes within the White House. For early in 1969, Nixon's political tutor, the late Murray Chotiner, called on me to say that the new President wanted friendly relations and that the resources of the White House would be available to me for hard-to-get information. All I needed to do whenever I had to reach the President, or wanted information, was to call Murray.

I used Chotiner's good offices on occasion, as when I wanted the Justice Department's file on the tax investigation of George Wallace, and for a time Chotiner was as good as his word. But when, in the inevitable functioning of my role, I began to publish exposé items about the new Administration, the olive branch was withdrawn. I found that access to White House cooperation was for sycophants only, not for reporters.

The Nixon Modus Operandi

Richard Nixon came to power with the conviction that he had gotten there by circumventing the working press and could govern successfully only so long as he continued to do so. Reporters were to be given comfortable accommodations, fed with daily trivialities, and occupied with diversions; but they were to be kept away from the news.

His presidency was to draw a curtain of secrecy between its internal operations and the outside world unprecedented in the memory of Washington observers. The President did not want the acts and policies of his Administration to reach the people through what he considered the distorting prism of the press. What he wanted known, he would communicate directly via television talks or other tightly controlled mechanisms he had developed.

Not only was the press distrusted. The millions who composed the permanent government were suspect, too. The highest military officers were to be denied the kind of critical information it was previously considered essential to have. Even the President's own appointees, the top few thousand in government, were to be given minimal initiative and not trusted with sensitive information in their areas. This denigration of the regular institutions of government was in part aimed at the press; what officials did not know they could not leak.

The history of the hostility between the President and his critics is too large and tangled a topic to be treated here. Suffice it to say that, from the beginning, grievous injustices had been done on both sides. Nixon had cut

and had been cut; he had suffered and had survived and
had won. Now he was to consolidate his victory, and
woe unto those who would not accept that victory. A
statement attributed to Egil Krogh reflects the attitude
inside the White House: "Anyone who opposes us we'll
destroy. As a matter of fact, anyone who doesn't support us we'll destroy."

Suspicion and a sense of lifelong grievance—all too
often confirmed—were accompanied in President Nixon
by a desire for solitude and a craving for an orderly environment undisturbed by trivial interruptions or inter-
necine discord. In the past he had made mistakes and
lost elections by trying to direct everything personally.
He would never again spread himself too thin. He would
gain the information he needed in the most efficient way
—by reading, not rapping. He would encapsulate himself from unnecessary turmoil, dealing regularly only
with those select few who had learned not only to resolve
conflicts, but to modulate their personalities so as not to
jar his sensitive vibrations. And so he came to act
through other men, who aped him and tended, in the
way of young men, to out-Nixon Nixon.

The trouble with all this was that a seething enterprise
like America cannot be compartmentalized, cordoned
off, and led from a glass bubble. Bureaucrats who are
denied trust will become untrustworthy. Officers who are
sealed off from information they need will find ways to
acquire it. Subordinates blocked from access to the
President will grow uneasy and begin to connive at office politics. Some of those barred from talking to the
press will begin to leak information wholesale. Suspicion
and hostility at the top will at length permeate an organization with apprehension, jealousy, and moral rot.

The Nixon way could not work for another, more important reason. There is a fundamental conflict between
uniformity and diversity, between politician and press,
that is built into the American character and system.
This latter conflict is more than an American phenomenon; it is a universal juxtaposition that has always pitted
the ferreter of fact against the mobilizer of opinion.

Alexander Solzhenitsyn has written: "For a country to have a great writer is like having another government. That is why no regime has ever loved great writers, only minor ones." We in America do not have, nor need we rely upon, a literary and moral giant comparable to that Russian immortal. In our Lilliputian practicality and historic good fortune, we have evolved an entire institution to undertake the mission that in a tyranny falls to the lonely genius and hero.

What is this mission? To give the people an alternative to the official version of things, a rival account of reality, a measure by which to judge the efficacy of rulers and whether the truth is in them, an unauthorized stimulus to action or resistance.

Long before Americans could vote directly, in effect, for their Presidents or their Senators, before the vote was given to the poor, women, blacks, and youths, before presidential nominating conventions or our present political parties existed, the role of the village editor and dissenting pamphleteer—as monitor, arbiter, critic, and rival of the politician—was imbedded as a fundamental of the American system. It was of this role that Jefferson spoke in his eternally repeatable declaration that if he had to choose between a government without newspapers and newspapers without a government, he would take his morning paper.

From its primitive state when any wanderer, if he was cantankerous enough, might set up his press and begin to assail his townsmen, the press as an institution has evolved through alternating chapters of disgrace and sublimity, of prostitution and martyrdom, of somnolence and vigilance, taking form in a thousand press rooms, in billions of miles of teletype tape, in the numberless newsrooms of radio and television, gradually assuming the role and shape that confronted Richard Nixon as he sought and finally won the Presidency. Theodore White has described its function:

The power of the press in America is a primordial one. It sets the agenda of public discusion; and this sweeping political power is unrestrained by any law. It determines what people will talk and think about—an authority that in other nations is reserved for tyrants, priests, parties, mandarins.

No major act of the American Congress, no foreign adventure, no act of diplomacy, no great social reform can succeed in the United States unless the press prepares the public mind. And when the press seizes a great issue to thrust onto the agenda of talk, it moves action on its own—the cause of the environment, the cause of civil rights, the liquidating of the war in Vietnam and, as climax, the Watergate affair were all set on the agenda, in the first instance, by the press.

In a fundamental sense, today more than ever, the press challenges the Executive President, who, traditionally, believes his is the right to set the agenda of the nation's action . . .*

President Nixon came to think he could stand against or outside of that historical process. He thought he could play to the friendly press and put the hostile press in a bottle. For a while it seemed to be working, on the surface. But under the surface, the press was beginning to sizzle in an investigative ferment. What it couldn't get the easy way, it began to go out and dig for. And the underbelly of his Administration was becoming a sieve. It was to be, ironically, the day of the investigative reporter.

While I was working on the stories that ultimately have become the chapters of this book, I considered that they were traditional stories such as I have worked on for twenty-seven years. I did not know at first that I and other investigative reporters were involved in a mortal battle, that each damaging story we published was creating a frenzy within the Administration, causing it to strike back in ways that soon exceeded the limits of the law. Most of the White House horrors that have by now effectively destroyed the presidency of Richard Nixon —and at this writing have made impeachment a strong possibility—were committed in reaction to or in an attempt to influence or circumvent some specific act of the press.

Many of the exposures that have brought the Administration low were leaked to the press by persons within

* *The Making of the President 1972* (New York: Atheneum Press, 1973)

the government who did so as a silent protest against the Nixonian approach to government. Some of those exposures would not have been published, or would not have been sought so diligently, were it not that the Nixon presidency inspired in the press an adversary relationship that went beyond the Constitutional requirement.

Plugging the Leaks

The government does not own the news, but every president has tried to control its flow. President Nixon kept such a tight nozzle on the news, however, that the official pipelines sprung unaccustomed, multiple leaks.

The White House began to go bananas over the inability of the regular law enforcement agencies to find and block the leaks. The crisis of distrust between the President and the press was, in the next several months, to reach a climax.

On May 9, 1969, for example, the *New York Times* revealed that, contrary to official U.S. statements, our B-52 bombers were carrying out raids on the territory of neutral Cambodia. The story, though true, was officially denied, and the Administration retaliated by ordering wiretaps placed on thirteen government officials and four newsmen, in order to find and punish those involved in the leak.

Even more extraordinary was the reaction to a minor item I published on December 21, 1970, about Pentagon officials joking over the Christmas firing of Defense Department personnel. When the story was denied by the Pentagon, I proved it was true by publishing segments of tape recordings I had obtained of the Pentagon meeting.

Instead of resignedly accepting leaks of the bizarre as unavoidable, the Administration launched a manhunt by FBI and military investigators. Suspects were grilled and subjected to lie detector tests, and their neighbors were interrogated. The wrong man, Gene Smith, a $13,500-a-year Pentagon clerk, was fingered and dragged before a grand jury. The charges were eventually dropped, but in the process poor Smith sustained bleeding ulcers, a high-blood-pressure condition, and was fired from his job for a trumped-up reason. Of such cruel absurdities are born vendettas between governments and reporters.

For the past quarter century, I have published news from classified documents. I have been less willing than other correspondents to accept the government's right to classify whatever it wishes. All too often I had found that the government used its classification powers to censor the news. Brass hats and bureaucrats stamped as "Secret" what properly should have been marked "Censored."

I continued the practice under the Nixon regime, to its increasing distress. I reported on March 24, 1971, for example, that despite White House assurances that the Vietnam War was being wound down on schedule, the Pentagon had prepared detailed plans for bombing North Vietnam and mining Haiphong harbor. Six days later, in the face of official denials that American ground troops were operating inside Cambodia and Laos, our column cited secret messages giving the exact number of Americans who had been killed during these incursions.

These secret military reports were more detailed, perhaps, than I would have published in earlier times. But such had become my resentment of the government's lies and venalities that I did not trust the Administration to act in the vast latitude of secrecy, and felt that it must be curbed by the force of informed public opinion. Other newsmen and publishers, clearly, felt the same way.

For on June 13, 1971, the *New York Times,* which ten years before had withheld its knowledge of the forthcoming Bay of Pigs operation because of its respect for the prerogatives of government, began publication of the Pentagon papers, recounting the top-secret history of America's involvement in Vietnam.

The leaker of these explosive papers, Daniel Ellsberg, withheld the section dealing with the secret diplomatic negotiations to end the war. When the White House put out misleading information about its diplomatic efforts,

I obtained the sealed section from other sources and published the highlights on November 30, 1971. As was established in court, nothing damaging to the national security was revealed in the Pentagon papers, but the credibility of the American government and many of its former luminaries was damaged.

Up to that time, the Administration had at least entrusted its reprisals to the authorized agencies under the cover, presumably, that such acts might one day be ruled permissable by a fully Nixonized Supreme Court. These agencies—the FBI, CIA, NSA, etc.—operated with the conditioned wariness of established bureaucrats. They put limits on the irregularities they would permit, even for a President who would be gone when they, hopefully, would still be there. They demurred from out-and-out crimes. Their results, therefore, were unsatisfying.

Such instruments were deemed insufficient to implement the wrath of the White House against Ellsberg, which had been roused to a fever pitch by his noble airs and his lionization by the liberal press. The Administration would put Ellsberg on trial, which was their right. But they also wanted to counteract the press buildup he was getting by obtaining and peddling smear information. When the FBI failed to produce what was wanted, and when a CIA "psychological profile" on Ellsberg turned out rather favorable to him, it was the last straw —the culmination of more than two years of frustration.

So the White House went into the second-story business under Egil Krogh and David Young. They brought in men who promised quick results—G. Gordon Liddy and E. Howard Hunt. Thus began the trail of bag-jobs, forgeries, frame-ups, break-ins, rough-ups, and buggings. Because the purpose was to plug news leaks, these White House thugs called themselves "plumbers."

They set up their command post in Room 16 of the basement of a White House annex known as the Executive Office Building. They were just settling down to their work of lawbreaking in July of 1971 as I was embarking upon an investigation that would receive their special attention.

On Saturday, July 17, my associate and coauthor, George Clifford, spent part of the day with Donald Nixon. I do not normally permit my associates to misrepresent themselves, but the only way George could get near the President's brother was to pose as a businessman. The loquacious Donald, who was wearing blue trousers and a light blue, open-necked sports shirt with a monogram on the breast pocket that looked like a jelly smudge, talked about his deals. The conversation began in a pastel building off the Los Angeles–San Diego freeway and continued over cheeseburgers and chocolate milk shakes in a nearby roadside restaurant. By the time George departed, he knew a lot about Donald's dealings with financial tycoons Howard Hughes and Robert Vesco.

Unknown to us, meanwhile, Donald Nixon had been under White House surveillance. The President had his own brother bugged and followed after receiving a "sensitive case report" from the Internal Revenue Service about Donald's association with two Howard Hughes aides, John Meier and Tony Hatsis, who were in tax trouble. The same report disclosed that a tax audit of Larry O'Brien, the Democratic National Chairman, had uncovered a close relationship with the Hughes organization.

President Nixon, twice burned in elections because of the Nixon-Hughes connection, was eager to prevent any more unfavorable publicity. His brother was consorting too openly with the two Hughes aides for the President's political comfort. This led to an intense, undercover effort to break up Donald's association with the Hughes organization. It wasn't Donald's closeness to Hughes, apparently, that the President minded; it was the risk that his bumbling brother might get caught. For at the same time that the President was doing his utmost to keep Donald away from the Hughes aides, presidential confidant Bebe Rebozo was arranging to receive a

$100,000 cash contribution from Hughes. The money, earmarked for the President, was delivered in two $50,000 consignments at San Clemente and Key Biscayne by Hughes emissary Richard Danner.

The Howard Hughes problem was entrusted to the three men closest to the President—staff chief H. R. Haldeman, aide John Ehrlichman, and Rebozo. What gave them nightmares was the possibility that O'Brien, through his relationship with the Hughes organization, might learn of the Nixon-Hughes dealings and use the information in the 1972 campaign.

Haldeman directed White House counsel John Dean and security man Jack Caulfield to find out how close O'Brien was to the Hughes crowd. Ehrlichman asked Caulfield also to keep Donald Nixon under surveillance. And Rebozo got hold of Danner and asked him to terminate the relationship between Donald and the Hughes aides. When the White House later learned through the surveillance that Donald was meeting Meier at the Orange County airport in California, Rebozo was quickly notified. Before the pair left the airport, Rebozo was on the phone to Danner demanding to know what was going on.

All of these precautions, however, did not prevent us from uncovering the story. On August 6, 1971, I was able to reveal that $100,000 of Hughes gambling casino profits, in two $50,000 cash bundles, had been delivered to Rebozo by Danner. In the same column, I quoted from a memorandum that Hughes had handwritten to his top man in Nevada, Robert Maheu. "I want you to go to see Nixon as my special confidential emissary," wrote the rich recluse in 1968. "I feel there is a really valid possibility of a Republican victory this year. If that could be realized, under our sponsorship and supervision every inch of the way, then we would be ready to follow with Laxalt as our next candidate." Hughes apparently believed that Paul Laxalt, then the Republican Governor of Nevada, was already in his pocket.

Our revelation of the $100,000 Hughes gift, I was told, caused panic inside the White House. The following month, Las Vegas publisher Hank Greenspun mentioned to White House aide Herb Klein that the $100,000 Hughes gift "may have later been used in the purchase of San Clemente." This report got back quickly to Ehrlichman, who asked the President's personal attorney, Herbert Kalmbach, to call upon Greenspun in Las Vegas. Kalmbach quietly sounded out the publisher about his information and assured him that no campaign cash had gone into the purchase of the San Clemente estate.

We moved on, meanwhile, to new revelations. On December 13, 1971, our column began a series of articles revealing the calculated subterfuges of the President's India-Pakistan policy, in which he favored Pakistan at the risk of involving the United States in war, while feigning neutrality. The response by the President to these articles has been recorded by Theodore H. White.

The President was to be driven to an extremity of anger at the publication of National Security Council minutes on the war in Bangladesh by columnist Jack Anderson, an unguided missile with multiple warheads likely to strike anywhere. Quoting dialogue from critical meetings, the Anderson columns stripped bare the essential privacy of national-security planners as never before . . .*

White, in an account rather sympathetic to the President, saw the Nixon Administration "moving, undercover, through a number of branches, to convert its feud with the adversary press into a full-scale guerrilla warfare, espionage and harassment."

I came back on January 24, 1972, with another "Washington Merry-Go-Round" column, drawn from our collection of secret Howard Hughes papers. I replayed the August 6, 1971, story, exploring in more detail the financial relationship between Nixon and Hughes, in order to stimulate the interest of the investigative press.

* *Ibid.*

Not long afterward, on February 3, 1972, the *New York Times* reported that the Howard Hughes papers were in the safe of Hank Greenspun, publisher of the *Las Vegas Sun* (although our copies came from another source). The February 3 date is significant, for on the following day, G. Gordon Liddy met for the second time with Attorney General John Mitchell to push the plans for burglarizing and bugging Larry O'Brien's Watergate offices. Nixon aides John Dean and Jeb Magruder were also present. According to Magruder's testimony, Liddy was instructed to "review the situation to see if there would be potential . . . for an entry into Mr. Greenspun's office."

Liddy dutifully went ahead with a plan to loot Greenspun's safe and thence to make a getaway flight to Mexico in a plane to be provided by Howard Hughes. The Watergate break-in finally was approved at a third meeting on March 30 at Key Biscayne, but the raid on Greenspun's safe was abandoned.

Still, the Howard Hughes angle may explain a mystery that has baffled Watergate investigators. What did the White House burglar hope to find that would justify breaking into the Watergate? Why would they take such foolish risks to burglarize and bug the offices of a Democratic Party factotum like Larry O'Brien? The inner Nixon circle was worried sick that the Nixon-Hughes relationship would become an issue again in the 1972 campaign, that O'Brien might be able to obtain in the incriminating details from his Hughes contacts, and that the Hughes papers might be ticking like a time bomb in Greenspun's vault. It was to cover up the Nixon-Hughes connection, some investigators strongly believe, that the Watergate crimes were conceived.

By this time, I was deep into the ITT scandal. I published the Dita Beard memorandum on February 29, 1972, touching off a brouhaha which boiled for months and whose end is not yet in sight. There has been sworn testimony that Gordon Liddy secretly spirited the distraught Dita Beard out of Washington one step ahead of the FBI and a Senate subpoena. She surfaced in a Denver hospital, where she was medically sealed off from investigators. There she received a secret midnight bedside visit from Howard Hunt, disguised in makeup and a reddish wig* and using his favorite Watergate alias, Edward Hamilton.

There is no transcript of what White House messages Hunt delivered to Dita, but after his visit she reversed herself and denied the authenticity of her memorandum, which she had previously authenticated. It was this colorful memo, you will remember, that recounted the terms by which an antitrust suit against ITT would be settled in return for a $400,000 political contribution.

John Mitchell, meanwhile, had just resigned as Attorney General to take over the Citizens Committee for the Re-Election of the President (CREEP). But for critical months he was torn and partially immobilized by the developing ITT scandal, now being ably abetted by daily contributions from the *Washington Post,* the *New York Times,* the *Washington Star-News,* the newsweeklies, and the network news shows. CREEP drifted, and during this period of intermittent leadership, the fatal steps were taken that launched "Operation Gemstone" and led to Watergate. Moreover, the Administration, in riding out the ITT scandal, sustained damage to its reputation and used up part of its arsenal of evasive tactics, which would be less effective in the future because they had been seen before.

About this time I became aware that I had become the object of certain discomforting attentions. I did not know then that there was a White House "enemies list," but I did know that I was on someone's list. I was hearing from people who had talked to me on the phone, who said that since the telephone call they were being snooped upon. I knew that persons in the Pentagon and the White House, suspected of having contact with me, were being subjected to phone taps, lie detector tests,

* Hunt contends that an impartial viewing will reveal that the wig in question is brownish and that the description of it as "reddish" is just another facet of the organized campaign to make him appear ridiculous.

and other indignities. My house was under surveillance by men with binoculars in parked cars, and I was conscious of being tailed.

In March, 1972, the *Washington Post* did a feature article, based on its sources within the government, which detailed how the White House was "coordinating a continuous effort to discredit Anderson." It was conducted by the Internal Security Division of the Justice Department, the FBI, elements of the White House staff, and the Republican National Committee. All told, dozens of government agents, presidential aides, and political flunkies were assigned to investigate us, to prepare attacks on us, and to plant stories in the press against us.

Moreover, the Administration was secretly cooperating with the world-famous private investigating firm, Intertel, which ITT had hired to probe us. Whatever Intertel could dredge up was added to the government's own file and was offered surreptitiously to the press.

My name was also posted prominently on a wallboard in the plumbers' basement sanctum, as a voodoo meant to inspire the occupants against the foe. Their efforts produced one unexpected result. They evidently learned that I was acquainted through the Mormon church with a Navy yeoman on Henry Kissinger's staff. The notorious plumbers zeroed in on Yeoman Charles Radford, using everything but rubber hoses to get a confession out of him. They bullied and browbeat him for three weeks. They put him through four lie detector tests; they screamed obscenities at him; they tapped his telephone. They finally got their confession—not that he had passed on Kissinger's secrets to me but that he had spied on Kissinger for the Joint Chiefs of Staff. He had even rifled through Kissinger's briefcase, he confessed, to get sensitive documents his military superiors wanted to see.

The White House campaign against me, if it succeeded, could destroy a reporter by scaring off his sources, undermining his credibility with readers and editors, and immobilizing him in time-consuming self-protection measures. As best a private citizen can, I tried to strike back—to find out precisely who my pursuers were and to turn the tables against them. I called in due notes from sources within the FBI, the Justice Department, and the White House itself.

Information came bootlegging in: That Assistant Attorney General Robert Mardian directed the "get Anderson" effort at the Department of Justice. That Acting FBI Director L. Patrick Gray had unleashed his men on an illegal field day with my telephone calls. That Attorneys General John Mitchell and Richard Kleindienst were obfuscating the official record to discredit my ITT stories. That presidential counselor Charles Colson was pushing bogus charges, apparently his specialty. (In an "Eyes Only" memo, dated November 11, 1971, to John Dean, the irrepressible Colson said: "You know my personal feelings about Jack Anderson." He then outlined a preposterous charge that I had been paid $100,000 to write favorable stories about the erstwhile Cuban dictator Batista. "It now appears," continued Colson, "as if we have the opportunity to destroy Anderson's credibility.")

And from within the Justice Department, I got tipped on such things as the license tag numbers and makes of the cars that were staking out my home. I followed it all up as best I could and struck back in the column and in the courts and in testimony before congressional committees. But the information I was getting was too fragmented and struck at persons either too high to catch red-handed or too low to matter much. I was not getting through to the operational middle where the laws were being broken in convictable form and where, still unknown to me, Hunt and Liddy cavorted, deploying their Cuban assault troops.

Winston Churchill once said that nothing in life is more exhilarating than to be shot at—and missed. In that spirit, my favorite Liddy exploit:

G. Gordon Liddy had flair; even his detractors will concede that. A month before the fateful Watergate break-in, during a dry run at McGovern headquarters, Liddy had pulled out his pistol and shot out a street light so that entry could be made under proper cover of darkness. He was a fast draw.

For a mercifully brief period, Liddy thought he had been instructed by Jeb Magruder to kill me, a mission whose merit he divined automatically and embraced without question. En route to consummation, he mentioned his mission to an aide of Magruder; that prescient gentleman spotted a possible failure of communication and told Liddy to hold up a minute. The aide apprised Magruder of Liddy's supposed assignment. Magruder, who himself was once threatened with violent death for laying a hand on Liddy's shoulder, agreed that Liddy had been laboring under a misapprehension. Whatever had been said to the man was only a figure of speech, not to be acted upon literally.

Liddy took the countermanding of his orders like a soldier, but he was disturbed about Magruder's unmilitary imprecision of speech and cautioned him against further misnomers. "Where I come from," he grumbled, "that means a rub-out."

The Watergate That Was

Were it not that something epochally sinister had happened later that night, I would likely not remember the day of June 16, 1972. As it is, the day of Watergate will always recall to my mind a personal coincidence which, had it been graced by luck, might have prevented the Watergate that was.

As I reconstruct it now, June 16 began as a routine Friday spent in my Washington office plotting forthcoming news stories with my staff and nailing down the last details for columns that must go out on Fridays to beat the weekend mail lag. In late afternoon, I hurried off to National Airport to catch a plane—a commonplace repeated one hundred times a year in pursuit of a scoop or a lecture fee.

Outside the terminal, as I headed for the entrance closest to where my Cleveland flight was already loading, I spotted a familiar face bobbing hopefully above the incoming bustle, a face at home in the world's depots of eternal expectations.

Frank Sturgis had been a friend and source for many years. I knew him as an authentic soldier of fortune, a flyer and gun runner, a romantic who bloomed ill-betimed in a programmed age, a seeker whom humdrum could never quite assimilate. Once, in his youth, he had confounded the odds and had become part of a legend —one of the ragged few who had persevered in the mountains with Fidel Castro and had come on to glory. But in the sourness of the dream realized, this American had defected from the Revolution to become again the longshot gambler against the house.

Henceforth he would risk his neck against Castro in foredoomed ventures of the Cuban "freedom fighters." We kept in touch over the years, but he would periodically drop out of sight, forever chasing adventure, usually finding misadventure. But now, here he was again, Big Frank, little changed by the years, with three companeros in tow and on his earnest face the old look of expectancy.

"Frankie!" I hollered, waving him down. He turned and a look of unease crossed his eyes, resembling an errant husband who at the point of rendezvous bumps into a well-meaning neighbor. But he came over, shook hands warmly, and we chatted for a moment in the banalities of airport encounters.

"What brings you to Washington?" I asked.

"Private business," he said. But he could not resist an exaggerated smile, a telegraph that he was off on one of his peculiar missions. He introduced me to a companion; the other two confederates hung back. We parted jovially, talking of getting together soon. Then Frank and his group disappeared in the direction of the taxicabs. They would momentarily depart for the Watergate Hotel where they had two rooms reserved under aliases.

On the plane, in the enforced idleness of waiting for our turn in the take-off pattern, a loose chord jangled in my head, agitating to be plugged in. One of the Cubans who had hung back, his face turned away, I knew from somewhere. Yes. Sturgis had introduced me to him in Miami years before. Barker was his name. Bernard Barker. "Macho," Sturgis had called him.

"Macho" was born in Cuba, but of American parents, and had always manifested a dual loyalty of fierce proportions. He was said to be the first Cuban-American to volunteer in the U.S. Army after Pearl Harbor, and during the war he served sixteen months in a German POW camp. After the war he returned to Cuba, where he became an undercover agent for our CIA after Castro came to power. Later, he was a key figure in the Bay of Pigs operation.

I wondered what the four Cubans were doing in

Washington. Something murky, I thought, probably for the CIA. As soon as I got back from Cleveland, I planned to check back with Sturgis. There might be a story in it.

Our plane rose in a diagonal line over Washington and wheeled to the west. Below, part of the Capital city still gleamed white in the late afternoon sun; part had surrendered to the encroaching shadows. Shadows, it has since seemed, that shall not fade.

When I returned from Cleveland on the following morning, Frank's "private business" was already public. Eight hours after our airport encounter, Sturgis, Barker, Eugenio Martinez, and Virgiolio Gonzalez had been arrested at gunpoint in the act of burglarizing and bugging Democratic National Committee headquarters at the Watergate Hotel. Arrested with them was James McCord, a former CIA wireman.

The *Washington Post* printed the story of the arrest as its "second lead," devoting eighty-three column inches to a matter which received little attention elsewhere. Shortly thereafter, the *Post* linked Howard Hunt to the burglary, plus the fact that he operated out of the White House.

At the White House, the fateful decision had already been made to fight disclosure of any tie-in between the Nixon Administration and Watergate, setting in motion the cover-up process that would lead from crime to crime. Ron Zeigler announced the official line: "I am not going to comment from the White House about a third-rate burglary attempt."

As I read the account, I remembered ruefully that, for two months before the dramatic arrest, I had been investigating a tip that the Democratic headquarters was about to be bugged by some part of the Nixon reelection apparatus. The tip had come to me from an old friend, William Haddad, a New York businessman.

As he heard it and reported it to me in a letter dated April 12, 1972, a Nixon adjunct called the November Group was to do the bugging. That was the clinker in the tip. The November Group was a consortium of advertising and media specialists, housed in New York and responsible for the political advertising in the Nixon campaign. I lost crucial weeks digging into the November Group, learning more about it than I should ever want to know. For it, of course, had nothing to do with the bugging plan.

Had I not followed Haddad's tip down a blind alley, and had I kept in closer touch with Sturgis, the events on the night of June 16 and early morning of June 17 might have been deflected. Yet, in a larger sense, what Watergate has come to represent could not have been deflected. It was inevitable. Its origin lay, not in coincidence, but in intractable substances forged during the rise of Richard Nixon.

I will not take the space here to recount how the press dug out the dark Watergate secrets and exposed them to the sunlight. Two young *Washington Post* reporters, Robert Woodward and Carl Bernstein, deserve the most credit. Yet we were not altogether asleep at the typewriter; our stories linking Haldeman to the cover-up, reporting that Mitchell had received Gemstone wiretap reports and exposing the attempt to bribe the Watergate defendants, added a few jigsaw pieces to the Watergate puzzle.

Still, President Nixon won reelection by the greatest popular vote margin in our history. His circumvention of the press, by which reporters were at one point reduced to watching one of his campaign appearances on closed-circuit television in contrast to the wide-open McGovern campaign, which was daily riddled by the reporters, was triumphant. The White House tactics of concealment, denial, and cover-up—of asking the public to believe the President and not the press—had won.

But unlike a political opponent, reporters cannot be finally defeated on election day. The battle resumes anew each morning; and in a free country, a press humiliated is a press dangerous. If press revelations had not convinced the public, they had rendered the U.S. Senate and the federal courts gravely suspicious. It was clear that matters would not be allowed to drop.

Finally, James McCord, facing a stiff sentence from Judge John Sirica, stated that higher-ups were involved in Watergate, that perjuries had been committed at the trial, and that he would henceforth cooperate with the court and the Senate Watergate Committee. This broke the dam. The united front caved in and a dozen involved persons, fearing they would be sawed off at the end of a long limb, began to confess to various authorities. Each day now brought the publication of new leaks in the major papers, on the television networks, and in the great newsweeklies.

The White House had one hope that could keep public knowledge of its Watergate involvement to a minimum. This was to confine the process to the grand juries, where secrecy was enforced and the Administration still held sway. Some Administration individuals might eventually be indicted and have to stand trial in the years ahead, but the sordid mess that enveloped almost the entire presidency could be kept from public view, confined to the realm of rumor, leak, and, as they liked to put it, "innuendo." Thus, the President remained steadfast in his refusal to let any principals in his regime appear before the Senate Committee.

I felt it was of overriding import to bring out of the shadows what McCord and the others were testifying. On April 2, 1973, I printed verbatim transcripts of McCord's secret testimony before the Senate staff, describing how the bugging of the Democratic National Committee was planned in the Attorney General's office by Mitchell, Dean, Magruder, and Liddy. This was the first direct documentation of the Watergate charges.

Shortly thereafter, I gained access to the transcripts of grand jury appearances by the principal White House and CREEP figures. Normally, I would have hesitated to publish such transcripts, for I respect the hallowed place that secrecy of grand jury proceedings holds under our system. But years of accumulated distrust of the Nixon presidency convinced me that it could not be trusted to prosecute its own members honestly unless the major facts were publicly and authentically known.

Moreover, the President's plan to prevent his aides from testifying before the Senate, on television where the public itself could see and judge, would be rendered untenable once their grand jury testimony had been let out of the bag and it became known how deeply they were involved. So on April 16, 1972, I began printing verbatim reports and continued to do so, day after day, through the testimony of McCord, Hunt, Haldeman, Strachan, Chapin, Magruder, and others.

The Watergate prosecutors, meanwhile, protested that my publication of the transcripts was hampering their investigation. I immediately paid a call on them to listen to their objections. I told them I felt they had held back during the Watergate trial. After listening for two hours to their arguments, I was persuaded that they were now seeking the full truth. Anonymous tipsters were refusing to appear as witnesses, they told me, for fear of being identified in my column.

Therefore, I announced on April 25, 1973: "I have agreed not to print further verbatim excerpts from the Watergate grand jury hearings. I do so because I have become convinced that further verbatim disclosures would not be in the best interests of the investigation. However, as a journalist, I have an obligation and a right to continue to report any and all pertinent information on this sordid scandal that so many people in high places have worked so hard to keep from the public."

The President, meanwhile, decided he would no longer try to prevent his aides, past and present, from testifying before the Senate. The show was on the road.

There are still many Americans who see the seemingly endless revelations of Watergate, as the White House once described it, as "a third-rate burglary." But the burglary has been lost in the plethora of dirty deeds; it was merely the key to a Pandora's box.

The Nixon coterie encroached upon the powers of Congress, trampled upon the rights of the press, violated our most basic freedoms. With eyes as cold as the marble around them, they sat in the witness chair in the

Senate caucus room and arrogantly asserted what they called the President's right to steal and wiretap and rig court cases. They justified it all in the name of national security.

They goaded dissidents, encouraged demonstrations, rejoiced over a report that there might be violence at a presidential function. "Good," scrawled Haldeman in response to the report that demonstrators "will be violent; they will have extremely obscene signs." Then, to protect the nation from such demonstrators, the President and his people claimed the right to violate fundamental freedoms.

The White House crowd, in short, has put national security ahead of the Constitution. The language of the Constitution—the people, justice, tranquillity, welfare, liberty—would protect the people from the government. The language of the Nixonites—law and order, secrecy, surveillance, executive privilege—would protect the government from the people.

FROM ITT TO
WATERGATE

The Informer

"What's Dita Beard got against you?"

As I recall that question now, asked by my long-time associate Opal Ginn, it was oddly prophetic. But at the time, January 28, 1971, it did not register. We were at my offices on K Street in Washington. I reflected for a moment, trying to pinpoint that unusual name among a long list of likely ill-wishers.

"I don't know," I said finally. "I can't place her."

"Well, she knows you," Opal replied.

On the previous afternoon, Opal had attended a farewell party in honor of Bill Burazer, a waiter of local renown, who was retiring after twenty-five years at the nearby Sheraton-Carlton Hotel. Many of Burazer's assembled admirers did not know each other, and during recurring rounds of introductions, Opal was presented to Dita Beard with the identifying tag, "Opal works for Jack Anderson."

Without pausing even to frown, Mrs. Beard weighed in with: "Your boss is a son of a bitch. I wouldn't touch him with a ten-foot pole." Similar accosts in the past had steeled Opal. She fired back an appropriate salvo from her own scatological repertoire and moved on, while all around the jovial circle smiles wilted in half bloom and highball glasses froze in mid-ascent.

The incident probably was not worth noting, I thought. Just as an actor has hosts of unknown admirers, so the muckraker collects legions of hidden haters. Yet, there might be something more specific behind this.

"Who is this Dita?" I asked. "Describe her for me."

Opal described a large woman, fiftyish, a face once

handsome but showing hard mileage, a raspy, whisky voice, a commanding manner, careless attire. "She's a lobbyist for ITT," Opal concluded.

Mention of the International Telephone and Telgraph Corporation made Dita Beard suddenly more interesting. Several weeks earlier we had charged in our column that an "aura of scandal" hung over ITT's acquistion of the Hartford Fire Insurance Company. The column had revealed the contents of a secret transcript we had obtained of Securities and Exchange Commission proceedings. The testimony recounted how the Connecticut insurance commissioner, William Cotter, after first vetoing the merger as contrary to the public interest, had reversed himself. His change of heart followed private meetings with ITT officials and the intervention of a politically active Hartford lawyer ITT had hired to press its case behind the scenes. The column also questioned the action of the Justice Department in approving the merger (after it, too, had first opposed it). Continuing, we wrote that the S.E.C. was quietly investigating personal trading in ITT stock by several top company executives who might have been tipped off on the terms of the Justice Department settlement with ITT weeks before any public announcement was made. It is a crime for executives to trade their own stock on the basis of information not available to ordinary stockholders.

If that column was the cause of Mrs. Beard's distemper, perhaps it had pinched the nerve I was groping for. For besides being a valid news story, our column of December 9 was a lure. I suspected that a pattern of improper influence had been exerted by ITT, first on the Connecticut insurance commissioner, then on the Department of Justice.

There were some curious similarities in ITT's tactics. Just before Commissioner Cotter abruptly changed his attitude toward the merger, ITT promised to bail out Hartford's lagging urban renewal program by opening a company office and building a new ITT-Sheraton hotel in the eyesore neighborhood. What was good for Hartford was good for Cotter, who was planning to run for Congress in Hartford. And while the Justice Department was in the throes of reversing itself on the merger, ITT-Sheraton secretly pledged upward of $400,000 in Boston money to make it possible for the Republican National Convention to be held in President Nixon's chosen city, San Diego, after local businessmen had failed to ante up.

Grist for suspicion, by all means, but concrete proof was needed linking the favor to the favorable decision. How does an investigative reporter find such links? There is a limit to what can be dredged up from interviewing obvious suspects and studying such records as are available to the public. The principals rarely admit to wrongdoing, and the pertinent documents are either classified, falsified, or strangely absent from the files. Moreover, the reporter is hobbled by self-imposed limitations. Unlike the government, the newsman has ethics that prevent him from wiretapping, burglarizing files, intercepting mail, buying information, or planting paid spies. There are legitimate ways by which he can develop sources and pursue leads. But when he reaches the place where the trail vanishes, he is lost unless some unknown insider comes foreward with the missing clue. I have never found anything unethical in trying to tempt the insider to come out into the cold.

In this respect, muckrakers are like the sirens of Greek mythology, who, by their seductive singing, enticed unknowing wayfarers to abandon the cramped boredom of safe passage for a hazardous try at strange excitements and gratifications. Somewhere within ITT or the Justice Department or the S.E.C. was a person who had access to the corroborating proof and a motive for revealing it. There is always someone somewhere. In our column of December 9, by showing our interest in all facets of government involvement with the ITT-Hartford merger, by showing indeed that we were interested enough to print even minor revelations, we were singing our siren songs.

I had a feeling the leak might come from within ITT. Our column had already developed one source inside the ITT hierarchy, and although that source was of only limited value in the present instance, he had alerted us to serious disaffection within the company. Some of it stemmed from the destructive pressures common to Executive Suite, where some must fall in order that others may rise. But at ITT, these pressures were exacerbated by the crotchety tyranny of Harold S. Geneen, the corporate panjandrum since 1959. Anecdotes abounded about Geneen. "Get rid of two bodies, one male and one female," read one of his personnel orders. Or, there was the meeting of ITT executives he opened by saying, "Gentlemen, I have been thinking. Bull times zero is zero bull. Bull divided by zero is infinity bull. And I'm sick and tired of the bull you've been feeding me."

The stories uniformly portrayed a man who was tough, abrasive, and dictatorial. He had risen by dint of ferocious single-mindedness from Wall Street runner and night-school accountant to the world's highest paid executive with a salary of almost $800,000 a year, plus extras. To get where he was he had sacrificed almost his entire personal life, and he demanded similar dedication from the host of top executives he had assembled to rule ITT's $9 billion empire. They were paid top dollar and given all the material perquisites that status seekers covet. But if they stumbled or showed signs of wearing out or otherwise ran afoul of Geneen, they began to experience the corrosive fears best known to those whose inflated life styles depend upon the caprice of one man.

On the fifth floor of the ITT Building in New York City there is a limbo known to its inhabitants as Death Row. Here executives who have fallen into disfavor are shunted aside. They have been stripped of their badges of honor—their limousines, their silver water pitchers, their private telephones, their place on the routing list of Geneen's personal memoranda. If they are tempted to depart and go elsewhere—before management is ready to let them loose with whatever information about ITT they may have—they know ITT can move in mysterious ways to retaliate against errant executives. They are therefore trapped. Here they await their fate, with little to do but plot how to get back their place in the pecking order, or how to undo the persons who displaced them. Even in this immobilized posture they serve the company—as a deterrent for those still among the blessed who may resist staying in line.

Yet tycoons who on Monday play God with the lives of others and on Tuesday conspire in nefarious acts are asking for trouble. Formidable though its security apparatus may be, any organization in which men must connive to court the favor or dodge the obloquy of one eccentric ruler is bound to be a spawning ground for one of the most valuable species in American life—the informer.

In an age marked by corrupt law enforcement and Madison Avenue imagery, the informer is our principal protection against the designs of public and corporate wrongdoers who have built massive walls to hide their activities from citizen and stockholder alike. I have been cultivating informers for twenty-five years; I know something about the psychology of one who has a dark secret and is teetering on the awful brink of disclosing it. His motive may be noble or base or just human; he may seek to protect the public from fraud, to advance a good cause, to discredit a rival, or to avenge a personal grievance. To the reporter the motive should be secondary, except as it bears upon the validity of the information.

The informer is often a stranger to the glare of publicity and is full of doubt and fear. He usually does not know the news business. He does not know just whom to go to or whether his disclosure will be deemed newworthy. Maybe, he fears, they will just yawn or even laugh at him for trying to peddle such trivial stuff and he will have exposed himself for nothing. Most of the time, the informer wants to stay hidden. Exposure will cost him his livelihood and lay him open to the most depressing harassments, for our society has not yet outgrown the hoodlum ethos, which honors the man who covers up his boss's crime above the employee who exposes it. Can he trust strangers to protect his anonymity? He knows vaguely that above the typical reporter are editors, lawyers, publishers—perhaps with advertisers to protect—any one of whom can kill the story after he has exposed himself or his cause to a widening circle. And so for weeks he hangs immobilized between visions of derring-do and nightmares of retribution. Most of the time he never comes forward; and even when he does he may turn back. I have had informants before me who, in the midst of their story, have begun to jabber, broken out in a sweat, and edged for the door.

I like to keep a light burning in the window for the storm-tossed informer. I signal to him from afar by championing his cause, by regularly printing exposés akin to his, by being accessible to the hushed voice on the phone, by periodically making public pledges to go to jail rather than reveal a source, by scandalizing the mighty so pervasively as to leave no doubt that whether it's a peccadillo or a state secret, the Washington Merry-go-Round is interested. I try to convey to the doubter out there that he has but one man to convince, and if he proves his case, the door is at once opened to 950 newspapers.

But several weeks passed, and no wayfarer appeared. I got no reaction of any kind from within ITT until Dita Beard's ourburst at the Burazer party. Hers was not quite the reaction I was looking for, but at least it indicated that the effort had made an impression there, if only to create a furor. If our man was on the premises, the furor might have given him ideas.

How to Succeed in Business

I had reasons for keeping watch on ITT.

There had been a pattern of influence-peddling in ITT's dealings with the government. In one decade under Harold Geneen ITT jumped in rank among American industrial corporations from fifty-first to eighth. This growth was not achieved by the traditional routes to corporate success: developing new products, introducing revolutionary marketing techniques, or doing anything related to making a better mousetrap, a cheaper one, or a better-packaged one. It was done almost exclusively by buying up existing companies, at an ever-accelerating pace. During Geneen's first decade at ITT the company acquired 110 domestic and foreign corporations. In his eleventh year alone, ITT completed or initiated 61 new mergers. By 1970, ITT had 331 major subsidiaries; even the subsidiaries had subsidiaries—708, to be exact. The company ran about 500 substantial installations, half in the United States and half abroad. It had 390,000 employees and operated in 67 countries on six continents. Naturally, the more companies ITT acquired, the higher its sales figures rose; under Geneen, its annual sales jumped from $811 million to over $7 billion.

My interest was not so much in its growth, however, as in how that growth was achieved. The basic merger tactic was to acquire 51 percent or more of a target company's stock by exchanging ITT stock for it, thus gaining control of 100 percent of that company's assets. To induce major stockholders to sell, ITT generally paid about 20 percent more than the stock was worth on the market; to get existing managements to acquiesce in these takeovers, ITT increased their salaries. In acquiring Avis Rent-a-Car, ITT paid 53.2 percent more than the market value of the stock; for Hartford Fire, ITT paid 28 percent more, in the currency of a newly created issue of ITT preferred stock.

This raised a question in basic economics: How long can you continue to pay more for stock than it is worth, and more for management than it is worth, before you start running into trouble?

Geneen's answer was superior, centralized management. Through the one thousand executives he brought together to run the ITT empire under his personal direction, new efficiency and vision was introduced which made the operation pay. To support his claim, he could point to increases in regular earnings averaging 11.6 percent each quarter for forty-seven consecutive quarters. Among the great corporations, only IBM, the innovator, had a better earnings record.

But a growing number of critics took different views. The American Institute of Certified Public Accountants accused Geneen of using accounting procedures to create the appearance of statistical gains that did not really exist. Students of tax loopholes pointed out that by manipulating its tax payments, ITT in 1970 paid only 2.1 percent on its earnings as opposed to the statutory corporate income tax rate of 48 percent.

Congressional antitrust investigators accused ITT of "reciprocity," meaning that one of its subsidiaries would throw its business to another subsidiary and vice versa, thus illegally freezing out competition from outside the "family." During the Johnson Administration, government attorneys charged that Geneen and other ITT officers had made misstatements on issues of major importance, so that even with subpoena powers it was difficult to tell what was really going on inside ITT. The Federal Trade Commission had cited ITT-Continental Baking for deceptive advertising.

And incorruptible Ralph Nader had zeroed in on ITT, charging it with an ugly record that included everything from reciprocity to vertical foreclosure and high-pressure tactics on government officials to manifesting a low regard for the law and bad faith in judicial proceedings.

To each of these charges, batteries of company lawyers and public relations men issued denials. The denials were usually as artful as the machinations that led to the charges.

For instance, when the Federal Trade Commission was trying to get ITT-Continental to clean up its fraudulent advertising, the government's position was attacked in a series of learned speeches by Professor Yale Brozen, a University of Chicago economist; then the Brozen speeches were reprinted in full by *Barron's,* the financial weekly. Then full-page ads, containing the text of the speeches, appeared in the *New York Times* and other newspapers. Then, just in case someone had missed it, hordes of ITT PR men called on financial editors all across the country to acquaint them with Professor Brozen's views. Finally, of course, it turned out that Brozen was on the payroll of the PR firm handling ITT-Continental's account and that he had been paid for making the pro-ITT speeches which got such miraculous attention.

Such defenses often arouse more alarm than the charges themselves. But it is not our purpose here to render a judgment on peripheral disputes. We cite them only to show that ITT's spectacular rise was increasingly accompanied by charges of unethical and even illegal conduct made by responsible spokesmen for the public interest.

But the issue of most concern to us was this: Is ITT using its growing wealth and power to get preferential treatment from government agencies charged with regulating corporations in the public interest?

We keep our own financial charts on corporate activity; they graph not the statistics found in business journals but the corporate handouts to politicians. On this indicator, ITT showed a rising curve in the 1960's that kept pace with its climb on Dow-Jones. ITT discovered

Senator Thomas Dodd's receptivity to corporate favors long before we did. The papers brought to us by his employees showed that even when he was just an obscure freshman senator, he was important enough to ITT to merit speaking fees, a free holiday at Boca Raton, tax-free testimonial gifts, campaign contributions, and a great deal of personal attention from ITT Vice President William R. Merriam, whose name appeared often on Dodd's appointments diaries.

The company was accustomed to operating at all levels of politics. In 1955 ITT prevailed upon Secretary of State John Foster Dulles to use his influence with British Prime Minister Harold Macmillan in behalf of its proposed cable under the Atlantic Ocean. For the same mission, Admiral Ellery Stone, an old Macmillan friend, was retained for a fee. ITT had had on its payroll leaders of national and international stature: Trygve Lie, former Secretary-General of the United Nations; Paul Henri Spaak, former Belgian Premier and Secretary-General of NATO; John A. McCone, ex-director of our Central Intelligence Agency; and numerous members of the British House of Lords and the French National Assembly. One might say that ITT almost managed to give influence-peddling a good name. Almost.

The nature of the company's interest in statesmen was clearly revealed by Hal Geneen early in his presidency. According to a sworn deposition given by ITT Vice President J. T. Naylor (retired), he was approached in 1960 by William Marks, another vice president. Marks explained that ITT was raising political contributions for both parties in the presidential race "to butter both sides so we'll be in a good position whoever wins." Marks continued, "Hal and the board have a program that is very important to political protection and business development. Hal has given me a selected list of top executives to contribute to the election campaign. You are down for $1,200. This can be financed for you by the company if necessary . . . you will be expected to recover the amount by covering it up in your travel expense account."

Naylor was brought to Bobby Baker and, as requested, gave $1,200 to the "Texas Business and Professional
Men's Committee for Johnson for Vice President." The
check was deposited two days after the election. Naylor
was uncomfortable about the matter, however, and declined to milk his expense account; instead, he took the
loss like an ordinary citizen. This, Naylor testified,
caused consternation in the company. Geneen re-
proached Naylor, saying, "Everybody does it, and the
board wanted it this way. It is paying off big in Washington." (Although these activities, as related by Naylor
in his deposition, constituted a clear violation of the
Corrupt Practices Act, the Justice Department adhered
to its unblemished record of never having brought a
prosecution under the act.)

One example of what Geneen meant by "paying off
big" occurred in 1963. ITT was having troubles with the
Japanese government, which was insisting that the company pay its taxes plus penalties for nonpayment. ITT
went to the Treasury Department in Washington and
persuaded it to intervene in the dispute with the Japanese government. As a result, the tax claim was reduced
from $7 million to $4.5 million.

It was under Geneen that the company opened its first
Washington office, in the new ITT Building five blocks
from the White House. The main purpose of the Washington office was to bring pressure on the government.
Like the branches of the armed services and the great
Cabinet departments, ITT had its Office of Congressional Liaison and its Congressional Relations Section. One
side of the Congressional Relations Section worked the
Democrats, the other side the Republicans—giving
away free plane rides, cut-rate vacations, touring cars
for congressional junketeers abroad, legal business to
the law firms of public officials, and other forms of
gravy including, as we have seen above, a highly organized program of campaign contributions.

In turn, ITT would call on its powerful friends for
discreet favors, in the form of behind-the-scenes interventions to help get government contracts or to avoid

government regulations. But occasionally, in moments of great stress for ITT, secret interventions were not enough. Then the congressional freeloaders would be called upon to perform in public.

So it was in 1967, when Lyndon Johnson's Justice Department was opposing ITT's acquisition of the American Broadcasting Company before the Federal Communications Commission. Three hundred senators and representatives of both parties joined to rebuke the Justice Department in a dismaying bleat of bipartisan solidarity. This congressional pressure helped persuade the F.C.C. to resist the Justice Department and approve the merger. But the wounds sustained in the battle by ITT and ABC finally caused them to abandon it.

Again, in 1971, a new crisis brought ITT's political allies into the open. Richard Nixon's Justice Department filed five antitrust suits against conglomerates, three of them against ITT. Congressmen are not normally noted for their scholarship in the field of corporate law, but lo and behold, two dozen members of the House of Representatives began making speeches, inserting learned opinions into the *Congressional Record* and introducing identical pieces of legislation—all aimed at revising or scrapping the laws and policies being used against the conglomerates. Later it was learned that most of these originated in the Washington offices of ITT.

The *modus operandi* was familiar; it had a trial run in Hartford. ITT's takeover of Hartford Fire, as previously mentioned, was first opposed by William Cotter, Connecticut insurance commissioner. He properly vetoed it in conformance with his statutory duty to protect the integrity of insurance operations. But ITT gave no thought to accepting this as the final verdict. It announced a new merger plan and immediately began to mobilize the Connecticut business and political community against the commissioner. The great Geneen began touring the Connecticut bush to whip up local chambers of commerce. There were also private trysts with Connecticut politicos who had leverage with Cotter.

New windfalls were offered Hartford Fire shareholders and officers. False representations were made that ITT would use its resources to strengthen Hartford Fire, when the opposite was the reality. A Democratic clubhouse lawyer was retained. A new hotel and corporate headquarters were dangled before Hartford pols who had a floundering urban-renewal boondoggle on their hands. Finally, the public hearing on ITT's latest plan was stacked with proponents; no one representing the public interest appeared.

Commissioner Cotter's instinct was to stand his ground. He called on Ralph Nader for help, telling him that no one had come forward to plead the public case, that tremendous pressure was flooding in on him from both the business and political communities of Connecticut, and that his staff was not up to the task of combating mighty ITT on the financial and fiduciary impact of the merger. He said ITT was also having him investigated (as General Motors had once investigated Nader). Nader and his brilliant associate Reuben Robertson answered the call and provided the requested data.

But though Nader and Robertson would continue the battle, Cotter abandoned it. He was, after all, young and ambitious, getting ready to run for Congress and hence vulnerable to local pressures. He complained that on a typical afternoon he would get forty to fifty irate phone calls from area businessmen primed by ITT with visions of bonanza. So he quietly caved in. Now he is firmly ensconced in Congress.

ITT, then, was a habitual offender; it had no conscience about undermining the decisions of regulatory tribunals; whenever it encountered a public body in its path, whether a state insurance commission or a federal regulatory agency, or even the Justice Department itself, the company's programmatic reaction was a multiple offensive aimed at undermining the tribunal that stood in its way.

In our book, here was a cat that needed a bell tied to it.

The Politics of Justice

Granted that ITT was incorrigibly promiscuous, granted that the omnipotent Justice Department had reversed itself no less mysteriously than the lonely state commissioner, the proof of wrongdoing would be elusive in something as hard to pin down as the effect of influence-peddling on a complex legal decision. Our small staff, with a column to put out seven days a week, cannot invest large blocks of precious time in a single story unless there is a strong cause for suspicion. The Justice Department assembled by Richard Nixon in 1969 fulfilled this requirement.

When law enforcement becomes entangled with party politics and when the party managers are appointed to administer justice, then justice becomes vulnerable to the political fix. For this is the currency that campaign managers use to pay off their obligations to the big contributors and the political wheeler-dealers.

Lyndon Johnson had been scrupulous about not naming his campaign aides to the Justice Department, but of the eight top Nixon appointees, seven were either campaign functionaries or defeated ex-candidates or both. Attorney General John Mitchell was, of course, candidate Nixon's 1968 campaign manager; his legal background had been almost entirely in the narrow field of municipal bonds. Mitchell's assistant, Kevin Phillips, had been the Nixon campaign expert on how to appeal to ethnic groups; by his own admission, he had no interest in the law except as a political stepping stone. Deputy Attorney General Richard Kleindienst was a chronic campaigner who had won battle stars as field director of the Goldwater campaign in 1964 and, four years later, of the Nixon campaign; he had also been an unsuccessful candidate for governor of Arizona and a lawyer for the Republican National Committee. Will Wilson, head of the Criminal Division, was an indefatigable Texas office seeker who turned Republican after being badly trounced as a Democrat in races for governor and senator; earlier, he had won election as a judge, but he was so little respected on the bench by the Texas Bar that he was known to lawyers there as "the lay member of the court." Robert Mardian, head of the Internal Security Division, was known not as a legal mind but as a right-wing political ideologue. Jerris Leonard, head of the Civil Rights Division, was another defeated politico, having been routed in a bid for the United States Senate by Wisconsin's Senator Gaylord Nelson. William D. Ruckleshaus, head of the Civil Division, was another political loser, beaten in an Indiana Senate race by incumbent Birch Bayh.

The hazard of populating the Justice Department at its upper levels with ex-campaign managers and wounded political warhorses is described by Warren Christopher, the former Deputy Attorney General under Lyndon Johnson:

Our whole philosophy has been that you have to de-politicalize this operation as much as possible. When the Attorney General was the President's campaign manager, the Deputy Attorney General was a campaign field director and gubernatorial candidate, and three assistant attorneys general recently ran for office, you are politicalizing things, no matter what kind of face you try to put on it. We've avoided people of this sort like the plague. Once they've run for office, even unsuccessfully, they are likely to want to run again. That is, they lost the gal last time, but they are going to get her next chance they have. That creates the danger that the way civil rights, criminal and antitrust suits are handled will be less than pure. Once the Department becomes political, of course, the mission of justice must suffer.

The dedication of the new men to administering justice could be judged by the transience of their tenure. Before the Nixon Administration's first term was over, Mitchell and Mardian had left the Justice Department to manage the next presidential campaign; Phillips quit within a year to set up a campaign-counseling business and become a political analyst and commentator; Wilson exited under a cloud that our column helped create. Ruckleshaus moved to the more politically glamorous Environmental Protection Agency, which specializes in excusing powerful business interests from compliance with the antipollution laws. Of the seven, only Kleindienst and Leonard were left by the spring of 1972, and both of them had been repeatedly accused by subordinates of political manipulations.

It was a Justice Department that, predictably, put politics first. This virus infected every area of responsibility. For transparent reasons, civil rights laws were not enforced or were enforced selectively. As part of an effort to intimidate the news departments the television networks were threatened with an obscure antimonopoly action, while far more conspicuous corporate octopi were left undisturbed. Prosecutions of militant pacifists, such as the Berrigan group, were launched with ferocious fanfare but conducted with such disgusting incompetence that the defendants looked more credible to the juries than the government, as the verdicts showed.

Amnesty from prosecution was routinely accorded to lawbreakers who were either politicians or political fat cats. Among them were the twenty-one G.O.P. finance chairmen for the 1968 campaign who patently violated the reporting provisions of the Corrupt Practices Act; the Maryland contractor whom the U.S. Attorney for Maryland found had entered into a bribery negotiation with several prominent congressmen; Senator Thomas Dodd, whose prosecution for criminal income-tax evasion was vainly requested by the Internal Revenue Service after a two-year field investigation; several corporations, whom low-level federal investigators found had made illegal contributions to members of Congress.

But in the first springtime of the Nixon Justice Department, back in early 1969, talk of politicalization was dismissed as sour grapes from the losers. The exhibit invariably held up to illustrate the legal integrity of the new department was President Nixon's eighth appointee, Richard W. McLaren, head of the Antitrust Division. McLaren was neither a political fund-raiser nor a frustrated candidate, but a lawyer of excellent reputation who specialized in antitrust work. He had an upright look and demeanor about him. Indeed, McLaren made impressive statements about the evils of economic concentration, and he followed through by filing antitrust suits against great conglomerates such as Ling-Temco-Vought and ITT.

The presence of Snow White among the seven dwarfs demanded an explanation, and there were several going the rounds.

Theory No. 1 was that President Nixon's roots were in Main Street, not Wall Street; that while he had his particular sugar daddies, he was not indebted to big business as a class, particularly the Eastern business establishment. It was said that before joining the Administration, McLaren had extracted two pledges from Nixon and Mitchell—that they would support his anticonglomerate stand and that he would be free of political interference. Proponents of this theory cited a speech Mitchell made which parroted McLaren's views:

The danger that super concentration poses to our economic, political and social structure cannot be overestimated . . . The Department of Justice may very well oppose any merger among the top 200 manufacturing firms . . . or by one of the top 200 manufacturing firms with any leading producer in any concentrated industry.

Theory No. 2 was that McLaren was a decoy set up to divert attention from the otherwise sinister cast of the department. Its adherents recalled that during Mr. Nixon's "great comeback," when a new image was being fashioned for the 1968 campaign, he surrounded himself with impressive, young intellectuals who contrasted with his entourage of the old Murray Chotiner era. The bright new people were occasionally put through trots in the yard before the press, and they helped to launch a new Nixon of broader gauge, deeper thought, and loftier vision. But the showcase thinkers never got through to the war room, where the old California gang still held sway. They were regularly intercepted by John Mitchell, a process later detailed by one of the decoys, Richard Whalen, in his book, *Catch the Falling Flag*.

Theory No. 3 was that Mitchell & Co. could afford to have a Snow White on the premises because it really didn't matter what McLaren said or did; whenever necessary, he could be turned off by the political men in the department. Of all the men who headed the divisions of the Justice Department, only McLaren could not seek court orders to restrain or temporarily enjoin illegal acts. The others could act on their own authority; McLaren needed the approval of the Attorney General. So why not let him putter away with his theories?

Theory No. 4 was that Nixon and Mitchell were using McLaren to go after that segment of Big Business that had never been really a part of the Republican establishment. This theory has been described by Columnist Milton Viorst:

There is, generally speaking, Democratic business and Republican business—and the interests of the two are often in conflict. There was such conflict in the last decade when the big conglomerate builders—the Ben Heinemans of Northwest Industries and the James Lings of Ling-Temco-Vought, for instance—were challenging the entrenched economic power of the "blue chip" corporations like steel and railroads. The conglomerate builders were new-money parvenues, free-wheelers and usually Democrats. The commercial and industrial establishment was old-money, aristocratic and almost invariably Republican. The two had little in common . . .

So it was not inconsistent that President Nixon—though patently pro-business—chose as his antitrust chief a distinguished lawyer named Richard McLaren who advocated an all-out attack on conglomerate power.

A variant of Theory No. 4 held that McLaren was being used for the old Washington game of "rainmaking." Under the accepted rules of rainmaking, the government threatens action against a certain practice or group without really planning to follow all the way through. The wrongdoers then come forward with a campaign contribution. If these belated supporters have been Democratic contributors in the past, not only have you found a new friend, you have cost the enemy an old supporter.

Whether McLaren would turn out to be the bold champion of vigorous antitrust action or the dupe of politically motivated men would have to wait upon events. The record of the Justice Department, meanwhile, was building slowly.

When Attorney General Mitchell and his team took office in January 1969, they inherited an antitrust action against the El Paso Natural Gas Company. El Paso's West Coast gas monopoly had been declared in violation of the antitrust laws, and the Justice Department was in the midst of an action seeking a tough divestiture order from the Supreme Court. To Justice Department watchers this would be an early test of the director of the new leadership. Would they follow through on the divestiture action their predecessors had initiated, or would they adopt a softer line?

It happened that El Paso was a client of the former Mitchell law firm (Nixon, Rose, Mudge, Guthrie, Alexander and Mitchell). Mitchell, therefore, "disqualified" himself from participation and put Kleindienst in charge of the case. The substitute quarterback knew what play to call. Six days after the Administration took office, the Justice Department withdrew its support from the action before the Supreme Court and went over to the other side, now joining El Paso in opposition to a new divestiture order. But a private citizen, California's former Attorney General William Bennett, persevered in bringing the action before the high court. The Court upheld him and ruled in favor of the proposition the new Justice Department had abandoned.

Later in 1969 McLaren testified on Capitol Hill against a bill that would permit joint newspaper operations in twenty-two cities to fix prices, pool profits, and allocate markets, in violation of existing antitrust law. He spoke for the Nixon Administration, he said. But then Richard Berlin, head of the Hearst Corporation, visited President Nixon, and suddenly the Administration was marching down the hill. Through the Commerce Department the President endorsed the bill McLaren had testified against, and it became law.

Soon after, McLaren requested Mitchell's permission to seek a preliminary injunction against a merger between ITT and Automatic Canteen Corporation, the leading manufacturer of vending machines. It happened that ITT, through its Continental Baking subsidiary, was a client of the former Mitchell law firm, so Mitchell "disqualified" himself and put Kleindienst in charge of the case, and he refused to permit McLaren to file the complaint. McLaren later was permitted to file suit against the merger, but only after it had been consummated—a circumstance which disadvantaged McLaren and left ITT in possession of Canteen Corporation during the years of litigation.

In 1970 McLaren asked Mitchell for permission to intervene against the merger of Warner-Lambert with Parke-Davis, two giants of the drug industry. It happened that Warner-Lambert was a client of the former Mitchell law firm, so Mitchell "disqualified" himself and put Kleindienst in charge of the case. Kleindienst refused permission, and the merger went forward undisturbed.

In 1971 McLaren asked Mitchell's permission to intervene against a merger of the fourth largest American steel firm (National) with the eleventh largest (Granite City). They wanted to form a new firm that would be the third largest. It happened that neither National nor Granite City was a client of the former Mitchell firm, so Mitchell did not disqualify himself. He handled the case personally, allowing the merger to go through.

In 1972 McLaren was preparing to go before the Supreme Court to oppose three ITT mergers, the biggest antitrust case in history. It happened that ITT was a client of the former Mitchell law firm, so Mitchell "disqualified" himself and put Kleindienst in charge of the case. But we're getting ahead of our story.

The Quixotic Crusade

Seen against the backdrop of ITT's lobbying prowess and the Justice Department's irresolution in enforcing the law, the doggedness of Richard McLaren's campaign against the largest merger in history seemed, at the beginning of 1972, like some death-defying marvel that confounded the probabilities. Within months, the anti-ITT suit would likely be heard by the Supreme Court, and even the ITT lawyers expected McLaren to win. As he teetered but ever righted himself on the trembling high wire, keeping his balance against the unseen push and pull of mighty interests, inching his way forward the few more yards to his goal, all the false starts of the past, all the locker-room theories about decoys and rain-making, were forgotten. Who could do other than applaud?

From almost the day McLaren assumed office in 1969, it had been foreordained that ITT would make or break his career in the department. He had begun by declaring war on a merger wave that had caused a hundred and ten of the five hundred leading industrial corporations to disappear via merger in the previous six years. As McLaren took office, fifty corporations controlled one-third of all the manufacturing in the United States. He issued a public warning against any merger among the top two hundred firms, or between any of the top two hundred manufacturing firms and any "leading producer" in a concentrated industry. Scarcely had he stated this policy than the board of directors of ITT, the ninth largest industrial firm, authorized acquisition of twenty-two domestic and eleven foreign corporations.

Among them were Hartford Fire, second among fire insurers; Automatic Canteen, first in the vending-machine industry; and Grinnell, first in the sprinkler fire-prevention field. ITT already controlled Continental Baking, the largest baking company in the United States; Levitt, the leading residential construction firm; and Sheraton, one of the two largest hotel chains in America.

A corporation that controlled all these diverse but complementary firms was in a position to destroy lawful competition in a hundred ways through what is known as reciprocity. The hotels could discriminate in favor of ITT-owned food products, rental cars, and vending machines; the thousands of ITT employees regularly traveling on company business could be directed to Sheraton hotels; the homebuilders could give the inside tract to ITT-owned insurance companies (in 1968, 83 percent of Levitt home buyers purchased credit life insurance through ITT's life insurance outlets); the great fire insurer and the great fire prevention equipment manufacturer could work together for common profits; the ITT-owned insurance and finance companies represented sources of capital for ITT enterprises that might not be equally available to competitors. Moreover, this sort of inside advantage would force other companies to seek similar alliances in self-defense. The possibilities for the spread of this distortion of competition throughout the American business structure were unlimited. McLaren on the high wire filed three separate suits against ITT's proposed mergers with Hartford Fire, Canteen, and Grinnell.

There is a rather depressing legal tradition surrounding antitrust suits. Invariably, the government loses in the lower courts. The first defeat comes when the government goes before a district judge seeking a preliminary injunction to prevent the merger from occurring in the first place. The big business bloc in Congress has fixed it so that the Justice Department cannot appeal these initial defeats; it must wait until the merger is consummated before filing suit in the same court to break it up. This suit, involving the same issue before the same court, naturally loses again. But this time the government can appeal directly to the Supreme Court, and just as invariably, the government wins on appeal. The uniformity of these Supreme Court victories reversing lower-court defeats suggests something very wrong with the federal district courts of this nation.

Why do the lower judges remain so oblivious to the Supreme Court dictum? Our view is that federal district judges are usually chosen not for their legal brilliance and integrity but, on the contrary, for their past services to the political machines and allied business interests that select federal judges. When the federal trust busters go into a community like Hartford to undo a merger, they are usually tackling what looks like a bonanza for local businessmen and their client politicians. The biases and interests of these groups are reflected by the men they have made into judges, so much so that they ignore the uniform policy of the Supreme Court.

A more charitable explanation, but one not essentially different, has been given by the distinguished legal authority on antitrust matters Professor Harlan M. Blake of Columbia University:

. . . District court judges are accustomed to dealing in the "hard" facts of mail fraud, drug distribution, damage claims, and the like. They find it difficult to "find" so nebulous a fact as that a merger causes a "probability of injury to competition," the criterion of the merger law. The Supreme Court, more attuned to questions of public policy, has no such difficulties. Furthermore, lawyers representing defendant corporations in the trial court are the best in the locality, and even in the country, often well known to and respected by local judges. Frequently, in terms of sheer manpower they outnumber the antitrust staff many times. Too, district court judges, often chosen from among successful local attorneys, are likely to share a similarity of outlook on business matters with their former colleagues.*

Therefore, when McLaren lost the first round of all three of his anti-merger actions against ITT, it was con-

* *Harper's* magazine, June 1972.

sidered par for the course. In each case he readied appeals to the Supreme Court, where his prospects for victory were bright. As the *Wall Street Journal* has pointed out:

In the last two decades, the government has never lost an antitrust case in the Supreme Court. Every appealed district court opinion in favor of a defendant has been reversed, and every appealed opinion in favor of the government has been affirmed.

· ITT was as apprehensive as McLaren was confident —so much so that in August 1970, Harold Geneen made an expedition to Washington and toured the backrooms, from the White House to the Justice Department, to bring pressure on McLaren to settle. Geneen had a "friendly session," according to an internal ITT memo, with the Attorney General on August 4. Three days later, ITT's Edward Gerrity, who had served with Spiro Agnew in the 10th Armored Division during World War II, wrote to his old military buddy about ITT's antitrust troubles. In the meantime, in the midst of its string of lower-court victories, ITT offered a settlement. It was communicated to McLaren by Attorney Ephraim Jacobs. Under its terms, the government would drop its three antitrust suits and ITT could keep Hartford Fire. In return, ITT would give up Canteen, part of Grinnell, all domestic operations of ITT-Levitt, and three ITT-owned insurance companies (ITT-Life of New York, ITT-Midwestern Life and ITT-Hamilton Life). Moreover, ITT would agree to prohibitions against the use of reciprocity devices in the future.

The heart of this settlement offer was that it would permit ITT to keep Hartford Fire. ITT had business projections for 1971 showing that Hartford Fire would provide 25 percent of ITT's total earnings in that year, a ratio that was likely to rise in future years. Profits from ITT's other subsidiaries seemed to be stretched as far as they could go. To maintain its earnings at 11 percent and its Class A borrowing power—both essential to continued expansion—ITT had to retain Hartford Fire.

But it was McLaren's stated purpose to halt the expansive power of ITT that Hartford Fire was fueling. And so he rejected Ephraim Jacobs' offer. "We discussed the Jacobs proposal with the staff, and we agreed to reject it," McLaren later explained. "I called Mr. Jacobs and told him of this and told him I could see *no reason for any such settlement as they had proposed.*"

Through the winter and into the spring, McLaren hewed to his course; in his public statements, he continually sounded the anticonglomerate tocsin, predicting that his ITT cases could well break new legal ground for the application of the Clayton Antitrust Act. But in April he fell silent on the great anti-merger crusade. Sherlock Holmes, had he been with us, might have seen a tell-tale clue in that silence, as he did in the case of the dog that didn't bark. The all-quiet at the Justice Department coincided with the ITT visit in April to the White House, where Geneen conferred with Pete Peterson, a presidential aide who later became Secretary of Commerce. The appointment was arranged, interestingly, by the then Secretary of the Treasury John Connally, whose former law firm had collected fees from ITT before Connally joined the Cabinet. Suddenly, on July 31, the Justice Department announced it had dropped its suits and settled out of court. McLaren had fallen off the high wire.

Had we known then about the Jacobs offer, the settlement would have aroused an immediate furor because the terms announced now were almost identical with those which, only eight months before, Ephraim Jacobs had proposed and Richard McLaren had scornfully rejected.

Like the Jacobs offer, the final settlement provided that the Justice Department would drop its three suits and that ITT would keep Hartford Fire. Like the Jacobs offer, the final settlement called for ITT divesting itself of Canteen Corporation, part of Grinnell, and Levitt. Like the Jacobs offer, there were restrictions on reciprocity and on the role Hartford Fire could play in ITT operations. Both versions permitted ITT to retain the profits from its illegal activities of previous years and to make the required divestitures in ways that, as Geneen announced, "will require the *reinvestment*—not loss—of certain of our earnings and assets into other areas of activity. . . We are confident of our ability to sell these assets and reinvest the proceeds advantageously."

There were differences, but they tended to cancel each other out. The Levitt divestiture was strengthened to include foreign holdings, but weakened to permit ITT to retain the most attractive of Levitt's domestic projects in terms of future profits, the Florida Palm Coast Development. ITT agreed to divest Avis Rent-a-Car, which was not part of the Jacobs offer, but was permitted to retain Midwestern Life, which was. The major difference was a provision in the final settlement that for the next ten years ITT would have to get Justice Department approval for giant acquisitions. But as Ralph Nader pointed out, the provision would likely prove a dead letter—in the tradition of most federal regulatory oversight—because the standards surrounding this approval were nebulous and the regulatory resources of the Justice Department nonexistent. Consider, too, as antitrust experts have, the possibility that ITT, anticipating a mortal battle over Hartford Fire, acquired Canteen and Grinnell mainly for the plea-bargaining purpose of surrendering them later in a "compromise settlement."

But even without such speculations, even without knowledge of the recent Jacobs offer, the cave-in by the Justice Department was transparent even to pro-business observers such as *Business Week,* which, in an editorial entitled "The Antitrusters Cop Out," said:

The sudden settlement last weekend of the government's package of antitrust cases against International Telephone and Telgraph Corporation is a singularly unsatisfying end to an important episode in government-business relations.

The ITT cases were promoted by the Nixon Administration as an attempt to establish a clear judicial definition of the limits on corporate growth in a modern society. By suddenly agreeing to accept the settlement, the government antitrusters have thrown away the chance to do that . . .

If McLaren and his lawyers feel that the mushroom growth of the conglomerate corporations threatens the U.S. economy and infringes the antitrust laws, then it is their duty to push the point with the courts until the law is esablished beyond question. It is not fair either to the companies involved or to the public to keep on brandishing the antitrust gun without ever proving that it really is loaded.

McLaren did not explain this stunning reversal of policy, or why his anticonglomerate speeches had stopped. Justice Department press releases, claiming victory, treated the matter tersely. The files that might have explained it were not available to the press or public. We were in the position the government always likes to have us in: we had to take their word for it. Government has grown very knowing about the press—about its limited resources, its short attention span, its difficulty in portraying complicated matters like corporate litigation, its inability to function when information is cut off.

And so the matter passed—with only unanswered questions to vaguely tempt our interest on a quiet day. McLaren's anticonglomerate crusade, like a block of cement heaved over the Fourteenth Street Bridge, had vanished out of sight.

The Lucky City

An occasional putrefying remnant bubbled up from below now and again to pother the calm surface, marking the spot where McLaren's brave crusade had disappeared.

In September it became known that ITT-Sheraton had put up the financial backing which earlier in the summer had made it possible for San Diego to be selected as the site of the 1972 Republican National Convention. The ITT pledge of $400,000 (partially refundable if local contributions reached a certain level) mercifully ended a presidential and civic embarrassment that during the spring had brought many a guffaw from the irreverent. At the time, there were hints that President Nixon wanted to stage his renomination rites in San Diego, a city that had been witness to his early struggles and triumphs, and had historically given him a higher vote than any other comparable metropolis. But the burghers of San Diego were oblivious to the honor President Nixon held out; the city fathers voted against even submitting a bid for the convention.

Presidential embraces, however, are not that easily eluded. The final date for bids was postponed to give San Diego another chance. The requirement for hotel rooms was trimmed from eighteen thousand to twelve thousand, to put it within San Diego's range. The required cash contribution by the host city was pared to fit San Diego's pocketbook. When the city still failed to react positively and a presidential humiliation loomed, a small army of White House and G.O.P. aides ganged up on the town. Bob Finch and Bill Timmons of the White House, G.O.P. Chairman Robert Dole, Patricia Reilly Hitt, and others began pressing California officials to influence San Diego. But still the locals balked. They didn't want their placid city to be disrupted by rowdy delegates and camp followers, nor their respectable tourist trade displaced by "brown baggers," a phrase Mayor Frank Curran defined as people who sleep in their cars and live on sandwiches. San Diego businessmen failed to come forward with the cash guarantee, and the City Council saw fit to appease popular sentiment by voting that no tax dollars could be used for the convention.

But rejection only heightened the President's ardor, a characteristic that throughout his life had proved the secret of his success. On June 1, San Diego's Washington representative William Harrington, telephoned City Manager Walter Hahn to relay instructions from Timmons and Dole on just how the city's bid should be submitted. On June 3, the harassed Hahn received an even more ominous message from Harrington: "I have just received word from the White House that Bob Finch and possibly Bill Timmons are en route to San Diego to confer with city officials. The President has said that he wants the convention in San Diego. It appears that it will be here."

The White House tone of command was made possible by an offer from Harold Geneen to fill the financial void left by San Diego's business community. For on that very day, area Congressman Bob Wilson revealed to the convention planners that he had lined up a $400,000 pledge. He did not, however, identify the donor. A few recalcitrant councilmen complained of being manipulated by outsiders, but on June 29 the city submitted a bid. Three weeks later San Diego was formally designated as the convention city. Not only the President's wish but his dignity was thus salvaged.

Because ITT's convention role was as yet secret, no connection was made when eight days after the selection of San Diego, the Justice Department announced the dropping of its suits against ITT. But the news would out, and in the meantime other fragments were surfacing.

In August Richard Dudman had reported in the *St. Louis Post-Dispatch* that ITT officers were under investigation for selling their ITT stock in the weeks just before the settlement was announced.

In September Reuben Robertson, Ralph Nader's associate, protested to McLaren over being denied information about the ITT settlement. "We wish to object most strongly to the veil of secrecy that has been drawn over the Antitrust Division since announcement of the decree, which has made full evaulation of the settlement . . . a virtual impossibility. There is no way to ascertain what considerations may have gone into the negotiations unless access is provided to the records of negotiations or to the government's evidence, all of which has been denied. These are historical records and we believe that there is not justification for secrecy as to their contents."

In November Robert Walters, a top investigative reporter for the *Washington Evening Star,* wrote an article which publicly raised the question of a connection between the legal settlement and the convention pledge. ITT responded with an ambiguous statement denying Congressman Wilson's version of a $400,000 pledge and saying it had pledged only $100,000 as a business investment, and expected to get part of that back. There was another reaction. The Walters story prompted Democratic National Chairman Lawrence O'Brien to ask in a letter to Attorney General John Mitchell: "Are you able, through a candid exposition of all the facts, to allay any suspicion that there is a connection between ITT's sudden largesse to the Republican Party and the nearly simultaneous out-of-court settlement of one of the biggest merger cases in corporate history—to ITT's benefit?"

The letter was answered by Kleindienst who claimed that he and Mitchell had no knowledge of the ITT gift and that anyway the ITT settlement had been "handled and negotiated exclusively" by McLaren. The ignorance claimed for Mitchell, who was rightly known for his tight control over both the Justice Department and G.O.P. political affairs, seemed a bit beyond belief.

In December another mysterious irregularity revived fleeting thoughts of the all but forgotten settlement. It was learned that McLaren had resigned; he had been instantaneously confirmed as a federal judge for northern Illinois and had gone off to Europe on a junket. It seemed an undistinguished end for so eminent a government figure and so heralded a career. Moreover, it was accomplished with suspicious haste and privacy. Normally, the process of judicial approval by the Senate— clearance by the two home-state senators, favorable examination by the Senate Judiciary Committee, and final confirmation by the entire Senate—takes months. But for McLaren, the entire confirmation process was compressed into four hours. At noon on December 2, 1971, the nomination was sent to the Senate from the White House, hearings were waived, key approvals were gotten by telephone, and by four o'clock in the afternoon McLaren was a judge, without public notice of any kind. To accomplish this, key senators were lied to, according to Senator Adlai Stevenson, III.

As an Illinois senator, his approval was indispensable. He has since described how it was obtained:

I was told at the time that the district court in Chicago faced a backlog of cases—and that Judge Hoffman was requesting immediate senior (part-time) status. The Congress, I was told, would soon recess for Christmas, and so immediate action on the nomination was necessary.

I now find that there was no backlog of cases and that Judge Hoffman did not want immediate senior status. I do not know the real reason for McLaren's hasty departure from the Justice Department.

As 1971 drew to a close, only some unanswered questions kept the door from closing entirely on the ITT matter, questions we tried to keep alive in our previously mentioned column of December 9. Why was the Justice Department hiding the record? Was there any connection between the ITT contribution and the ITT settlement? Why the unexplained contradiction between ITT's version of its pledge and the G.O.P. version? Had ITT executives been tipped off on the settlement terms weeks before the announcement and did they profiteer from this inside information by trading their own stock? Did McLaren's resignation have anything to do with disillusionment over the collapse of his anticonglomerate campaign? Was the hustled confirmation designed to foreclose the normal hearing that might have revived questions about the ITT settlement?

But news stories are generated by answers, not questions. With the fuel of vital information cut off by the government and the conglomerate, the tiny flame of interest flickered and went out. By February 1972, so forgotten was the ITT case that Richard Kleindienst, nominated to suceed John Mitchell as Attorney General after Mitchell formally resumed command of the President's reelection campaign, sailed through confirmation hearings without an unfriendly question being asked and emerged with a unanimous vote.

Then, in late February, a document that would answer the nagging questions came into our hands.

The Lady Is a Lobbyist

Whenever a reporter writes the history of an exposé, he is invariably hobbled by his duty to protect sources. Concealing a source goes far beyond hiding his name or other obvious data that would identify him. The government agencies and corporate empires I write about maintain sophisticated intelligence and counterintelligence systems; a seemingly harmless detail, like the approximate time or place a tip was received, or even the medium through which it was passed, might enable them to identify the source or at least to narrow their list of suspects. In order to guard against innocent slips, I do not reveal even to my colleagues on the column the sources or circumstances through which I receive information, and I do not require them to reveal such things to me. Suffice it to say, then, that at a certain point in time the column had developed two sources within ITT, that certain verbal information was passed along with the promise that I would receive two dozen supporting documents. I am able to say that on February 22 I received what was to become famous as the Dita Beard Memorandum.

The memo read as follows:

PERSONAL AND CONFIDENTIAL

WASHINGTON OFFICE

1707 L Street, N. W.
Washington, D.C. 20038
Tel. (202) 296-6000

Date: June 25, 1971

To: W. R. Merriam
From: D. D. Beard
Subject: San Diego Convention

I just had a long talk with EJG. I'm so sorry that we got that call from the White House. I thought you and I had agreed very thoroughly that under no circumstances would anyone in this office discuss with anyone our participation in the Convention, including me. Other than permitting John Mitchell, Ed Reinecke, Bob Haldeman and Nixon (besides Wilson, of course) *no one* has known from whom that 400 thousand commitment had come. You can't imagine how many queries I've had from "friends" about this situation and I have in each and every case denied knowledge of any kind. It would be wise for all of us here to continue to do that, regardless of from whom any questions come: White House or whoever. John Mitchell has certainly kept it on the higher level only, we should be able to do the same.

I was afraid the discussion about the three hundred/four hundred thousand commitment would come up soon. If you remember, I suggested that we all stay out of that, other than the fact that I told you I had heard Hal up the original amount.

Now I understand from Ned that both he and you are upset about the decision to make it four hundred in *services*. Believe me, this is not what Hal said. Just after I talked with Ned, Wilson called me, to report on his meeting with Hal. Hal at no time told Wilson that our donation would be in services ONLY. In fact, quite the contrary. There would be very little cash involved, but certainly some. I am convinced, because of several conversations with Louie re Mitchell, that our noble commitment has gone a long way toward our negotiations on the mergers eventually coming out as Hal wants them. Certainly the President has told Mitchell to see that things are worked out fairly. It is still only McLaren's mickey-mouse we are suffering.

We all know Hal and his big mouth! But this is one time he cannot tell you and Ned one thing and Wilson (and me) another!

I hope, dear Bill, that all of this can be reconciled—between Hal and Wilson—if all of us in this office remain totally ignorant of any commitment ITT has made to anyone. If it gets too much publicity, you can believe our negotiations with Justice will wind up shot down. Mitchell is definitely helping us, but cannot let it be known. Please destroy this, huh?

Despite the abbreviations, first names, and inside allusions, this remarkable document—out of the mouth of ITT's lobbyist-in-chief—answered in a flash the very questions we had vainly pursued for months. According to Dita Beard: McLaren's superiors at Justice and the White House had decided in the spring of 1971 to restrain his anti-ITT zeal; the $400,000 commitment was a contributing factor; Mitchell was fully informed of ITT's gift and was playing a pro-ITT role in settling the case; the identity of the phantom donor was kept secret for months because "if it gets too much publicity you can believe our negotiations with Justice will wind up shot down"; the confusion as to just what Geneen had promised was occasioned by his attempt to alter the original understanding; inside information about the forthcoming settlement was so widespread among ITT officials at the time the stock selling began that Mrs. Beard had to protest loose talk. Little wonder that McLaren suddenly abandoned his three-year dream and resigned while he could still at least be a judge, or that his confirmation was muscled through without any opportunity for an examination of his record on the ITT cases.

Important as it was, the Beard memorandum was only a springboard to the story we were after. I knew it to be authentic because of the circumstances under which I had obtained it, but since I could never reveal those circumstances it would have to be authenticated by other, demonstrable means. For one thing, Mrs. Beard would have to be inveigled into acknowledging the memo as genuine. Then, everyone named in it who would talk to us would have to be interviewed. And all the leads thus developed would have to be run down and checked out.

Our initial approach would probably make or break the story. Should we go to Dita Beard first and risk precipitating an immediate denial? Or should we try to encircle her by first seeking corroboration from others at ITT, at the risk of touching off a trip wire that would alert the entire ITT organization and assure that Dita would be forewarned and waiting for us, probably with a canned alibi?

Such questions required some calculations about what kind of a person Dita Beard was, and the type of immediate environment she operated in. At the outset, I knew little more about Mrs. Beard than that she was the sole registered lobbyist in Washington for the world's largest conglomerate, and that no less an authority than *Fortune* magazine regarded her as one of Washington's most influential corporate representatives. But a little excavating—simplified by Dita's habit of late-afternoon tippling and storytelling at a Republican hangout called the Capital City Club—fleshed out the picture.

Dita Davis Beard turned out to be an old Washingtonian, the daughter of an amateur opera singer and an Army general of some social standing. Her father, a rollicker and a sportsman, raised her like a boy on a Montana range, and she seems to have always had in her a frisky touch of the wild jackass. But at twenty-one, she bowed to Washington socialites as a debutante, with all the usual society-page flummery about her natural charm and her love of tennis, Bach, dancing, Chanel No. 5 perfume and so forth. A photograph of her taken in 1939 hints at the conflict-torn personality that was to evolve. Decked out like the conventional belle of the times, she has a face with a determined and rather prominent chin, sensual eyes and mouth, and an expression of mocking humor that belies the dainty, artificial flower in the pompadoured hair.

In any event, she bloomed brightly for her season of balls and parties. Tall, shapely, and gamesome, fond of liquor, sea voyages, and liaisons, she kept many a swain on a string and would later boast of having betrothed herself to three of them at the same time. Her own descriptions of her wartime service as a Red Cross girl could have come out of *M.A.S.H.* But reality has a way of setting in, and by the time she was forty the calliope had fallen still and she was alone with two broken marriages behind her and five children to care for.

She turned up as a campaign aide at Nixon headquarters during the 1960 presidential race. This experience, combined with an earlier one as a secretary on Capitol Hill, must have taught her something about the tainted relations between politicians and corporations, for when she moved to ITT's new Washington office in 1961 she immediately shone as a natural at congressional relations. Agile and energetic, she proved adept at plying cooperative politicians with entertainment, company planes, speaking fees, financial contributions and the rest of the standard paraphernalia without which the typical congressman cannot seem to exist. She was soon making $30,000 a year in salary, plus a $15,000 bonus and a $3,000-a-month expense account. According to the reports we received, she reveled in besting the men around her at their own games, not only at office skulduggery but at all the male devices for escape and time-wasting—whisky drinking, cursing, hunting, riding, shooting, snowmobileing, card playing and the like. So far, what we had was not worth much—a portrait of the meretricious triviality that passes for success in the tinsel zone where business meets politics.

But among this chaff was an occasional kernel of investigative grain. Dita's rapid rise at ITT had alarmed her nominal superiors. She soon had an office as big as her boss's, a matter which in corporate circles is freighted with ulcer-bearing significance. She traveled hither and yon without bothering to get higher approval. She quickly became a favorite of Geneen's; that impatient tycoon was said to be impressed with her unobsequious bluntness and her gruff faculty for instantly getting down to brass tacks. She rose so high in his favor that she could obtain an audience with him whenever she asked. When her projects were being frustrated by those above her, she would simply go over their heads.

Insensitive to the consternation this caused, she compounded it by making no secret of her contempt for her immediate bosses, such as the dignified Vice President William R. Merriam, whom Dita was wont to call "that stupid shit Merriam." Other evidences of the Beard candor were abroad in Washington. This particular senator was "a little bum"; that regulatory commissioner was "a mother"; even the imperial Geneen was not spared gravel-voiced imputations that he was not above welshing on an agreement or playing both sides of the street. There was intelligence to the effect that in 1970, while Dita was ill, the vice presidents who stood between her and

Geneen, envious and fearful over being upstaged and perhaps soon displaced, had conspired to get her fired. But Geneen, according to the report, would have none of it.

And so the seeds of intraoffice division were here—a woman who regards herself as superior to the men around her, and who occasionally proves it by trying, aggressively and recklessly, to push ahead of courtiers who are mediocre but skilled at the serpentine game of bureaucratic survival. I delight in the news of disaffection in high, walled-in places, the way a corporate lobbyist brightens at learning of a free-spending senator who has fallen into debt.

Informants who reported to us on how Dita's intimates appraised her used such phrases as "highly emotional," "strong-willed," "fiercely independent," and "can't stand lies." If so, she was in the wrong business, a buffalo loose in a glass factory. There were other phrases that could be significant—"Mother Beard," "a generous heart," "a sympathetic shoulder to cry on." It was a fact that she had raised and educated five children by herself, without financial assistance from her ex-husbands. And a fine, close-knit family it was, by all accounts. To be sure, one daughter worked at the Finance Division of the Republican National Committee, but all the others seemed to be engaged in legitimate pursuits.

Apparently, beneath her boozy exterior, Mrs. Beard possessed elements of courage, pride, candor, and generosity of spirit—qualities that do not jibe with the security requirements of corporate lobbying. I kept returning to such phrases as "can't stand lies" and "tells the truth even when it hurts." Should we confront her with her own memo her initial instinct might be to tell us the truth, whether out of honesty or that sort of braggadocio that refuses to slink and hide, hoping to muddle through in a way that would salvage her pride as well as her job.

Or, we could assume that her standard of truth was merely a "private" thing—for friends and family only —and that she wouldn't hesitate to lie to Jack Anderson about a business matter that could damage her or her company. Even so, she might still be vulnerable to the right kind of interview. From what I could find out, she was not knowledgeable about the press and avoided it like the plague. One proof of this was her anonymity. Every day the women's pages are full of stories about the inane doings of empty-headed, inconsequential women, but Dita Beard, an important and colorful figure on the Washington scene for twelve years, was unknown outside the circle of politicians and businessmen she was in cahoots with. When *Fortune* magazine did its 1967 article on Washington's top lobbyists, she resisted inclusion and in the end gave only minimal cooperation.

There was wisdom in her attitude, for lobbying is a perverse plant that thrives best in darkness; but it is the kind of wisdom that is likely to leave one ignorant of the finer points of journalism. There was only one tactic she could pursue that would be a real obstacle to us: To deny authorship of the memo, to claim it was a fake. The amateur at trying to deceive a reporter—confronted with one of her own memos in black and white—would likely contrive an explanation to show that the memo was really innocent, that it didn't mean what it seemed to mean. But however ingenious such an explanation might be, the very making of it would give the game away and provide us with the *sine qua non* of our exposé—confirmation that whatever the memo meant, she had in fact written it.

In any case, her first reaction—before she could be surrounded by all the paid obfuscators sure to be promptly mobilized by the company—would be crucial. Possibilities of reactions both glorying and mawkish opened up. Supposing she told the whole truth, spiced with her favorite four-letter words, about how she got her company off the government hook! Or would we see instead an abject middle-aged woman, challenged in the public spotlight to live up to the bluntness she had espoused, cowed into swallowing her words for fear of losing her place in life? As a witness to not a few such dilemmas, I inclined to the latter prediction. It is one thing to be brassy and candid on the barstool at the

Capital City Club and quite another on the witness stand. But in our business, we hope for the best.

One more preliminary question remained: Who on our staff would have the best chance of creeping up on Dita Beard's blind side and getting the admissions we needed? Much would depend on just how she was approached. I talked the matter over with Opal, my counselor during sixteen years filled with ticklish situations. We agreed that if I, the monster, went personally to Mrs. Beard's office, she would be all hostility and there would be no hope for the kind of dialogue I wanted. What was needed was an easy approach, not a three-alarm confrontation.

I have five associates, all excellent newsmen, composing what I believe to be the best news investigative staff in the country. One is Brit Hume, age twenty-nine. Tall and lanky, with unlined, guileless face, refined manners, stylish clothes, and a transparently idealistic and sympathetic nature, he looks more like an acolyte than the hard-nosed investigative reporter he is. Perhaps Brit could disarm Dita's fears, arouse her motherly instincts, and encourage the sly old trooper to believe that here was a callow youth she could con. Opal and I agreed that Brit was the one for Mother Beard.

For the next several days Brit's adventures were the main topic around our shop. There were innumerable discussions over strategy, regular briefings by Brit on his progress, phone calls among us at all hours of the day and night. My associates have wide latitude in doing their job in their own way. There are decisions that only I can make, but there are sources, insights, and advice that all of us chip in. But from the time Opal dropped the Beard memo on Brit Hume's desk, the task of developing the story fell mainly on him.

A reporter in Hume's situation must succeed by his wits. Getting a voluntary admission that unlocks a great scandal—in this case Dita Beard's acknowledgment that her memo was authentic and not a forgery—is almost always a game of bluff. You must pretend to already have the proof you are dying to get, for if your prey senses you are in doubt you will never get it. You must get the answer without even asking the question. It is a game played on the enemy's terrain, so you must tiptoe through an unknown minefield filled with potential gaffes that might at any time explode in your face. Your only advantages are that the other side (1) is sitting on a powder keg far more ruinous than you can imagine and therefore is scared; and (2) does not know the nature of the one fact which, above all others, you are seeking.

Such considerations were much on Brit Hume's mind when, memo in pocket, he waited for Dita Beard at the ITT conference room. He could not ask her to authenticate the memo, for that would reveal his need for her to do so; nor could he announce that he knew it was authentic, challenging her to deny it, for that would be too obvious a ploy. Moreover, the meeting was to be chaperoned by two company public relations men, Bernie Goodrich and Jack Horner, a circumstance that would gravely inhibit deep probing. He would therefore ignore the question of authenticity, as if it were a fact established beyond need of further mention. He would brandish the memo under her nose and count upon his very possession of it to indicate an access to ITT sources that made it futile for her to lie baldly. He would ask only for clarification of various segments of the memo, the answering of which would ipso facto place Dita Beard in the position of either acknowledging or disowning the memo.

Brit's first glimpse of Dita made quite an impression on him, as he recalled later:

. . . after a few minutes, Dita Beard bustled in through a door behind me. She was an astonishing sight. A large woman in her mid-fifties, she had gray hair that showed traces of having once been red or blond, or dyed one of those colors. Her skin was leathery and puffy and she wore no makeup. A paper clip held her horn-rimmed eyeglasses together where one of the hinges had broken. She had on a chartreuse, short-sleeve sweatshirt and a pair of soiled yellow cotton slacks. Her flat, slip-on shoes were battered and dirty. Her voice had an edge of raspiness that might have been the result of the Chesterfield Kings she chain-smoked. The impression she gave, though, was not of a brokendown woman but of middle-aged tomboy. She moved and spoke with self-assurance, and it occurred to me as we shook hands that she must have considerable influence in that office to get away with being dressed as she was in the middle of the week. She reminded me of Tugboat Annie. I liked her.*

Brit said he was there to give her a chance to refute any misleading impressions in a memo of hers that had come into his hands. He said he wanted to give her the opportunity to check it out against other correspondence on the subject so that it could be seen in its proper context. Then, heart pounding but face feigning nonchalance, he withdrew the document from his coat pocket, slowly unfolded it, and slid it down the table in front of her. For a moment she read in funereal silence while the public relations men arched like cats at the approach of a strange and ominous-looking dog. Mrs. Beard's first reaction was to talk *around* the memo, disclaiming its unhappy implications but not disowning the memo itself. On the contrary, she acknowledged that the penciled initial at the top was "my own little 'D.' " Brit was halfway home.

The buoyancy slowly drained out of her as she finished reading her incriminating statements of eight months before. When she raised her face, Brit detected apprehension and resignation there. "All right," she sighed. "What do you want to know about it?"

Brit moved to a seat beside her, and they began going through the document together line by line. His questions were gentle, and he avoided pressing her about the most damaging sentences. As long as Goodrich and Horner were hovering around her, Goodrich kicking her under the table and both spieling the ITT line at every opportunity, nothing was to be gained by trying to back Dita against the wall. That could come later. Besides, Brit was getting exactly what he wanted from the initial interview. Every time Dita Beard identified a set of initials or a first name, every time she explained the context of a paragraph from her memo, she was again confirming the genuineness of the document. At length, Brit departed, giving them a copy of the memo and his assurance that he was not about to rush it into print. They would have plenty of time he said, to check things out carefully with their files and with company officials before he conferred with them again. Our objective was to talk to Dita alone, and to preserve a climate favorable to discussion.

The next night Brit called me at home around nine o'clock. He had just come home and had received a message from our office that Dita Beard had left word she wanted to see him "urgently." Since the hour was late, Brit's intention was to call on her first thing in the morning. But the tone of her message had a ring familiar to me—an intimation of anxiety and perhaps vulnerability that had better be probed before it passed. Brit agreed and called Mrs. Beard to say he'd be over immediately.

Two things happened—one as he entered the Beard residence, the other as he left two hours later—which indicated we were on the right track in our hunch that Dita would feel she could outfox an amiable young man like Hume and take him into camp. She opened the interview with a surprise accusation.

"I know you got this from Jack Gleason," she said. When Brit honestly answered that he had never heard of Jack Gleason, she shot him a suspicious glance, which Brit took to mean, "You can't fool me, boy. I have been around too long to be spun by any comment like that."

And on the way out, after a most lugubrious hour, Mrs. Beard embraced Brit, acting as if she expected him to kiss her goodbye as a son would his mother. But Brit Hume had neither been outfoxed by poses nor muddled by sympathy. During the questioning he had not taken notes, judging that to do so would have inhibited Mrs. Beard. The minute he got home, he typed out the interview while it was fresh in his mind. The next morning I read it in the cold light of day. It gave me everything we could have hoped for.

FEBRUARY 24, 1972.

Memo for record:

I reached Dita Beard at her home tonight after failing to get in touch with her today. She returned my call and left the home phone. She wanted to talk with me in person. I took her address and drove immediately to her home in South Arlington. The address is 2313 South June. I arrived sometime shortly after 10 p.m. She was with her son, Bull, a friend, Walter someone, and her secretary, Beverly someone. We talked in her kitchen. She sipped a drink and chainsmoked Chesterfields at the counter where we sat on wooden slat stools. At first, we just talked generally about how unfortunate it was that she had been with the two ITT press men during our meeting the day before. She went into a long discussion about her life and the difficult time she had which ended with her telling me how she landed a job with ITT in Washington in the early 1960's. She said she has five children, has been married twice, the second time to a Randy Beard, a man she described as alcoholic. She had been drinking and was very emotional. She wore the same clothes as when I had seen her at the ITT offices the day before, a chartreuse sweatshirt and cotton slacks (yellow). She looked weary and as if she had been crying, which she did several times during our conversation. Because she was so upset, I felt it would be unwise to produce a notebook for the discussion.

When we eventually got onto the subject at hand, the memo, she repeatedly promised to tell me the whole truth, but also kept asking me if I wanted to "destroy" her. She told me one of her assignments was to drum up business for the Sheraton Hotel division of ITT. She said the first thought of having the GOP convention in San Diego came during a conversation she had with Ed Reinecke in about January of last year. She said he considered it a possibility and mentioned it to her. She said he later reported on a meeting with John Mitchell on the subject in which Mitchell, told there was a $400,000 commitment to back the convention in S.D., asked, "From Whom." "From Dita Beard," she said Reinecke answered. "Humph," she quoted him as quoting the A.G. as replying.

She explained her memo as an effort to "put some sense into the head of the stupid shit Merriam," or words to that general effect. Her conversation was laced with four-letter words, including "fuck." She said Merriam had brought about much of the unfavorable publicity on the ITT convention arrangements by letting slip a comment at the Metropolitan club to the effect that Geneen had had a conversation with Bob Wilson and the outcome of the anti-trust cases then pending had been assured to go ITT's way. She said the remark had been overheard by Richard Dudman of the St. Louis Post-Dispatch.

She said the first real step toward getting the convention into San Diego came at a Luau dinner at the Half-Moon in San Diego following the ITT annual meeting in the Spring. She said it was May. She said she brought up the subject at dinner in the presence of Geneen, Bill James, head of the Sheraton division, Bob Wilson, the Congressman. She said it was the first any of them beside herself and Reinecke really knew of the idea, except that it had long been known that President Nixon had wanted the convention there. She said that after her conversation with Reinecke earlier she had flown to S.D. and searched the city high and low for hotel space to get an idea if it might be possible to have the convention there. She said Bob Wilson acted in astonishment at the idea because it was news to him. Indeed, she said, he was annoyed by the whole thing a little because he had not been told about it. She said Geneen reacted by saying, get Bill James over and then said something to the effect that ITT would certainly support the convention, underwrite. She repeatedly referred to the cash the company is putting up as "seed money." She also said that when Reinecke had first discussed the matter with her, he had said something to the effect that he felt S.D. could accommodate "this kind of a convention," not something like Miami.

She said the Half-Moon session was the place Geneen made his original offer, but she did say that he later had a phone conversation with Wilson. She said this was what the memo meant when it mentioned "his meeting with Hal."

She explained that the memo was also an effort to straighten Merriam out on the actual terms of the convention offer which he had got confused and mentioned to a guy named Gleason at the White House. She said when she talked to Merriam, he mentioned this to her after my appearance at her office. She said both on the phone and at her home that she believed this guy Gleason was the source of the leak. She said Merriam had told her he didn't remember what he had done with the memo.

Finally, we began to get into the subject of Mitchell. She said the PR man wanted her to tell me that she made the whole thing up. But she said that would be a lie and she wouldn't lie like that. She said when I kept pressing her about it, that she had called Louie Nunn and he couldn't remember any conversation that might have had to do with Mitchell. I kept pressing her. She said things like, "If I tell you the truth, will you use it to destroy me." She was becoming increasingly emotional. I tried, gently, to continue to press. I asked her if there was a way she could tell me the facts and we could keep her name out of it. She shook her head. She was really upset at this point. I recited my surmise about what had occurred. Namely, that the fix, if there was one, took place before the settlement proposal was drafted and before the negotiations began. I said I thought the influence must have come while the matter was still in danger of going to trial.

I finally began to press her to tell me if there had been an agreement of this kind. She was weeping now. She nodded yes. I asked her if it was negotiated by her. Again, a yes nod. With Mitchell? Again, yes, nodding. She was broken down now, her head in her hands and she darted into the bathroom just behind the stool where I sat. I paced the kitchen while she was in there. It was just about 11 o'clock.

When she came out, she again asked if we were going to ruin her. I said I didn't know, that I wouldn't know what we would do until we had the facts. She then told me this story. She was invited, as she had been in the past every year, to go to the Kentucky Derby. This year, her friend Gov. Nunn mentioned that John Mitchell would also be one of his guests at the governor's mansion after the race. She said she mentioned this to E. J. Gerrity the New York Public Relations chief of ITT in a memo. She said before she left, they talked by telephone and Gerrity told her what the company wanted most if she and Mitchell should get onto the subject of the merger cases then in court.

She said that after the derby, she went to the Mansion for a buffet dinner and mentioned that Martha Mitchell was putting it on and she said some unkind things about Mrs. Mitchell. She said this was her first meeting with John Mitchell. She said that as they were going in to get in the buffet line, Mitchell took her arm and took her aside. It was just the three of them then, she said, Mitchell, herself and Gov. Nunn. She said that Mitchell proceeded to give her a scathing, hour-long scolding in the bluntest language for putting the pressure on the Justice Department on the mergers via Capitol Hill and other means instead of coming to see him. She said Mitchell said he had been told she was the "politician" in the company and he had heard much about her long before coming to Washington. She said he knew about all the speeches she had written and gotten delivered by friendly members of Congress. She said Mitchell knew all about her, even asked about son Bull's grades. She said she had gotten speeches delivered in both houses of Congress. She estimated about a dozen. She said Mitchell told her he had gotten a call from Nixon saying "lay-off ITT." Later, she changed this to something, like Nixon saying "make a reasonable settlement." She said Mitchell told her he was sympathetic but that his great problem was McLaren, whom she described as a "shit." She said she did what she could to fight back, but she was overwhelmed by Mitchell's diatribe. She blessed Louis Nunn for staying at her side during the whole thing. Finally, she said she asked him, "Well, do you want to work something out," or words to that effect. She said he replied in the affirmative. She said he said, "What do you want," meaning what companies did ITT wish to retain in the merger case settlement. She said she told him they had to have the Hartford Insurance Company "because of the economy." And she added that they also wanted "part of Grinnell." She said she couldn't remember what else she asked for, but it was exactly what the company got in the settlement.

She said the agreement was reached, actually, as they went through the buffet line and then sat down to eat. She said that Harold Geneen knew nothing of the fix with Mitchell, and that he still does not. I pressed her repeatedly on this, saying I found it hard to believe but she stuck to it all the way. She said this was the only meeting or conversation she has ever had with JM. She said that their discussion had nothing whatever to do with the convention negotiations and later said that her conversation with Reinecke about Mitchell's reaction to the proposed San Diego location came after the Kentucky session. She insisted this was correct, although I pressed her and said it would have seemed more likely Reinecke would have gotten the reaction he got from Mitchell before their meeting.

She said the only other person inside ITT who knew of this at the time was Gerrity. She said she had reached him on vacation prior to her meeting with me at home and that he urged to pull the big sob story about the kids and everything in an effort to talk me out of doing a story. She spoke with great admiration and gratitude of Geneen repeatedly.

She said that after the meeting in her office, she came in the following morning to find that the ITT security men from New York had gotten there first and were destroying all her files. She said they said they feared they might be subpoenaed after our story came out. She said they were destroying them by putting them through a document shredder. She said they even destroyed some of her personal files.

She said the PR types I had seen the day before had told her to get out of town and stop talking to me.

She insisted throughout that the merger fix was entirely a separate matter from the convention deal.

This interview, added to the original memo on June 25, 1971, both of them coming from a high official of a great corporation, constituted in themselves a highly newsworthy and valid story. But we now undertook to strengthen it by finding separate corroboration of the key details.

We tried to obtain interviews with all of the people mentioned by Dita—except President Nixon and his chief of staff, Bob Haldeman, who were out of the country. We knew, of course, we would be questioning what lawyers call "hostile witnesses." We did not expect them to admit having taken part in a felony, but we hoped they would confirm a detail here and there. We were not disappointed.

Congressman Wilson confirmed Dita's version of the time, place, and circumstances in which the $400,000 offer was made by Geneen—on May 12 at the Half Moon Restaurant in San Diego. He also backed up Dita's account that Merriam was confused over the terms of the agreement. Dita had told us this was one reason for her memo. Her other reason for the memo—concern about loose discussion between Merriam and the White House of the ITT commitment—was confirmed by Jack Gleason, who turned out to be an ex-White House aide turned ITT PR man. Gleason told us of conversations on the matter between Merriam and Bill Timmons of the White House which Gleason said had so alarmed Dita that in addition to writing her scornful memo to Merriam, she called Timmons and bawled him out. Records of expenditures by the Republican National Committee, available at the Capitol, showed that the G.O.P. had paid Mrs. Beard's travel expenses to San Diego, apparent proof that party and company were working in tandem on the convention.

Attorney General John Mitchell would not talk to us. His assistant, John Hushen, confirmed that Dita Beard and John Mitchell had a conversation at Governor Louie Nunn's Kentucky Derby party. But beyond that, Hushen tried to con us out of publishing the story with tired old ploys that slowed us down for a few hours. First, Mitchell refused a direct quote of any kind while holding out the promise of a response at some future time. Second, he had Hushen tell us that he could "prove" the falsity of our information. Powerful public officials employ these subterfuges because there are reporters and editors who can be either convinced or intimidated by them, particularly when they come from the Attorney General of the United States. But we were not sufficiently impressed with either Mitchell's veracity or his omnipotence. When a few hours passed and the promised proof did not materialize, we proceeded with our story.

ITT's reaction was that of an organization up to its armpits in guilt. Although the company knew exactly what was in the memo in our possession, days passed and we could get nothing out of its Washington spokesmen but "no comment." Meanwhile, the company had fed thousands of documents into a document shredder and had advised its lobbyist-in-chief first to lie to us and then to get out of town.

Other interviews helped us to explode the two cover stories put out by the Justice Department when the first news of the ITT convention pledge had leaked out: (1) that Attorney General Mitchell had no knowledge of any commitment from anyone, and (2) that Kleindienst had played no role in negotiating the settlement, which he said had been "handled and negotiated exclusively" by the unimpeachable McLaren. Dita Beard had told Brit Hume that California's Lieutenant Governor Ed Reinecke had conferred with Mitchell about the $400,000 pledge soon after the pledge was made on May 12. We could not reach Reinecke, but his aide, Edgar Gillenwaters, told us that he was with Reinecke at a meeting with Mitchell on May 17, 1971, when Reinecke explained to Mitchell the ITT-Sheraton offer in detail and received Mitchell's blessing. And Felix Rohatyn, an ITT director, told us that he had met privately with Kleindienst several times on the case and had "handled some of the negotiations and presentations to Kleindienst and McLaren."

We were ready to go to press.

Senate Sparring

We compressed the findings and conclusions gleaned from more than twenty interviews, plus countless private documents and public records, into a story that ran in three daily columns.

The first column led off:

We now have evidence that the settlement of the Nixon Administration's biggest anti-trust case was privately arranged between Attorney General John Mitchell and the top lobbyist for the company involved. We have this on the word of the lobbyist herself: crusty, capable Dita Beard of the International Telephone and Telgraph Company. She acknowledged the secret deal after we obtained a highly incriminating memo, written by her, from ITT's files.

The memo, which was intended to be destroyed after it was read, not only indicates that the anti-trust case had been fixed but that the fix was a pay-off for ITT's pledge of up to $400,000 for the upcoming Republican Convention in San Diego . . .

She said she met with Mitchell at the Governor's Mansion in Kentucky during a dinner reception by Republican Governor Louie Nunn last May after the Kentucky Derby.

Confronted with the memo, Mrs. Beard acknowledged its authenticity . . . Mrs. Beard insisted the subject of the G.O.P. Convention never came up with Mitchell and was never a factor in the anti-trust case. But this clearly contradicts her memorandum, which was written about six weeks after the Kentucky Derby dinner.

This opener was followed with a second column two days later:

We have now established that Attorney General-designate Richard Kleindienst told an outright lie about the Justice Department's sudden out-of-court settlement of the Nixon Administration's biggest anti-trust case . . .

Denying any connection between the convention cash and the anti-trust settlement, Kleindienst insisted that the Justice Department's anti-trust staff had been free from any political pressure from above.

"The settlement between the Department of Justice and ITT was handled and negotiated exclusively by Assistant Attorney General Richard W. McLaren [then head of the Antitrust Division]," Kleindienst said in a letter to Democratic National Chairman Larry O'Brien.

However, we have now learned that Kliendienst, himself, had held roughly a half-dozen secret meetings on the ITT case with a director of the company before the settlement was reached.

The director, Wall Street financier Felix Rohatyn, conceded to us that he met in private with Kleindienst, who was then Deputy Attorney General, at the same time McLaren was negotiating with ITT's lawyers. "I was supposed to make the case on the economic side of it," Rohatyn told my associate Brit Hume. He said he particularly stressed to Kleindienst ITT's arguments for keeping Hartford Fire.

The third column followed immediately:

The Justice Department and International Telephone and Telegraph are now trying to lie their way out of the scandal over the suspicious, sudden settlement of a landmark anti-trust suit against ITT . . .

The statement says the Attorney General "was not involved in any way with the Republican National Committee convention negotiations and had no knowledge of anyone from the Committee or elsewhere dealing with anyone from International Telephone and Telgraph."

This is false. Last year, California Lt. Gov. Ed Reinecke and an aide, Edgar Gillenwaters, met with Mitchell in his Washington office to discuss efforts to hold the convention in San Diego.

We could not reach Reinecke, but Gillenwaters told us he and Reinecke personally informed Mitchell that ITT had offered to put up as much as $400,000 to support a G.O.P. convention in San Diego.

"He liked the idea of having the convention in San Diego," Gillenwaters said of Mitchell. "He didn't need any persuading. He said, 'if you can do it, more power to you.' "

ITT also issued a statement that only its lawyers were authorized to deal with the Justice Department on the anti-trust cases. "Neither Mrs. Beard or anyone else except legal counsel was authorized to carry on such negotiations," the statement said.

This is also false. Felix Rohatyn, an investment banker and director of ITT, told us he held a series of half a dozen secret meetings during the merger negotiations with Deputy Attorney General Richard Kleindienst. Rohatyn said he was specifically authorized to "make the case from the economic side" by ITT President Harold S. Geneen.

Published on February 29, March 2, and March 3, these columns provoked the swiftest official and unofficial response I have encountered. All the major newspapers immediately began to treat our columns and the reactions to them as front-page material. On March 1 Dita Beard fled Washington for points unknown. On the same day, Kleindienst asked to testify before the Senate Judiciary Committee in rebuttal to our charges. By March 2 the hearings were actually under way!

Among reporters who love the republic and know the Congress, the prospect of congressional hearings must ever inspire mixed feelings.

Hearings will focus a national spotlight on the abuse we seek to end. Some of the principals will be required to testify under oath. Some documents will be made public that otherwise would forever remain "classified" or otherwise hidden from the people. The media will assign top reporters to cover the hearings. This will stimulate competition, and for a short while the press will function as the watchdog and debunker it ought always to be instead of the tranquilized conveyor belt for government press releases and "backgrounders" it normally is.

Yet, for all these pluses, one should not lightly provoke a congressional hearing into high crimes. Once in a generation, as in the Walsh probe of the Teapot Dome or the Watergate hearings when atypical circumstances conjoin, it will be an exemplary inquiry, but usually it turns out to be a more palpable public disgrace than the acts being investigated. If the alleged offense is grand enough—not something trifling like subversion or welfare chiseling, but something massively destructive like the suborning of the Justice Department and the White House by a corrupt corporate giant—the majority of the investigating commitee is likely to be on the side of the miscreants. Senators will unashamedly reveal themselves, not as judges impartially but sternly searching for truth, but as a rooting section for the accused. They will ask friendly questions, praise evasive or perjured answers, hound honest witnesses, accuse sincere colleagues of political motivations, and in the end, they will kill efforts to subpoena key witnesses and vital documents and force the probe to a premature close. A minority will press the investigation honestly, but such senators invariably seem to be short on power within the committee. When the showdown comes, they will not have the votes needed to force the production of key witnesses and documents. Their efforts, genuine though they may be, usually achieve little except to create the facade of an honest investigation.

Thus there is always the risk that instead of exposing and deterring corruption, a Senate hearing will legitimize and encourage it by exonerating the offenders and by teaching all the unschooled swindlers and unshaped politicians out there in the national audience how easy it is to get away with boodling, how much support it has in high places, and how transient are the embarrassments of getting caught.

Moreover, there is the personal attrition to consider. To any muckraker of mature years, average sensitivities, and emotions as depletable as the next fellow's, the news that the circus is again assembling heralds another unpleasant testing of the verities upon which he has founded his career. Long ago he convinced himself that good will overcome evil if the actors are seen and the facts known, and so he became a scandalmonger; but he must always fight back insidious doubts which might prompt him privately to entreat: "Call off the hearing; let well enough alone; don't let children and civics teachers see corporation officers and U.S. senators in action!"

But he has invested his life in the proposition that pollution must be seen and smelled to be combated, that

corruption hidden is corruption heightened, that our institutions are still vital enough so that scandal will bring
not demoralization but reform. Thus, at the announcement of the Senate hearing, after a certain initial queasi-
ness, the old juices commence to rise in him, and when
the first gavel falls he is at his place at the press table,
notebook in hand.

It was with such ambivalent musings that I received
the news that Mississippi's Senator James O. Eastland,
the Senate Judiciary chairman, had called a hearing at
which Attorney General-designate Richard Kleindienst
would be examined on the charges in my columns. The
immediate circumstances surrounding the hearing gave
off the familiar odor of whitewash. For one thing, there
was the unseemly haste. The hearings would begin on
Thursday to examine charges that had started to come
out on Tuesday. This allowed no time for those senators
who really wanted to investigate or for the press to even
begin to master the questions at issue.

An official inquiry into charges such as those raised
by the Dita Beard memo and the subsequent interviews
requires certain preliminaries—the staff interrogation of
scores of witnesses, the taking of dozens of sworn depositions, the examination of thousands of subpoenaed
documents (a process requiring weeks or months of organized effort by a skilled staff)—before senators are
ready for public hearings. We were offered instead a
hit-and-run hearing, at which carefully chosen Administration and ITT spokesmen could soulfully and indignantly profess innocence before a panel of unprepared
senators and an audience of uninformed reporters.

Chairman Eastland's definition of the subject under
investigation also gave off a whiff of lime, as did the
unaccustomed alacrity with which the full Judiciary
Committee, usually inert in the face of public alarums,
had bounded onstage to take jurisdiction. A number of
subcommittees in both houses, with skilled investigative
staffs, are equipped to probe antitrust scandals, political
briberies, corruption of administrative officers, break-

downs of regulatory law and other such matters alleged in the Beard revelations. But these investigative units were all circumvented by Eastland's swift claim of jurisdiction for the full Judiciary Committee, a group not equipped by any standard for the task.

For instance, there would be no committee counsel to organize and conduct the questioning, as Rudolph Halley did for the Kefauver crime investigation, or Benjamin Fern for the Senate ethics inquiry into Senator Thomas Dodd. What Chairman Eastland had in mind was a disjointed round robin, in which the sixteen senators on the committee would do the questioning themselves in bursts of ten minutes each—a format which invited ineffectiveness by preventing a sustained, calculated interrogation. Moreover, the chairman had prejudiced in advance a real free-swinging inquiry by his definition of the question to be investigated. Had Kleindienst lied when he told Larry O'Brien that the settlement between the Department of Justice and ITT was handled and negotiated exclusively by Assistant Attorney General Richard McLaren?

Well, we had charged that Kleindienst had lied, but this was really a peripheral issue. The basic revelations contained in Dita Beard's memo and interviews went far beyond Kleindienst to a vast constellation of White House aides, Cabinet level officials, ITT executives and political figures, among them a governor, a lieutenant governor and a congressman.

Kleindienst was not even among the ten political and ITT figures indentified in the Beard memo as participants. By defining the purpose of the hearings so narrowly, Senator Eastland appeared to be setting up a rationale by which the committee could refuse to probe fully the most significant aspects of the Beard memorandum's revelation that the highest Administration figures had quashed the case against ITT in return for a $400,000 convention commitment.

Kleindienst could have been at most a tool in this arrangement. But Eastland was making him the principal figure. Why? This was especially curious in view of Eastland's known closeness to Kleindienst. I suspected that the chairman's intention was to make Kleindienst the issue in order to divert attention from the uglier implications, to get him on and off the stand in a day or two, to clear him before a real investigation could take root, and then, with a flick of his cigar ash, to declare the whole matter closed, leaving all the collaborators named in the Beard memorandum free and clear.

This suspicion immediately gained support from events. Before the hearings even began, the senior committee Republicans, Senator Hugh Scott and Senator Roman Hruska, declared Kleindienst innocent; Kleindienst had scarcely taken the stand to begin testifying when Eastland left the hearing room to tell the press: "This man had done nothing wrong"; and before they had even had a chance to ask a question, G. O. P. juniors like Ed Gurney and Marlow Cook were telling television audiences that no one had laid a glove on Kleindienst and that the hearings should be concluded at the end of the first day.

But even before these remarkable performances, the picture became clear to me when I learned who the witnesses were to be. Not a single "prosecution witness" was scheduled. Only high-up front men for the Administration and ITT were on the initial list—Kleindienst, Mitchell, McLaren, Geneen and Rohatyn. Naturally, they would deny any wrongdoing and each would corroborate the other's testimony.

Cabinet and corporate figures are in one respect like rare tropical birds. They have learned to communicate with one another through near-inaudible sounds, poses, and gestures. If there is to be a bribe between them, they do not blatantly come to terms about it. The arrangement is carried off through a process of almost imperceptible movements, coincidences, grunts, raised eyebrows, knowing smiles. There is not going to be an incriminating document, tape recording, or photograph left behind. So, unless there has been a thorough preliminary investigation, it is almost impossible to go behind their own accounts.

All serious investigations into matters of this kind must be based on defectors, lower-level participants who are willing to talk, subpoenaed records that can be pieced together painstakingly to show a pattern, the contradictions in secret depositions. But no time or effort was being taken to find and properly intimidate potential defectors; no lower-level participants, either from the government of ITT, were scheduled; the pertinent records had been shredded by ITT or classified by the Justice Department as a part of their "investigative files" and no depositions had been taken that might later yield telltale contradictions when the witnesses were called to testify. As would soon become public knowledge, key members of the committee were planning a one- or two-day performance at most, followed by a vote of confidence in Kleindienst that would conveniently dispose of the entire matter.

This committee strategy would dovetail with the tactics of both the Administration and ITT. The Administration's stance could clearly be seen from the pose adopted in the two days before the hearings began—consisting of laconic press statements by Mitchell, Kleindienst, and White House spokesmen. None of them, they said, knew anything about the $400,000 contribution, nor did they have anything to do with negotiating the settlement with ITT. Somehow they had become disembodied and detached from the administrative and political operations of the Nixon Administration and the Republican party, and they were floating in remote space. They could be confident that no one on the other side was in a position to challenge their version of their confidential conversations with each other, since they were prepared under the claim of executive privilege to conceal pertinent documents and to prevent the most sensitive witnesses from testifying at all. In the unlikely event that some random question by a senator struck home they had only to feign lack of memory and wait for the ten-minute period to expire.

As for ITT, our sources within the company were able to brief us on evolving strategy. Geneen and the other top ITT officials would claim total ignorance of Dita's memo or its implications. If this didn't work, they were prepared for Phase II. Although they had destroyed, so far as they knew, all incrimination documents that could support the published Beard memorandum, they still faced two hazards: (1) the possibility that Dita Beard would testify and tell the truth as she had told it to Brit Hume, and (2) the unchallenged authenticity of the Beard memorandum itself. At a strategy session at ITT's New York headquarters on Park Avenue, three alternate plans of attack were decided on, to be utilized as developments indicated: (1) to destroy the reputation and credibility of Dita Beard, (2) to undermine the authenticity of her memo, and (3) to investigate Jack Anderson in an attempt to discredit his reliability and his motives.

Already, stories were beginning to circulate among newspapermen about Dita Beard being unstable, a drunk, a liar, a self-promoter who faked the memo just to blow her own horn. Intertel was engaged to perform the hundredth or perhaps the thousandth probe of our humble operation. And science, or what passes for it in the legal game, was to be invoked. There are all kinds of pseudoscientists who, for a reasonable fee, will furnish "expert testimony" for or against the authenticity of any handwriting specimen, document, voice recording, mental condition, or any other phenomenon that may bear upon a trial or an inquiry. Soon some of these professional testifiers would be working for ITT on the Beard memorandum.

Thus, a vast effort undertaken by three of the most powerful institutions in America was under way to discredit a story that had a real potential to bring about reform and, in the process, to destroy my reputation as a newspaperman. Normally, when I have filed a story I am done with it. I don't try to promote it in the press or to manipulate reactions. Partly this is because we must always be at work on the next story if we are to publish every day, and partly it is because I feel a reporter should stay a reporter and not deteriorate into a backroom mover and shaper of events. But in this instance I deviated from the passive role. So much organized pressure was being exerted to sweep the Dita Beard memo under the rug that counterpressure had to be applied by someone. No one else was likely to come forward.

We evolved a plan of counterattack. We would invite other investigative reporters to share the information and insights our head start had given us, even to the extent of giving them our raw documents. Brit Hume was to be in charge of this effort, and the page-one treatment our revelations received from the start was largely due to skill in this role. I would work on the Senate, phoning and visiting senators to urge their attention on the matter and to offer information and help. Contrary to the popular impression, we have *some* friends on Capitol Hill. There are many other members, both of the Senate and of the Judiciary Committee, who would take due note—in measuring the pros and cons of what posture they should assume—of the fact that our column was taking a continuing interest in their performance. I told senators what I knew, offered assistance, assured them of the growing public indignation my mail revealed, and let them know I had other documents I would make public at the proper time. This was a friendly warning not to jump too quickly to the ITT-G.O.P. side lest they be burned by subsequent revelations.

Most of the ITT documents, including those we received later, involved the company's intervention in the affairs of Chile. We began to prepare a series of columns that would show ITT's attempts to block Salvador Allende Gossens from coming to power—and thus risk a grave international crisis—in order to suppress a government unfriendly to ITT and its exploitation of Chilean resources I would hold this series until I felt the need to hypo the ITT hearings; then I would run it and release all the supporting documents to the Foreign Relations Committee and to such papers as the *Washington Post* and the *New York Times*.

But the centerpiece of our effort to keep the ITT probe from being deftly smothered in the crib was a demand that we be allowed to testify at the hearings. There had to be some hostile witnesses to break up the love feast. What was needed was a disrupting influence, someone to contradict the smooth, coordinated alibis; someone to shout "Liar" and to remind the public of the evasions and contradictions the committee majority was swallowing, someone to bait pro-ITT senators for their condonation of scandal, someone to whom conscientious senators could address questions that would elicit information they wanted publicized, someone to keep the hearings going, to foul up the whitewash machinery and to give chance and circumstances and opportunity to create the chaos that sometimes causes even the best-staged hearings to slip out of control and run amok.

I was not eager to testify, with good reason. It would tie me up for days, perhaps weeks. I might come out a fool, particularly in view of the incendiary role it would be necessary for me to assume. My appearance on the stand would give the Administration agents on the committee, and several long-suffering targets of mine there, a chance to confront me with all the reportorial mistakes of a lifetime as well as with whatever personal embarrassments Intertel and the Justice Department and the White House wiretap and safecracking gang would be able to dredge up about me and my staff. It would expose Brit and me to charges of perjury, since our testimony would undoubtedly be in flat contradiction to that of the ITT-G. O. P. witnesses, and to prosecution for contempt, as we would have to refuse the inevitable committee demands that we reveal our sources within ITT.

But I saw no other way to wage effective guerrilla warfare against the combined strategies of the Judiciary Committee, the Nixon Administration, and the International Telephone and Telegraph Company.

And so I called Chairman Eastland, an old and respected adversary, and asked to testify. "I'm sure, Mr. Chairman, that you want to be fair about this and to get our side," I said.

"Of course we want to hear your side," drawled Eastland.

What this meant, in translation, was that I was threatening to create a public nuisance and holler "Foul" if we were refused. Measuring in his wise old way the disruption we could cause as witnesses against the righteous breast-beating we would do if excluded, Eastland decided to let us in the door while reserving the right to seat us at the least conspicuous place at the table and serve us last, after everyone had gone home.

I knew Eastland—crafty, cordial, flexible, courteous —a senator who has consolidated great power not by autocratic conduct but by knowing how to bend with the wind, ever so slightly, without losing his place. He is a Southern gentleman and would keep his word to call us as witnesses; but he would no doubt try to keep us off the stand, with ingenious excuses, until the Administration witnesses had made a compelling case and public attention had peaked and begun to decline.

That was his prerogative. But even as "scheduled" witnesses, Brit and I would have some status at the proceedings. While Mitchell and Kleindienst were giving their version inside the hearing room, we could be out in the hall in front of the television cameras—Brit modestly stating the unfortunate facts and sorrowfully deploring the misrepresentations going on inside, while I came on with the big brass drum and delivered the bastinado. Fair enough.

Ignorance Is Bliss

It will strike some as incongruous that I, a partisan in the hearings, should presume to analyze them here. Should not that juridical role be left to disinterested scholars? As a matter of fact, I orginally intended to end my story at the point where the hearings began—since the two-month hearing touched off by our columns was now part of the public record—but I abandoned this notion on the theory, perhaps self-deceiving, that to abbreviate would be to short-change the reader who had stuck with me thus far.

Such an account has obvious limitations. The testimony I have selected as significant is drawn from a transcript that runs to 1,750 pages; others would have selected differently. No doubt all who are characterized here as impostors could point to inspired ripostes in their testimony that I, with my jaundiced view, found unmoving and thus ignored. I add further that the motivations ascribed here to the witnesses were rejected in toto by the committee, which found all suspects blameless; the perjuries I see abounding everywhere have only belatedly aroused official interest because of Watergate.

The early testimony confirmed that the strategy of John Mitchell and Richard Kleindienst would be the one foreshadowed by their previous public statements: they claimed to know nothing of the ITT convention gift and to have played no role in the negotiation of the ITT settlement. Lesser figures, further removed from the President, would take up the burden of representing that there was nothing wrong with either the gift or the settlement. If unkind fate or the discovery of other unfortunate memos should explode either or both of these claims, the debris would not fall on the respective Attorneys General.

The claim of ignorance is the standard stratagem of most high officials under investigation. Whatever the alleged crime, if it was committed at all, expendable subordinates did it while their unknowing superiors were attending to higher responsibilities. So it was with Senator Thomas Dodd and Senator Daniel Brewster; so it would be with the wheat scandal, the milk scandal, the Watergate scandal. This inveterate official posture has all the strengths and weaknesses of the squatting position: simple to assume, cautiously protective, appropriate for what one has in mine, but rather unseemly for public display and a bit difficult to maintain gracefully.

In this case, the squatters could look forward to having all the best of it. There were no defectors to contradict them, no organized prosecution to combat all the "I don't recall" 's and "I don't remember" 's and "to the best of my recollection" 's. The committee had seen to it that minimal public attention would be focused on the unbecoming attitudes of the distinguished witnesses. A short hearing was planned; television cameras were banned from the hearing room; senators such as Marlow Cook, Hiram Fong, and Edward Gurney were alerted to smooth things over by nodding gravely and commenting sympathetically at the non-answers. Conversely, my strategy was to call the attention of all and sundry to the odd posture of the chief legal officers of the land so that, as embarrassment mounted around the ears, and strain increased on the tibia and fibula, the Honorable Mitchell and Kleindienst might lose their balance and come down with a crash.

Such jockeyings consumed the first weeks; we were not successful enough to topple the magistrates from their dogged positions, but we did succeed in defeating the attempts to shut down the hearings and in holding our own in the battle for public opinion, as the ITT-G.O.P. complaints of unfair press treatment attested.

The strength of saying "I don't recall" and "I was not

aware" resides in the difficulty it poses for the adversary, who cannot positively disprove something as subjective and nebulous as the claimed state of mind of a practiced witness. A cross-examiner thrives on the witness who contradicts himself; when all the witness gives him is a claim of ignorance, the interrogator is working with the minimum. There is, nevertheless, a weakness. To protect one's claim of ignorance of the crucial matters, one must guard his flanks by also claiming ignorance of all collateral matters, the knowledge of which would have led him unavoidably to the forbidden tree. Thus, if the challenge is pressed long enough and ingeniously enough, the witness is compelled to claim ignorance of so many things he must have known about that he is gradually perceived as either uncommonly stupid and negligent or as a man who is lying his head off.

The strength of this defense was exemplified by John Mitchell's testimony, the weakness by Kleindienst's.

When Mitchell took the stand, wearing his petulant air of affronted dignity and annoyance with the inconveniences of the democratic process, a formidable though circumstantial case stood against him. He was widely known to be Nixon's political manager, privy to every campaign decision of consequence, such as the selection of San Diego as the convention site. And as Attorney General, too, he had obviously been aware of all important projects undertaken by the Justice Department.

Here, as in the case of Peter Flanigan, the essential ingredients of a major scandal seemed to come together: cognizance at the higher level that a gift had been accepted from ITT at the moment its case had reached a crucial juncture in negotiations with the government. Even if the $400,000 pledge did not overtly influence the Justice Department turnaround, just for Mitchell to know his political arm had received a gift while his legal arm was deliberating whether to settle the anti-ITT suits constituted a scandal that could ruin careers and even topple the Administration. Once this double-cognizance was established in fact as it was in circumstance, the failure of Mitchell to reject the gift and take steps to dispel the suspicion about the integrity of the negotiations would surely prove an insupportable burden that would in time crush the Administration's case.

When Dita Beard rightly said in her memo that *public* knowledge of the ITT pledge would shoot down the settlement, she was unconsciously saying what everyone knows in his heart—that *private* knowledge of it by the G. O. P. high command *should have* shot the settlement down. Mitchell met the danger by totally dissociating himself from both transactions:

I was not involved in any way in any negotiations which led to the selection of San Diego as the site of the convention by the Republican National Committee. I have never talked to the Deputy Attorney General or the Assistant Attorney General in charge of the Antitrust Division about the San Diego Convention site or anything relating to discussions or negotiations with ITT or any of its subsidiaries. I do not recall when or how I first learned of the Sheraton Hotel Corporation's participation and support for the holding of the convention in San Diego, but I believe that I first read about it in the newspapers. I do not as of this date know what arrangements, if any, exist between ITT or the Sheraton Hotel Corporation and the Republican National Committee or between ITT or any of its subsidiaries in the city of San Diego or any agency thereof.

Men who knew of Mitchell's tight control over both his political and departmental fiefs found it hard to believe that he had not shared the anxiety of lesser Nixon politicos over the San Diego dilemma or their elation over its resolution by ITT. It was as if the manager of a heavyweight champion should profess no interest in the site of the title fight, the gate, the television arrangements, or the terms of the contract.

And if Mitchell had kept hands off the ITT matter, why had he agreed to confer with President Harold Geneen of ITT during Geneen's Washington rounds in behalf of reversing the government's antitrust policies? They discussed only general antitrust policy, said Mitchell beguilingly, theory which had no relevance to the specific problems of ITT. Just a little philosophical discussion between two theoreticians who happened to get together for an academic exercise, unmindful that their respective minions were negotiating a multi-million-dollar antitrust settlement.

Ignorance was Mitchell's defense, and since the only records available on his activities were those provided by Mitchell himself or his allies, none of his scattershot interrogators was able to put a dent in it. Having made his categorical denials, he settled back in a kind of discommoded imperiousness and, in effect, challenged the doubting fools on the committee to prove otherwise. The scheduling of witnesses greatly assisted him, and illustrated the way Chairman James Eastland stage-managed the show. As noted earlier, before Mitchell had announced his line of defense, we had obtained an interview with Edgar Gillenwaters, aide to Lieutenant Governor Ed Reinecke of California, in which Gillenwaters said he was present at a meeting where Reinecke told Mitchell the whole story of ITT's role in making possible a San Diego convention. Mitchell was quoted by Gillenwaters as blessing the deal: "Well, if you can get it, more power to you."

Shortly after Gillenwaters spoke to us, Reinecke himself told the same story to three other reporters. It seemed fitting, therefore, that Reinecke and Gillenwaters be put on the stand immediately to tell their story under oath. Fearing this would not happen, I issued a public challenge, just before Mitchell was to testify, pointing out the conflict between his and Reinecke's versions and urging that it be resolved under oath. The chairman was unmoved. He held off the appearances of Reinecke and Gillenwaters for five weeks until the public had forgotten who they were and wasn't much interested in being reminded. Yet the explanation given by the lieutenant governor will someday be of interest to archivists poking through the ruins so I reproduce it here.

The background was ably summarized by a news story in the California newspaper, the *Sacramento Bee*:

LIEUTENANT GOVERNOR REINECKE'S SHIFT ON ITT STORY

The startling turnabout in Lt. Gov. Ed Reinecke's story about press reports of a corporate financing offer to bring the Republican National Convention to San Diego, has. raised questions from Washington to Sacramento . . .

And Reinecke, the man who could resolve them, is no longer available to the press to do so. This conduct contrasts sharply with last week when Reinecke, an affable man with ambitions to run for governor in 1974, was easy to reach.

Now that it is clear that either version of his story contradicts former US Atty. Gen. John Mitchell, President Nixon's political strategist and confidant, the doors to Reinecke's office are closed.

"If you have specific questions we will answer them," said a staff aide. "He has said all he is going to say on this other than to answer specific questions."

The Bee has not yet received any reply to questions posed in writing yesterday.

Until last Friday, Reinecke and Edgar Gillenwaters, director of the Department of Commerce, had told numerous reporters, including a representative of the Bee, they reported to Mitchell last May in Washington on financial arrangements for bringing the convention to California.

Among the arrangements was a $400,000 financing guarantee by the Sheraton Hotel Corp., a subsidiary of International Telephone & Telegraph Co.

Mitchell, whose Justice Department settled an antitrust prosecution against another ITT subsidiary in July, has maintained he knew nothing of convention financing and that the offer had nothing to do with the settlement.

In an interview with the Bee last Thursday Reinecke was asked, "I understand you and Ed (Gillenwaters) talked to Mr. Mitchell sometime in May, was that right?"

"That's right," the lieutenant governor replied.

"Was Reinecke the first to inform Mitchell of the Sheraton underwriting offer?" Reinecke was asked.

"I discussed it with the attorney general," Reinecke replied. "Whether I was the first one or not I didn't ask him.

"But we did discuss it and he was very pleased to see the progress we'd made, not just with Sheraton but with getting the city and the county to come around [with more money], because the President had indicated apparently to him—never to me—that he would like to see it come to California, and so this . . . in other words, we were doing what they wanted to see done, and so they were delighted to hear it."

And in the same interview Reinecke mentioned seeing Mitchell during Reinecke's May trip to Washington to promote the space shuttle project:

"This was strictly a political thing between Sheraton and their desire to help get the convention to San Diego. The fact that I was talking to John Mitchell was not that he was attorney general. He was, you might say, the political arm of the administration.

"And so when I went to Washington on space shuttle business I made it a point to go there to see what we could do about bringing this convention to San Diego . . ."

That was Thursday.

On Friday Reinecke called a press conference for a clarification: "On the May 16, 1971, trip to Washington, D.C., we did not meet with Atty. Gen. Mitchell as I had previously reported," Reinecke declared.

The lieutenant governor went on to add a statement which had raised a major and still unanswered question.

The statement: "My discussion with Atty. Gen. Mitchell concerning the convention was at 9:30 a.m. on Sept. 17, 1971 . . . This would have been the first time either of us [Reinecke or Gillenwaters] discussed any such offer with the attorney general."

The question arises because of the timing in Reinecke's correction. San Diego was publicly selected as convention site last July 23. By then the financing offers were firm.

Why then would Reinecke be reporting to Mitchell on convention financing in September, and why would Mitchell be "delighted" at that date to hear of Reinecke's progress?

Other questions of credibility are arising in comparing Reinecke's statements with Mitchell's. Last week, for example, the outgoing attorney general told a news conference:

"I don't know the faintest thing abou* the convention financing . . ."

It was easy enough for Reinecke, after being clued in by Mitchell's office, to change the date of their meeting from May to September; but Reinecke had described to the press a conversation with Mitchell that would make no more sense in September than would a child's speculating on December 26 about what Santa Claus might bring. It would have been silly for Reinecke to report to John Mitchell on the progress he is making in clearing the path for the selection of San Diego if that selection had already been made two months earlier. And presumably, Reinecke would not, in September, say that the President "would like to see it come to California" or say that he had called on Mitchell "to see what we could do about bringing this convention to San Diego" when San Diego had already been selected way back in July.

Reinecke was questioned on this discrepancy by Senator Birch Bayh and Senator John Tunney. His answers brought laughter if not belief:

I believe it needs to be put in the proper perspective, Senator.

As Mr. Gillenwaters just indicated, that statement—that meeting did not take place in May. The particular position that I was in at the time that I responded to first an AP wire service call from Bill Stall, of the Sacramento Bee, and then from two gentlemen here, Bob Walters of the Star was one, and I am sorry I slipped the other name right now. Well, the first call from Bill Stall was when I was on vacation time; I was in Missouri finding out the whys and wherefores of artificial insemination of cows, and perhaps that had me all shook up. I don't know, but nonetheless I had accepted the information from my staff that I should call this gentleman and that they were the dates that we had the discussion and, of course, I was there knee deep in straw—

And:

The attitude or perhaps the tense of the verbs that I was using may have been unfortunate, I do not know. I do not recall the conversation specifically that you referred to and it is very difficult for me to say that I was talking in the future tense or whatever it might have been that you are referring to. I do not know that I can really offer much help in that area, Senator. All I know is the facts that I have and that I can establish, and if they sound unbelievable, I am sorry for it, but they are the best that I know and they are the ones that I intend to give because, as I told you, if you have nothing else in this business you have only your integrity to protect and I intend to do that.

But even if Reinecke's account of insemination and dissemination was to be believed, Mitchell wasn't entirely in the clear. He had been told of the ITT pledge, according to Reinecke, in September 1971, but as late as March 1, 1972, Mitchell was still claiming to know nothing but what he had read in the newspapers. He reiterated this position during his testimony. Reminded that Reinecke, after his recollection had been refreshed, claimed to have told all to Mitchell in September of 1971, Mitchell was unperturbed.

It is quite possible that Lieutenant Governor Reinecke mentioned the convention in San Diego and Sheraton Hotel or something else, but it would have made no impression on me whatever, I not having an interest in it.

How could a mere Senate committee penetrate such invincible ignorance? But if the credulity of the senators had been strained, they were too polite to challenge a man of Mitchell's power and prominence. He left the stand unscathed. In the hall, which was thronged with reporters and cameramen, he convened what members of the Nixon Administration have come to regard as a press conference; he made a statement for the cameras and then refused to answer questions. Mitchell denounced the press for unfair coverage, labeled the ITT story "a house of cards" and huffed off, leaving the questions reverberating in vain.

When the eminent philosopher with the open-door policy reached his car outside, a lady reporter approached him, asked a question, and held out her microphone for an answer. Mitchell's bodyguard pushed her out of the way as Mitchell got into the car. The lady rebounded with her microphone and her question. All that could be heard from the philosopher was, "Watch your arm!" as he slammed the car door and the car lurched off.

Harold Geneen followed the same strategy of ignorance and aloofness. His testimony went even more smoothly than Mitchell's, for he was not plagued with the indiscretions of a Reinecke. His only problem was to appear convincing in his new role as a permissive fumbler. For Geneen came to the stand carrying the reputation of the most exacting taskmaster in all industry, an organizing genius who had perfected a method for learning and correcting everything untoward that happened in his six-continent empire. A 1971 report of the House Antitrust Committee describes the old Geneen:

There is universal agreement that he demands an extraordinary amount of detail from subordinate officials; some problems, even quite minor, are solved at a higher level in ITT than at any other large company.

Forbes magazine describes Geneen's attention to detail as follows: "What is unusual about Geneen is the detail he demands. He demands monthly reports from all divisions. He studies them at monthly meetings attended by his key staff people and important line people. The monthly reports have to include not only major items on why a division is above or below quota but items as minor as a lost order. To insure that the reports are made in sufficient detail, Geneen has a staff that is constantly dropping in on operations to check on them, and line people know if Geneen finds out anything negative about a man's operation, no matter how petty from anyone else but the man himself, he explodes. So the reports are highly detailed."

The new Geneen, however, was as oblivious of happenings in his company as if he had just awakened from a Rip Van Winkle nap. He had only a slight recollection of Dita Beard and only a vague notion of what she did for ITT. He knew nothing about her memo and did not know of a single ITT official who had ever seen it. He didn't know anything about the document shredding, nothing about who had done it, or how, or why. He knew of no improper act by anyone at ITT in connection with the antitrust settlement. He had had nothing to do, really, with the famous ITT pledge to help finance the Republican convention, outside of once vaguely expressing interest in the idea to the responsible officer involved, Sheraton President Bud James.

What Geneen was ready to talk about was the twenty-year currency crisis of the United States and its balance of payments dilemma, which ITT could help solve if only the government would stop tying him up with lawsuits he didn't understand and let him get on with his business. The committee was highly deferential to Geneen, and the day passed without a rub—another success in an almost unbroken series of successful meetings for the great man.

"I Don't Recall"

Richard Kleindienst faced a far more difficult test of the amnesiac defense because it involved much more forgetting. Mitchell's defense was comparatively easy, for it dealt with things not committed to paper—the whisperings and winkings that attend campaign contributions, gossamer substances you can't put your finger on, like the reversible conversations of politicians. Kleindienst's defense, however, had to contend with more concrete realities. He was up against the paper tracks—appointments schedules, diaries, letters between attorneys, memoranda among Justice Department colleagues. What was said at a meeting can be fudged, but the meeting itself cannot be safely hidden, nor can things written on paper be denied lest in this Xerox age a copy leak out.

Not only was Kleindienst's role more taxing, but the timing was unfortunate. His testimony coincided with headline news that Dita Beard had disappeared, apparently in flight from an expected subpoena, with twenty-four FBI agents in five states trying to track her down. Moreover, our revelations that ITT had destroyed records pertinent to the inquiry by feeding them into a document shredder, combined with the refusal of the Justice Department to furnish the committee with the records of its relations with ITT, set a dubious atmosphere for Kleindienst's contention that nothing was amiss.

He also came to the stand burdened with his public statement that the ITT settlement had been "handled and negotiated exclusively" by Richard McLaren and his antitrust staff. This categorical assurance, given, as

116

we have seen, to Democratic National Chairman Lawrence O'Brien, had doused the first conflagration of press suspicion. But when our column revealed the six meetings with Felix Rohatyn, the artful dodge had turned into a dead cat that now hung heavy around Kleindienst's neck.

Rohatyn's words to us, spoken before he recognized their implications for Kleindienst, left the Attorney General-designate very little wiggling room. Rohatyn had said, "I, as a director of ITT and an investment banker, handled some of the negotiations and presentations to Kleindienst and McLaren." Rohatyn had added that he had been assigned by Geneen to "make the case on the economic side." It was on this basis that we had charged Kleindienst with lying. So Brit Hume and I awaited his explanation with some curiosity.

His method was to admit candidly what was already known and beyond hiding but to deny its logical implications. He admitted his meetings with Rohatyn while denying they had in any way constituted taking part in negotiations. He said that Rohatyn told him that if the government persisted in taking ITT to court, and if it won, dire financial consequences would follow for ITT and Hartford Fire, whose stockholders "would suffer a loss in excess of $1 billion in the value of their stock." The divestiture, "as a result of the manner in which they acquired the company," Kleindienst quoted Rohatyn as saying, "would have a very drastic effect upon the liquidity of the company," interfering with their "ability to perform on $200 to $300 million of contracts abroad."

As Kleindienst told it, Rohatyn was pleading not just for ITT, but for the nation, the flag, and the United States Marines. For if ITT was damaged, the result would have an adverse effect on the nation's economy, prosperity, and balance of payments. He said:

He [Rohatyn] then asked me if I would direct Mr. McLaren, the Assistant Attorney General in the Antitrust Division, to call a meeting of his staff, and any other experts that the Government might want to have with them, and economic experts of the I. T. & T. Corp. for the purpose of permitting I. T. & T.

to make this economic presentation to the Government, not a legal argument whether or not as a matter of law the position of the Department was meritorious, but in order for the Government to be able to have this information, and hopefully arrive at some kind of a settlement in these cases calculated to permit I. T. & T. to retain the Hartford Insurance Company and not be required to divest it.

Translated, this proposition from the preeminent investment banker to the acting Attorney General read to me as follows: "Look, Mr. Kleindienst, let's forget the question of whether this valuable property was illegally obtained. Let's forget that ITT was warned by the government from the start that if we acquired Hartford Fire, we would be hauled into court. Let's forget that we promised a federal judge that if he would not block the takeover, we would separate Hartford Fire's activities from ours in a way that we could divest it, if later directed, with minimal dislocation to anyone. Let's forget, Mr. Kleindienst, that we made false statements to the judge and are therefore in trouble. Tell your man to let us present this matter not in terms of the law but only in terms of how much it will cost us to give up Hartford Fire and how much our loss will hurt the general economy, we being the big spenders that we are."

Lest the reader think me fanciful in this translation, I quote from a memorandum from McLaren to Kleindienst dated July 17, 1971:

. . . ITT's management consummated the Hartford acquisition knowing it violated our antitrust policy; knowing we intended to sue; and in effect presenting to the court that he need not issue a preliminary injunction because ITT would hold Hartford separate and thus minimize any divestiture problem if violations were found.

Perhaps equally guilty is the trial judge, who listened sympathetically to defendants' plea that granting our motion for preliminary injunction would cost Hartford the $500 million premium ITT was paying for their stock. Obviously, if such a premium is being paid on an unlawful acquisition, the acquiring company may lose that and more if forced to divest, and will so plead if found guilty.

Kleindienst, to return to the hearing transcript, answered Rohatyn's request as follows:

I told Mr. Rohatyn that I would not direct Mr. McLaren or Judge McLaren to do that, but that I would call him and see if he would be willing to do that. I did. Mr. Rohatyn left. I did. And then I called Mr. Rohatyn and said that Mr. McLaren would be willing to have such a meeting.

The meeting was held, with Kleindienst present. The economic and financial consequences of divestiture were presented, as though they were not apparent to antitrusters who had been studying the matter for two years. McLaren, according to his own testimony, was persuaded by this presentation to reevaluate his position. While the reevaluation was going on, Kleindienst continued to have private sessions with Rohatyn while what Rohatyn called "parallel meetings" took place between their subordinates. The reevaluation soon led to a complete reversal of government policy and to the settlement which permitted ITT to keep Hartford Fire after all.

Well, didn't all this show that Kleindienst, contrary to his statement, had indeed taken part in handling and negotiating the case? Not at all, said Kleindienst. He came to the hearing equipped with three verbal lubricants designed to help him slide out from under the implications of the Rohatyn meetings: Rohatyn was not a lawyer; Rohatyn had discussed economic, not legal aspects; McLaren was only asked, not ordered, to hear Rohatyn's arguments.

From where I sat, there were three things wrong with these arguments. The suggestion that discussions with Rohatyn about the case could not possibly count as negotiations, since he was not a lawyer, must have amused investment bankers everywhere. For Rohatyn was the boss of many lawyers, including the ones who were negotiating with McLaren; he had behind him a prodigious career of putting corporations together and taking them apart; Geneen's purpose in dispatching him to Washington obviously was to raise the ITT argument to a more potent level than mere lawyers had been able to do. When Rohatyn was not educating Kleindienst, moreover, he was closeted with Mitchell, helping the Administration to prevent the collapse of Wall Street firms that had used their customers' money and couldn't pay up. So far as impact on the negotiations was concerned, it would have been better for the public weal if Kleindienst had negotiated with one hundred ITT lawyers rather than one Rohatyn.

Kleindienst's reiteration that he and Rohatyn had discussed only "the economic argument" sought to create the impression that the economic side was something abstract, ethereal, and divorced from the settlement, just as Mitchell's harmless discussions of antitrust law with Geneen were held to have no relation to the practical applications being visited upon ITT. Yet, as we shall elaborate when we get to McLaren, the basis of the resolution of the ITT suits was that the legal arguments were thrown out and the case was decided on the basis of the economic arguments Rohatyn first made to Kleindienst. The honest thing for Kleindienst to have said was that he had discussed with Rohatyn *only those questions that were decisive to the eventual settlement*—the dollar-and-cents arguments—and had not wasted his time talking about legal aspects, which were not to be the basis of the decision.

As for the distinction Kleindienst tried to make between *directing* McLaren to hear Rohatyn's arguments and *asking* him to do so—well, come now. When you are a man's boss, you don't have to order him—it's not even good form, expecially among lawyers—you just ask him. This is particularly true when what you want him to do is to forget about the law and concentrate on the "economic aspects."

Kleindienst had come to the hearings with the advantage of knowing that word of his private meetings with Rohatyn had gotten out; but he did not know what else, if anything, had gotten out. Should he volunteer to the committee a complete list of all his involvements in the

ITT case and put the most innocent face on them he could? Or should he withhold this information, in the hope that the press had already shot its wad and the lonely doubters on the committee had no further information?

He chose the orthodox course. In his opening statement to the committee, he did not admit anything beyond his relations with Rohatyn. His tactic, as it evolved, was to volunteer nothing unless the other side stumbled onto it; then he would recollect and admit that, yes, come to think of it, he had met with or corresponded with so-and-so, but had forgotten it because the contact was so trifling he did not regard it as being within the context of the hearings.

In this catch-as-catch-can fashion, belated acknowledgment of several other interventions was dragged out of him. He had discussed the case with John Ryan, Deputy Chief of ITT's Washington office—a conversation that led to his meetings with Rohatyn. He had been sent a letter by Reuben Robertson, one of the principal litigators in the case, which had asked him point-blank if there was any connection between the ITT pledge and the settlement. He had had phone calls and correspondence about the litigation with ITT Special Counsel Lawrence E. Walsh, who said he was contacting Kleindienst instead of McLaren because he was aware of Kleindienst's previous involvement in the litigation. At Walsh's behest, Kleindienst had by-passed McLaren to intercede with Solicitor General Erwin Griswold to delay the filing of an anti-ITT brief to the Supreme Court.

Although Kleindienst testified that he had had no conversations on ITT with White House aide Peter Flanigan, it turned out that (1) Flanigan had phoned Kleindienst to tell him of ITT's complaints about getting harsh treatment from McLaren; (2) Flanigan had phoned him again to tell him that he had received a Wall Street analysis that would support Rohatyn's presentation; and (3) Kleindienst was present when Flanigan delivered to McLaren that report, which proved so persuasive in causing McLaren to reverse himself.

Kleindienst's successive explanations of these matters, and of his failure to come clean about them until they had been otherwise revealed, grew thinner and thinner. He had not remembered his conversation with Ryan because it had occurred at a party. He had not been shown the letter from Robertson, because he did not have time to look at unimportant mail (though some might think a letter from a Ralph Nader partner raising the question of fraud had a certain potential for trouble in it that would have disposed the staff to put it on Kleindienst's desk). He just couldn't remember, despite "racking my brain," any of the three conversations with Peter Flanigan, though he did not now dispute they had occurred. He couldn't remember Flanigan delivering the Wall Street report, or why Flanigan would come to his office with it, or what they said to each other when Flanigan handed over the report which was so decisive in resolving a $2 billion legal action. And so it went. Little did the great Flanigan realize the nonexistent impression his conversations and visits were making!

The success of the amnesiac defense depends on getting on and off the stand relatively quickly, as Mitchell and Geneen had done, and not having to forget too many things. The mounting pressures which these gross implausibilities brought upon Kleindienst at length made his rigid posture insupportable, and he eased the strain by conceding that while he had not "handled" or "negotiated" he had "set in motion a series of events" which led to the settlement.

The Fix

Every national Administration ought to make it a rule to appoint three or four indisputably honest men, if for no other reason than their utility as character witnesses when the others are under suspicion. Richard McLaren was such a man, a Godsend in this hour when a believable figure had suddenly become indispensable. Almost alone among the Justice Department hierarchy, he was not tainted by past services as a political fund raiser or by partisan manipulation of his office. He was well regarded even by liberals who, in their predilection for good intentions, had made a minor hero of McLaren for his policy pronouncements and suit-filings, forgetting that he had permitted most of his great projects to ignominiously abort.

At the hearings, McLaren was positioned by the side of Kleindienst—indeed, fastened to him like an ill-matched Siamese twin. Earnest-looking, amiable, with an air about him of legitimate purpose and honest naïveté, McLaren undeniably added an appearance of rectitude to the proceedings.

His role in the defense was pivotal. If Mitchell or Kleindienst had not caused the reversal of the Justice Department's position, who had? If McLaren could provide a convincing answer, the holes in the previous testimony might be forgotten. It was well known that victory in the Supreme Court on the ITT suits was his central objective, the only way he could achieve vindication of his antitrust policy and an honored place in the history of America's effort to preserve free competition. The great victory had been within his grasp. He had predicted it, and ITT Special Counsel Lawrence Walsh had conceded it. His Supreme Court briefs were already written and filed. The venerable Justices were ready to act. What then, if not political pressure from superiors, had caused him to reverse a course he had hewed to for two years?

I sat on the edge of my chair awaiting his explanation. Solemnly, McLaren declared he had reversed himself and had abandoned his goal of a final Supreme Court clarification because ITT had made a persuasive case of "hardship" and because he had become apprehensive that the "ripple effects" of forced divestiture might harm the national economy. McLaren said he had been persuaded by the arguments presented to him by Rohatyn's men and, particularly, by an analysis of these arguments prepared by financial consultant Richard Ramsden which subsequently became known as the Ramsden Report.

Judge McLaren identified three factors in his conversion: (1) He had not realized, until Rohatyn's men enlightened him, that ITT and Hartford Fire stockholders might suffer as much as a 16 per cent loss on their shares, which would be punitive for them and might have an adverse effect on the stock market in general; (2) if ITT were denied access to the $1 billion annual cash flow of Hartford Fire, its credit rating and borrowing capacity would be lowered; and (3) if ITT were thus weakened, the effect on the United States' international balance of payments might be adverse.

On the face of it, this explanation did not have the ring of conviction. Certainly ITT and its stockholders would be somewhat dislocated if forced to give up illegal acquisitions, but that is one of the purposes of an antitrust suit. The Supreme Court had settled that in the Du Pont case when it ruled: "Those who violate the Act may not reap the benefit of their violations and avoid an undoing of their unlawful project on the plea of hardship or convenience."

The argument about general adverse effect on the

stock market and our balance of payments had an even flimsier substance. Even an infrequent investor like me knows that every year the market absorbs individual drops by companies comparable to ITT without noticeable effect. And with all due respect to ITT, its contribution to our balance of payments for good or ill is just a drop in the bucket. Legally, the argument amounted to the inadmissible claim that ITT was too big to be required to obey the law and that the law was in bondage to hypothetical fluctuations of the stock market and the trade market. Economically, it was an obvious counterfeit, even to a non-expert.

But before positively writing off McLaren, I recalled the periodic warnings of my attorney that I am inclined to legal quackery and oversimplification. Surely there were legal and financial experts who would read McLaren's testimony and pass professional judgments on it. And indeed there were.

Senator Birch Bayh invited an opinion from two distinguished professors at the famed Wharton School of Finance and Commerce of the University of Pennsylvania—Irwin Friend and Randolph Westerfield. The senior of the two, Professor Friend, is an internationally respected authority, bearing such formidable titles as president of the American Finance Association and chariman of the Business Economics Statistics Section of the American Statistical Association. Under the cheerless scrutiny of these gentlemen, the McLaren interpretation of the Ramsden analysis of the Rohatyn arguments was given about as much credence as the notorious autobiography of Howard Hughes.

I quote the significant findings of Friend and Westerfield:

To summarize briefly the more detailed comments below, the Ramsden report gives virtually no support to the position taken by Government officials that divestiture of Hartford might have severely damaged the nation's economy. Thus, Mr. McLaren refers to concern over "ripple effects" and "disastrous consequences" and Mr. Kleindienst to the raising of "a very serious question in terms of the economic impact" of the divestiture of Hartford. There do not appear to be any plausible reasons for expecting such repercussions.

The Ramsden report does provide some support for the conclusion that ITT stockholders would have been adversely affected by divestiture. However, the arguments made are not convincing and it is our impression that the report overstates the likely impact of divestiture on these stockholders. To the extent there would have been some adverse effect on stockholders, it is not clear why they should be protected from the consequences of assuming what might legitimately be regarded as a normal business risk associated with investment in a conglomerate. Even prior to the effective date of the merging of Hartford with ITT, stockholders were on notice of the U.S. Government suit and of the U.S. District Court ruling that pending trial of that suit, ITT was required to hold the Hartford business separate from the other businesses of ITT.

The first argument that divestiture of Hartford would adversely affect the United States balance of payments, as noted above, is tenuous and in any case not of any moment in view of the magnitude involved. The potentially more important second argument that divestiture might cause a severe and negative ripple through the stock market and presumably as a consequence through the general economy is not even mentioned in the Ramsden report and has virtually no justification.

Declines in stock prices of individual stocks, even of the 16 percent magnitude estimated by Mr. Ramsden for ITT would not be expected either from economic theory or from empirical evidence to have an appreciable impact on other stock prices. The much larger divestiture of General Motors by Du Pont does not seem to have had a major impact on the market either for these securities or for the market as a whole. Even the potentially much more dangerous Penn Central bankruptcy did not have too severe an impact on other stock prices.

Another verdict, examining the legal side of McLaren's argument, was later published by the eminent Dr. Harlan M. Blake, professor of law at Columbia University and co-editor of *Cases and Materials on Antitrust Law*, a legal textbook used in law schools throughout the country.

Of the Ramsden Report, Professor Blake said: "Most of it reads like the kind of research report on a company put out every day by the major brokerage houses. In addition, these are the kinds of arguments that every antitrust lawyer knows by heart and makes in desperation when his arguments 'on the merits' are not strong enough to prevail."

Professor Blake continued:

The possibility of an adverse effect on access to the capital market is not a factor that can be taken into account since it is present in every antitrust suit worth prosecuting; monopoly profits or cartel gains, at the expense of consumers, always improve the looks of financial statements and reduce credit risks . . .

The Ramsden report was equally weak in arguing excessive injury to stockholders. No shareholder has any vested right to stock values arising from anticompetitive circumstances. Furthermore, most of the risk to ordinary investors had been absorbed by arbitrage buying and selling during the previous year by sophisticated speculators betting, in effect, on the outcome of the litigation . . .

Most important, in the event that Hartford were to be ordered to be divested two or three years hence, the courts have plenty of discretion in choosing plans that prevent injury to the innocent (for instance by spreading small public offerings over a period of time) . . .

Finally, the balance of payments argument is the reddest and smelliest herring in the entire weaponry of businessmen seeking special treatment in antitrust matters. Even Ramsden's report described the possibility only as "some indirect effect." . . .

As an antitrust lawyer, McLaren must have known well that even if somehow troubled by one or more of these arguments, he could not accept them without violating every tenet of antitrust policy.*

Even Ramsden himself disowned the interpretations McLaren and Kleindienst claimed to have drawn from his report.

SENATOR BAYH: Now, Mr. Ramsden, does your report go into the details of the ripple effects?
MR. RAMSDEN: Absolutely not.
SENATOR BAYH: Does your report go into the disastrous consequences to the economy that were referred to by Mr. McLaren?
MR. RAMSDEN: Absolutely not.

* *Harper's,* August 1972.

SENATOR BAYH: Does your report go into the very serious question in terms of the economic impact that has been referred to by Mr. Kleindienst in sustaining the Government's position?

MR. RAMSDEN: I don't believe there is anything in any report of that nature.

I do not contend that even the opinions of such acknowledged authorities as Friend and Blake constitute the last word. They are persuasive to me, but there are experts and experts. What they *do* show beyond peradventure is that Rohatyn's "economic case" and Ramsden's supportive report were, to say the least, open to serious question, not only in themselves but as the determinants of one of the greatest antitrust actions ever instituted. The question that gets at the nub of the Justice Department's integrity in the matter is, What safeguards were employed to see that the pro-ITT arguments were subjected to rigorous, objective analysis? Kleindienst and McLaren are not children—they knew ITT was bound to be lugging in a self-interest plea; what did they do to make sure that they and the public were not being hoodwinked?

The answer was dragged out. McLaren did not go to impeccable and impartial experts like Professor Friend, whom a previous Department of Justice had consulted in the massive Du Pont divestiture of General Motors. After considerable jogging of his memory by Senator Edward Kennedy, McLaren remembered that he had called Peter Flanigan, the White House ambassador to big business, for the name of a financial expert. Flanigan suggested the name of Richard Ramsden, a young man from Flanigan's firm of Dillon, Read, which, by the way, held two hundred thousand dollars' worth of ITT stock. Ramsden had been helpful to the Justice Department in advising on another "hardship" settlement, one for Ling-Temco-Vought. After the phone call, McLaren mysteriously stepped aside. It was Flanigan who called Ramsden in and instructed him, mainly by handing him a brief whose authorship he did not identify but which turned out to be ITT. Ramsden was not paid by the Justice Department but by the Commerce Department; therefore he did not undergo the kind of check which would have revealed his employer's holdings in ITT stock. After two or three days' work, Ramsden brought forth a twelve-page report, which he delivered not to McLaren but to Flanigan. "Mr. Fix-It," as Flanigan is affectionately known in big-business circles, called Kleindienst and described the contents; subsequently Flanigan delivered the report to Kleindienst's office. At this point, McLaren turned up again. He later reviewed the arguments of Ramsden in seclusion. Astonishingly, Ramsden never once discussed his findings with McLaren. No *outside* expert was asked to look at the Ramsden Report, nor were any of the economic specialists *inside* the Justice Department asked for their opinions. They were, in fact, calculatedly excluded from deliberation. When Kenneth Elzinga, the Justice Department economist who would normally have been consulted but wasn't, finally got to read the Ramsden argument as a result of the hearings, he called it "a sham and a whitewash." Upon this suspect basis, one of the most ambitious antitrust suits ever brought against any conglomerate was dropped and a compromise settlement was entered into.

Brit and I waited patiently for our turn to testify. When there was a lull in the hearing, Chairman James Eastland would send an aide to whisper in my ear that the chairman wished to see me in his chambers. Eastland would explain with elaborate politeness why yet another delay was necessary. I would answer, with equal politeness, that I understood the chairman's problem and that we would hold ourselves ready for the chairman's convenience.

In the meantime, we would testify in our own manner, out in the hallway to the newsmen and the television cameras. As the only witnesses on our side of the fence, competing against two dozen witnesses that were in one way or another associated with the Republican party or ITT, I thought we should put aside the passive decorum normally expected of witnesses.

When our day to testify arrived, Brit was at my side. He was, of course, the legitimate witness, the one who had talked to Dita Beard and Felix Rohatyn and Edgar Gillenwaters. I was there as a sort of self-styled *éminence grise*.

I thought Brit was a sensation as a witness—precise, articulate, with almost total recall. He captivated and convinced the audience, if not the committee. His testimony was essentially a factual reiteration of material previously printed here, particularly in his memo on the Beard interview, so it need not be recapitulated.

What the hearings needed now, I thought, was a troublemaker, someone to stir things up and sharpen the issues. If the tactic of the other side was in part to put the spectators to sleep with obfuscations, ours must be to wake them up with accusations, get the other side mad in the hope that they would say foolishly memorable things.

My main candidate for the role of the fool was Senator Roman Hruska. A visceral supporter of the moneyed interests, he is quick to rise to battle in their defense, and he is none too bright. I had his blood pressure in mind as I testified or gave interviews he was likely to see on the television news.

When the ITT-G.O.P. witnesses would say they couldn't remember, I'd say they were lying; when they would use one or another of their executive privileges to deny information to the committee, I'd accuse them of taking the Fifth Amendment, and "Senators, wasn't that a terrible disgrace for members of the Justice Department!" When senators would volunteer as to how they couldn't see anything that ITT or the Justice Department had done wrong, I'd say that the country must be deeply troubled about the inability of its senators to tell right from wrong. When they would bring in rulings to show that it was perfectly all right for corporations to give money for political conventions, I'd say it was an out-and-out crime, and I would read the section of the law that said so.

That last one was what got to Hruska. I had felt he was getting closer and closer to the boiling point, and when I impugned the legality of corporate gifts he burst into steam. He asked me if I was a lawyer. I replied that I wasn't a lawyer but that I understood the English language. He responded that it took a good deal more than understanding the English language to interpret the law. Sensing a faux pas coming, I was abrasive with him. He proceeded with his proofs, but my bad manners had a cumulative effect on its victim. He lectured me:

SENATOR HRUSKA: ... You can have your opinions about it, but again I submit that the committee will probably have a pretty good idea of where the credibility lies with regard to whether the contribution by a corporation to support a political convention is a crime.

MR. ANDERSON: Well, I am aware that the attitude toward political contributions on the part of the politicians has been somewhat fuzzy.

SENATOR HRUSKA: It is not fuzzy at all. Conventions all over America are bought all the time by business communities, and everyone——

MR. ANDERSON: I subscribe to that.

SENATOR HRUSKA: Everyone in this room knows it.

To me that remark was worth a week of waiting in the Senate hearing room. What Hruska had done for the anti-Carswell forces with his defense of mediocrity and his affirmation that mediocre people deserve a representative on the Supreme Court, he had now done for us.

Dita's Last Stand

The time had come for Dita Beard to decide whether she was really different from the "little bums" she feigned to disdain. Was she the tough, spit-in-your-eye, can't-stand-lies, wear-no-man's-collar free spirit she portrayed herself to be? Or was she just another collapsible corporate tool who could whimper and lie with the worst of them when her salary was on the line? Most of us who have to make this decision are permitted to make it in private—permitted, if we so choose, to sell ourselves in half-compromises that can be disguised even from ourselves. But for Dita Beard, the decision would be unmaskable and must be taken on the public stage. She had written a memorandum. She had authenticated it. When it was published, she had let it stand unchallenged. She could get out of it now only by lying under oath at high noon in the town square. And it wouldn't be a simple lie. It would have to be the groveling kind, the outlandish kind that even her best friend couldn't believe. Would she do it?

It was human that she should seek to put off this decision. She had counted on a sympathetic reaction from her ITT superiors, as one who had been wounded in the line of battle might well expect. But she was denied access to Geneen, and something in the words and looks of her ITT colleagues caused her later to exclaim that they were pleased at the prospect of her destruction.

She sought refuge in flight. On the day the hearings started, with her own subpoena an inevitability, she took off incognito for points west after telling her friend Congressman Robert Wilson: "Where I am going, they won't be able to find me, and I won't be able to talk to them."

Whether she had discovered the way to sanctuary before she reached Denver, or whether fate intervened there, will remain a matter of conjecture, thanks to the Delphic medical statements and the contradictory diagnoses that followed. When she reappeared, she was safe in a coronary ward in the Denver Osteopathic Hospital. She was said to be suffering from an "impending coronary thrombosis," and the FBI agents who were just a skip behind her with a subpoena were barred at the door.

But though this enforced silence stayed the wholesale havoc that the cross-examination of Dita Beard might wreak, it left the distressing memorandum still intact. The memo hung palpably over the hearing room, mocking the clubfooted evasions and preposterous obfuscations of the witnesses. Senator Sam Ervin, a Southern Democrat essentially sympathetic to ITT's position, was moved to exasperation after listening to its officers testify. He exclaimed, "This is the worst presentation I have ever heard." During the questioning of ITT Senior Vice President E. J. Gerrity, the usually polite and charitable Ervin broke in to say: "Some people are good rememberers and some are good forgetters . . . perhaps a good forgetter is better than a good rememberer. We have witnesses here who possess both or neither of these qualities."

If the ITT-G.O.P. was to be extricated from what the *Washington Post* in its daily editorials had begun to call the Dismal Swamp, one of two things had to be discredited—Dita Beard's memo or Dita Beard herself. Since she had authenticated the memo to no less than four persons within her own circle, the former alternative seemed unlikely. The latter was now cranked up. I had learned of this plan and had publicized it hoping to lessen its effect. And I informed the committee in these words:

Our sources close to ITT tell us the company is planning an all-out effort to discredit Dita Beard. We understand that Vice President E. J. Gerrity is masterminding the effort to paint his only Washington staff lobbyist as a crackpot and a drunk. We are told that an effort will be made to show that her memorandum was not written last June but at some later time in a fit or irrationality. We understand the company may produce testimony to the effect that the memo was not typed on an ITT office typewriter. We anticipate an effort to show that the version of the Kentucky Derby dinner she gave my associate was inaccurate because of her mental condition.

Nonetheless this very process began to unfold. Chairman Eastland, with an unexpected flair for dramatics, told the press that he would soon produce "surprise witnesses" who would clear things up satisfactorily for those under suspicion. A special session was called to hear Mrs. Beard's long-time doctor, Hungarian-born Victor Liszka.

For several years, Mrs. Beard had been drinking excessively when under tension, Dr. Liszka testified. She suffered from periodic "distorted and irrational behavior." This "irrationality" sometimes affected her thought processes, her actions, and her sentences. It could be caused by the heart's failure during a sudden attack to pump enough blood to provide oxygen for the brain. In this condition "her thoughts do not flow in logical order. She would become so disoriented that she would be incapable of a legal act, such as signing a will or a contract . . ." Finally, with an assist from Senator Gurney, the incredible doctor came to the conclusion that fit the bill: "Having lost the facility of judgment, putting things together in an uncontrolled fashion, she could have written an inaccurate memo."

Other doctors expressed shock that Liszka would so violate the code of confidentiality as to publicly degrade his patient. The medical director of the American Heart Association dismissed Liszka's medical theorizing as "nonsense." Nobody writes memoranda during an angina attack," he said. Questioning by skeptical senators brought out the fact that Liszka had made two visits to the Justice Department just before testifying and that for years he had been reporting to ITT headquarters on Mrs. Beard's health (a company policy for top executives) without ever mentioning any mental or emotional problems. Then it surfaced that Liszka and his doctor-wife were being investigated by the Justice Department for Medicare frauds (Liszka was cleared, his wife indicted).

On the following day, surprise witness number two, former Governor Louie Nunn of Kentucky, was produced. Nunn had been the host of the Kentucky Derby party at which Dita, in her memo and in her interview with Brit, claimed to have discussed with Mitchell the deal which terminated the ITT suits. Nunn said he had never left Mitchell's side and could testify that Mitchell had repeatedly rebuffed Mrs. Beard when she attempted to talk about the ITT case. The governor described Mrs. Beard as an old acquaintance who drank heavily and was worried about losing her job. Toward the end of the evening Mrs. Beard collapsed in a stupor, he said. Not to be outdone by Dr. Liszka as a diagnostician, Nunn attributed her collapse to a combination of exhaustion, her heart ailment, and alcohol. The last time he saw Dita that night, they had "laid her out on the floor."

Kleindienst tied a ribbon on the neatly wrapped package. The only implication of misconduct, he said, "is in a memorandum written by a poor soul—it's just a sad situation."

Nunn's testimony, however, underwent a tortured metamorphosis as I apprised the committee of a sequence of events:

When our column on the Beard memorandum was first published, Mr. Nunn was called for comment by the Associated Press. He acknowledged having John and Martha Mitchell as his guests at the Kentucky Derby. But he said he did not know whether Mr. Mitchell had met Mrs. Beard at his home. The same day the Chicago Daily News quoted Nunn as saying "I never heard any discussion about anything except generalities." These two news organizations reached Mr. Nunn before he had read John Mitchell's statement about our column. Afterwards, he decided to comment no further. He issued a statement saying he stood on what the Attorney General said. However, Ward Sinclair of the Louisville Courier Journal persuaded Mr. Nunn to answer one question about the nature of the discussion between Mr. Mitchell and Mrs. Beard. Mr. Nunn's answer was that he was "unaware" of the topic of discussion. So, first Nunn didn't know if Mrs. Beard and Mr. Mitchell had even met. Thereafter, he acknowledged they met but didn't know what they talked about. Then, he came before this Committee with elaborate testimony about an embarrassing confrontation between Mrs. Beard and Mr. Mitchell. He now has full recollection of several efforts by Mrs. Beard to approach the Attorney General about ITT and the treatment the company was receiving from the Justice Department. He remembers how Mr. Mitchell fended off Mrs. Beard and how she later collapsed on the floor, the apparent victim of a heart ailment. He even remembers Mrs. Beard visiting him the next day to apologize for the incident and to seek his advice as to whether the embarrassment could hurt her company or cost her her job. Once he had described these events in considerable detail, Mr. Nunn's memory once again turned to molasses.

The ugliness of this combined assault appeared the more odious now that Dita Beard was no longer a fugitive from justice, but a patient in a hospital, a mother surrounded by her babes, seemingly unable to defend herself, while obvious charlatans trampled all over what was left of her reputation. In the eyes of many this assault did not rescue the ITT-G.O.P. from charges of dishonesty, it merely exposed their venality as well.

But if the campaign to portray Dita Beard as a lush and a mental case failed of the mark as propaganda, it was highly effective as intimidation. Reports from Denver said that Dita's condition (whatever it was) drastically worsened when she read the accounts. She must now have seen the end that lay ahead for her unless she entered into full cooperation with ITT—a woman alone, unemployable, isolated from all that she had known, turned into a laughing stock, ruined. There were subtle reminders, too: every year on the first Monday of March she was accustomed to being awarded a bonus, which had now reached $15,000; but the first Monday had come and gone and there was no bonus.

Perhaps her long silence did not betoken a struggle of conscience versus expediency after all. She may have hesitated because she thought it was too late to deny the memo. It was not just Brit Hume's testimony that she must challenge. There was testimony in the record of four other conversations she had had about the memo. In none of them did she deny writing it. Quite to the contrary.

She had told her doctor, Victor Liszka, "I was mad when I wrote it." She acknowledged to her immediate boss, Mr. Merriam, that the handwritten "D" on the memorandum was hers, and never denied its authenticity. In a two-hour showdown with her New York superior, Mr. Gerrity, she made no categorical denial of authorship, despite a concerted effort by Gerrity to elicit one. Gerrity later testified, "When I asked her, I said, 'Did you write this memorandum?' And she would say, 'Well, I guess I did, I think I did, but I could not have really because it is not true.' But she never categorically denied writing the memorandum." She also called on Congressman Wilson to discuss the matter, and according to a tape-recorded interview given by Wilson to journalist Robert Cox, she left Wilson with the impression that she had written it, all right, and that "enemies within ITT had leaked it to Jack Anderson." Shortly thereafter, according to Wilson's Senate testimony, Merriam called on him and told him that he (Merriam) had received the memo from Dita, had read it, and had given it back to her.

All this testimony and the weeks that elapsed since the publication of the memo, during which she had let it stand, made the task of belated repudiation difficult. But where there is a will—

In deep secrecy, White House undercoverman E. Howard Hunt, wearing a CIA-supplied disguise, flew out to Denver to confer with Dita.

The first public sign of the coming recantation was the announcement that a California attorney named David Fleming was now guiding Dita's affairs. Fleming shared a Washington law office with Republican National-al Committeeman Carl Shipley, and it was soon revealed that Fleming was being paid by ITT and had insisted on an initial retainer of $15,000.

The early signs were subtle but unmistakable. The campaign to discredit Dita suddenly ceased. Fleming began referring to "that alleged memorandum." He flew to Washington for private consultations with the Republican senators on the committee. Then on March 17, three weeks after the Hume interviews, Fleming read a statement in Dita's name branding the memo "a forgery, a fraud and a hoax." The pro-ITT senators, who two weeks before had been setting up Mrs. Beard as a zombie, now embraced her as the sole repository of truth in the matter. Nothing would do but that the committee must go to Denver to question Dita under a format to be worked out by her lawyers and doctors. Some of the Democrats smelled a rodent, but G.O.P. leader Hugh Scott threatened that until Dita Beard was heard he would boycott "that circus . . . based on fraudulent documents."

Long after the passage of time has caused these events to recede, I expect that Dita Beard's hospital-room scene will remain fondly in my memory, a tableau representing the complicity and the futility of the U.S. government in the face of corporate mendacity. In the center of the scene, propped up on pillows, is the once swashbuckling Dita, contrite, repentant, and wired up with all the artifacts of mortal illness, including a nose tube. The obscene harridan of a month ago, who by her own boast used to break up staff meetings by telling "the filthiest story I could think of," is now little girl lost. She describes herself as "a little lonely lobbyist," living only to redeem her honor and willing to answer all questions "as long as this thing keeps beating."

The understanding was that the visiting senators were to have nine hours of questioning—three hours a day for three days; the doctors could end it at any time their machines showed signs of distress. The proceedings began with the reading of Dita's prepared statement, which started right off with a whopper appropriate to this idiotic setting: "I have never sought to run away, hide, escape, or make myself unavailable to this Committee. It was my intention upon leaving Washington, D.C., on the morning of Thursday, March 2, 1972, to get some rest which I desperately needed because of my heart condition and on advice of my doctor." (Her doctor, Victor Liszka, testified that the last advice he would have given Mrs. Beard was to take a long airplane flight to high-altitude Denver.)

Then to the main argument: "I did not write, compose or dictate *the entirety* of the memorandum which Mr. Hume presented to me in the Washington office of ITT last month. I do recall similar language in the first part of that memorandum which I wrote some time in late June or early July of 1971, at the request of Mr. Merriam."

What she meant, as she later elaborated, was that she had indeed dictated certain paragraphs and sentences in the famous memo, but that some unknown intervener had ghosted in other paragraphs and sentences—the ones that caused all the trouble.

Then she explained how it came to pass that she had not immediately denounced the memo to Hume as a fraud. "I began to read it rapidly. Some of the language, the general subject matter of the first paragraph looked familiar. At that moment, I had no reason to assume that this was not a memorandum written by me. He asked me if I had written it. I had not yet fully read it or taken the time to study it. I acknowledged that it looked like my little 'D.' As I read on, I became shocked and obviously flustered. Some of the language brought back absolutely no recall because it set forth allegations about which I had no knowledge."

Why had she not then demurred from authorship of the memo? "I had had a heart condition for some years, and I was, frankly, afraid of what a prolonged encounter would do . . . I could picture the total ruination of myself, my family, or financial security . . . I was in a state of total despair. I know all too well the viciousness of some reporters in Washington and the fact that they care nothing of damaging human beings but only getting a 'story.' I began to drink. By the time Mr. Hume arrived I had a feeling of utter desperation."

Then the questioning began, and gaping holes immediately began to appear.

SENATOR COOK: When did you first realize that the Anderson memo was not the same one you had prepared?

MRS. BEARD: Well, the day in the office when I read the whole thing . . . I really tried every way in the world to figure what in the world it was, and then when I got to the second page and called Hal "big mouth" or whatever it was, I realized this is not mine. I wouldn't say anything like that.

She made the same point to Senator Hart: "In the first place, I would never call the man I think more of than anything in the world, Harold Geneen, whatever the word is in the back, blabbermouth or something." (A few days later, William Merriam testified that he had heard Dita refer to Mr. Geneen as "a big mouth" on a number of occasions.)

In her written statement, Mrs. Beard had said that she originally thought it was her memo because the initial on it looked like "my little 'D,' " but as she began to warm to the subject, she said this: "In the first place, I knew the 'D' was not mine, but I wasn't absolutely convinced of it, because I hadn't really studied it, and until the night I came out of the Intensive Care and Mr. Anderson was on television with 'Sixty Minutes,' and they happened to show a close-up, if any of you all saw it, a very clear close-up of the top section of that paper, and I just nearly jumped out of bed. I called the children. I called everybody to look at that. That is not mine."

Senator Phil Hart, the acting chairman of the Denver field group, with his gentlest bedside manner, asked two fundamental questions:

CHAIRMAN HART: I think it is on the mind of all of us—if even before you left Washington, you had concluded that the so-called Anderson memorandum had not been prepared by you, why in heavens name didn't you tell the world at that time?

MRS. BEARD: Sir, I had absolutely no one to turn to. I—the people in the Washington office were obviously delighted. I don't know what happened. I couldn't make them listen . . .

CHAIRMAN HART: Well, it is your testimony that you were convinced, after checking your expense accounts, diaries, etc., that it was not your memorandum. You told your associates in the Washington offices and you went to New York and you told your associates in the New York office . . . You are protesting at all times that this is not yours?

MRS. BEARD: I didn't say—No, not that strongly, because I worked so long with them all that I didn't think I was going to have to start beating on the desk.

The prepared statement was unraveled a bit further by Mrs. Beard's response to what was intended as a friendly question from Marlow Cook:

SENATOR COOK: Well, Mr. Hume also testified that during the meeting at your home on the 24th, you told him that you had negotiated the terms of the settlement of the ITT cases with Attorney General Mitchell during a party at Governor Nunn's residence on May 1. Now, did you ever say that to Mr. Hume?

MRS. BEARD: If I did, it must have been toward the end of the evening, sir, when I was so upset.

Having practically wiped out the carefully prepared written statement, the witness began to open up marvelous new vistas of inquiry. She said that her memo to Merriam, or at least those portions of it that had not been ghosted in, was occasioned by a call Merriam received from the White House in which Merriam was asked whether the $400,000 ITT was donating was going to the Republican Convention or straight into the President's campaign. Intimidated as they were by all the medical apparatus, the senators must have been seized—depending on their persuasions—with spasms of either hope or alarm. With two and a half days to go, who could tell where this examination would lead?

But it was to lead nowhere. Suddenly, Dita fell back on her pillows moaning, her face contorted with apparent pain, her arms outstretched to her doctors. The room was emptied. The doctors began ministering. Attorney Fleming promptly diagnosed to the press a "near-massive heart attack." Her doctor contented himself with saying, "She will probably never be able to testify as long as she lives." The visiting senators beat it back to Washington, and nothing more was ever heard of Dita Beard's subpoena.

A miraculous recovery immediately followed. Three days after the collapse, Dita was questioned, minus her medical equipment, on a nationally televised interview conducted by Mike Wallace. A week after the "near-massive heart attack" she gaily checked out of the hospital and vanished altogether. Three weeks after the collapse, on April 15, a statement was released by Dr. Joseph Snyder and Dr. Ray Pryor. These specialists were not Mrs. Beard's doctors but two Denver cardiologists chosen by the president of the Denver Medical Association to conduct an independent examination of Mrs. Beard's condition. They said they could find no evidence of heart disease. There were no positive findings from a physical examination, electrocardiogram, or chest x-rays. The only indication that Mrs. Beard had a heart condition, they said, was based entirely on her own description of chest pains, "which is subjective information."

Meanwhile, ITT was providing mathematical and scientific backup for Mrs. Beard's explanation. An ex-secretary was produced who claimed to remember having typed certain sentences, but not others, of the memo dictated nine months before by Dita Beard; her recollection of what was in that memo and what was not in it, did not, however, jibe with Dita's testimony. ITT added to the confusion by claiming no less than three Beard memos bearing the same date and concerned with the same subject. Then the company produced the inevitable report by paid experts who, for a thousand dollars a day, had made "microscopic, ultra-violet, fluorescent and highly sophisticated micro-chemical analyses." These analyses disclosed that the alleged June 25 memo published by our column had actually been typed six months later and, therefore, could not have been genuine. We had reached the shell-game stage.

I was certain that the only people who were falling for this planned confusion were those who wanted to be deceived, but I felt it should be countered anyway. At my request, Brit Hume took five lie-detector tests, given by Lloyd B. Furr, an acknowledged polygraph expert used frequently by the Justice Department. All five tests showed that on every point of Brit's account of the Dita Beard interview, he was telling the truth. It has been said that the most revolutionary thing in the world is truth. We had fun brandishing those tests and demanding that the other witnesses follow suit; but none of them, patriots that they were, wanted any part of that revolution.

The FBI discredited the "micro-chemical analyses" by releasing a report on its own tests of the Beard memo which showed that the document was typed with the same typewriter ribbon on the same typewriter as other Beard memos done on and around June 25, 1971; the only conceivable way it could have been typed six months later, the report indicated, would be if the alleged forger had removed the typewriter ribbon from the wastebasket and held it six months before committing his forgery.

The attempt to destroy the hearings by the use of manufactured confusion had now hit full stride. James Boyd, who learned about the derailing of Senate hearings firsthand as one of the exposers of Senator Thomas

Dodd, has explained how that process was applied to the ITT hearings:

The process by which a congressional investigation ultimately becomes confused and muted resembles that which changes a rooster into a capon: its digestive apparatus is stuffed to excess while its vitals are castrated. The ITT-GOP propaganda teams bloated the probe beyond recognition by pumping in artificial exhibits, while its former potency was excised with a legal scalpel called "immunity."

The public cannot focus if, for every ball it identifies in the air, two more are thrown up. It apprehends that it is being purposely confused, but it wearies anyway, and is at length diverted to other things. And so, however preposterous the stunts may look individually—the three Beard memos to confuse the real one, the opposed medical reports, the conflicting document analyses, the ATT gift to the Democrats to balance the ITT gift to the Republicans, explanations that a thousand conventions are "bought" each year all over America—when viewed collectively, they succeed. Aibel or Merriam or Griswold or Reinecke or Dole or Liszka or Nunn or McCone or Scott or Cook or Hruska may look idiotic for a day, when their ball is shot down, but their embarrassment is temporary and their victory comes at length when the crowd tires of keeping track . . .

The idea is to bring the public to a point of bewilderment at which people will say, "it's all political." At that point the investigation can be ended by a party-line vote, with minimum backlash from the public. And so it was.*

The Beard interview in the hospital room represented the highwater mark of public interest in the case. It had been sustained for much longer than was thought likely, but several weeks of calculated confusion had finally dissipated it. As public interest ebbed, and the ITT story dropped off the front pages and the lead-off segments of the network news telecasts, the strength of the pro-ITT-G.O.P. senators on the Judiciary Committee grew. On April 27, 1972, a motion that would have prolonged the hearings and pursued the more blatant perjuries was voted down, with Chairman Eastland casting the decisive vote. On April 27 the hearings ended. The committee then voted to clear the nomination of Richard Klein-

* Washington Monthly, June 1972.

dienst by a vote of 11 to 4. On June 8, 1972, the full Senate confirmed Kleindienst by a vote of 64 to 19.

As this book goes to press, the errant Dita Beard has been shifted from handling political deals in Washington to conducting "sales research" in Denver. Her harassed superior, William Merriam, has been dispatched to Europe to devote himself to international trade. Francis J. Dunleavy, a new corporate president determined to win good-conduct medals, took office on January 1, 1973. And a repentant Harold Geneen, though still number one in the corporate hierarchy, has offered public penance and put ITT's executives on their best behavior. "We are mindful," he has instructed them, "of our obligations as citizens in each community in each nation in which we live and work and do business." Whether all this is mere polish on the corporate image or genuine reform is a matter for cynical speculation.

A Gallup poll, meanwhile, reported that almost twice as many people believed our charges as believed the government's defense. But our system of representative government is run by men who know how to measure the effluvium of public opinion that is here today and gone tomorrow against the solid weight of the financial interests that will always be with us.

The Business Buccaneers

The financial empire Harold Geneen built stretches, like the British empire, beyond the world's sunsets. And like its holdings, ITT's loyalties also extend beyond any national boundaries. It has become a government unto itself, with its own foreign service, intelligence apparatus, secret codes, and other governmental trappings. Its $7 billion operation each year exceeds the annual budgets for most nations, and the corporate ruler is paid four times more than the President of the United States.

ITT ranks with the great oil and munitions and industrial combines, whose economic tentacles encircle the world. So great is the economic power of these multinational, multibillion-dollar consortiums that they have become a separate world force. Their representatives actually assemble on occasion, in the manner of the United Nations, to discuss on a world scale how to best promote and protect profits. They are the modern buccaneers, well tailored and turned out, whose quarry is the world. They have no real interest in the welfare of any one nation. They are concerned only with making huge profits, however they can, wherever they can.

Governments may rise and fall; wars may shake the world. But the dividends keep pouring in, remarkably unaffected by international boundaries and politics. In Vietnam, for instance, the oil companies that fueled the U.S. military machine also paid protection money to the Viet Cong. This information was extracted from U.S. officials by Senator George Aiken (R-Vt.); they admitted cautiously at a secret Senate hearing that oilmen were known to be paying "tolls" for access rights through Communist-controlled territory. The three oil companies that did business in Vietnam—Esso, Caltex and Shell —indignantly denied the charge. Esso officials mournfully informed Senator Aiken that the Viet Cong had destroyed 40 percent of their Vietnam shipments. The senator pursued this point at a subsequent closed-door hearing. How much oil, asked Aiken, had been lost in South Vietnam? General Earle Wheeler, then the Joint Chiefs chairman, supplied the answer. "Only a fraction of one percent," he said.

I had an opportunity to make a personal investigation during the Tet offensive in February 1968. On a reconnaissance flight over the battle grounds outside Can Tho, I asked the pilot to make a sweep over the nearby Esso refinery. The plant stood out, an industrial castle in the jungle, inviting attack. I spotted scars of battle in the area, but the refinery had miraculously escaped damage. Intelligence sources told me, further, that oil trucks were allowed to move unhindered and that service stations had been left largely untouched in South Vietnam. There had been some oil losses, of course. A Viet Cong attack on the marine base at Danang on August 5, 1965, had damaged the Esso bulk plant and had destroyed about a hundred and twenty thousand dollars' worth of oil. An observer suggested that the marines might have saved the oil by pulling off their guards and mounting huge Esso signs around the plant.

This strange sanctity for oil property had been brought to our attention earlier. Competent sources told us that the Central Intelligence Agency had banned attacks on Havana's three oil refineries during the Bay of Pigs operation. Destruction of the Esso, Texaco, and Shell refineries would have left Fidel Castro's tanks, trucks, and planes short of fuel, thereby impairing their effectiveness against the motley invaders. Yet on the eve of the invasion, a fighter-bomber, loaded with explosives, radioed that it was over the Esso refinery in Havana and asked permission to bomb it. The CIA command post ordered the plane to ignore the refinery and look for gun emplacements to bomb.

Like the oil giants, ITT has a record of putting profits ahead of patriotism. In the dark days before World War II, according to still-secret FBI reports, ITT invested heavily in the German airplane manufacturer Focke-Wulf as Adolf Hitler was building up the Luftwaffe. The head of ITT's German subsidiary was a dedicated Nazi, and he was accompanied on his trips to the United States by his secretary, identified by the FBI as a German spy. After America's entry in the war, ITT set up a marketing office in Switzerland and attempted to transship strategic communications equipment from the United States to the Nazi military machine.

The postwar congolmerates, although their world-wide corporate interests are seldom identical with national interests, seem to be able to work their way with most governments. In many countries, the U.S. embassies function virtually as branch offices for private business interests. The State Department, of course, is supposed to protect American interests abroad, but it is not required to adapt U.S. foreign policy to please the conglomerates.

At the risk of alienating the rulers of the Congo, for example, the State Department brought pressure on them to grant Standard Oil of New Jersey a license to build a refinery. I saw the secret cables to our embassy in Leopoldville bluntly instructing our diplomats there to help Standard of New Jersey.

In Ceylon the State Department fully succeeded in alienating the government over a few service stations owned by Standard of New Jersey and Texaco. For twleve years the two oil giants had stalled the construction of a refinery which Ceylon needed badly. In exasperation the government finally nationalized their service stations. The State Department subsequently invoked a foreign-aid clause, which permits shutting off aid to any country that seizes American-owned property and fails to pay for it within six months. Ceylon offered to reimburse the oil companies, but both firms delayed furnishing the necessary financial figures for six months. It had all the earmarks of a deliberate stall. One oilman gleefully remarked: "This will teach the Ceylonese a lesson." Instead, Ceylon stood her ground and turned to Russia for petroleum products.

ITT plotted even more drastic action against any government that dared to oppose the company's financial interests. There had been talk in Argentina, for example, of nationalizing the ITT telephone system; the conglomerate immediately began plotting a revolution. In 1968 the governor of Puerto Rico considered taking over ITT's profitable but poorly serviced telephone company; ITT threw its resources against the governor, who was defeated at the polls. In 1970 the Marxist Salvador Allende Gossens, campaigning on a platform of nationalization, won Chile's presidential election. Without waiting to see whether he would be able to keep his promises, ITT tried to stop him from taking power.

ITT owned 60 percent of the Chilean telephone company, and Geneen intended to keep it. On October 23, 1970, ITT's Washington vice president, William Merriam, sent a message to Henry Kissinger in the White House. It was a stilted, rather ungraceful demand for tough American action to stop Allende.

Kissinger's reply, dated November 9, was merely a short acknowledgment: "I have read it carefully and I have passed it to those members of my staff who deal with Latin American matters. It is very helpful to have your thoughts and recommendations, and we shall certainly take them into account. I am grateful for your taking the time to give them to me." Before passing Kissinger's note on to ITT's New York headquarters, Merriam typed a short message on the bottom. "Believe this is more than perfunctory," it said. "Things are brewing on the Chile matter . . ."

Indeed, ITT had been brewing trouble for Chile for several months, and a top Kissinger aide had been informed of the plot almost from the beginning. The giant conglomerate was scheming to create financial chaos in Chile, to put pressure on the Chilean congress to keep Allende from power, and to organize a coup to take control of the government. Participating in the conspiracy were the Central Intelligence Agency's clandestine-services chief for Latin America, William V. Broe, and the ambassador to Chile, Edward Korry.

Chile's highly respected president, Eduardo Frei, was not eligible to run again in 1970. Allende won a plurality, but not a majority, in the general election. Under the constitution, the Chilean congress had the final decision between Allende and the second highest vote getter, right-wing candidate Jorge Alessandri. The potential for violence was enormous. The militants of the right were blamed for some shootings. The militants of the left, certain they would gain the votes of most Christian Democratic deputies, were disciplined but determined to protect the first victory at the polls by a Marxist.

ITT made its first approach to the White House on September 11—an outrageous offer to help finance American intervention in Chile's internal politics. J. D. "Jack" Neal, ITT's director of international relations, telephoned Viron P. "Pete" Vaky, a senior State Department officer on Kissinger's Latin American staff. The conversation was described in a memorandum, dated September 14, from Neal to Merriam:

I told Mr. Vaky we are aware of Ambassador Corry's [sic] position re Allesandri being certified and then resigning in order for Frei to run again. Also, we have heard rumors of moves by the Chilean military.

Mr. Vaky said there had been "lots of thinking" about the Chile situation and that it is a "real tough one" for the U.S. I admitted we understand the difficulty of the U.S. position but we hope the White House, State, etc., will take a neutral position, or not discourage, in the event Chile or others try to save the situation.

I told Mr. Vaky to tell Mr. Kissinger [ITT President Harold S.] Geneen is willing to come to Washington and discuss ITT's interest and that we are prepared to assist financially in sums up to seven figures. I said Mr. Geneen's concern is not one of "after the barn door has been locked," but that all along we have feared the Allende victory and have been trying unsuccessfully to get other American companies aroused over the fate of their investments, and join us in pre-election efforts.

Mr. Vaky said to thank Mr. Geneen for his interest and that he would pass all of this on to Mr. Kissinger. He offered to keep us informed.

More details of the ITT plot were spelled out by two of the company's Latin American agents, Hal Hendrix and Robert Berrellez, in a September 17 report. Both formerly were respected journalists specializing in Latin American affairs. Their communication outlined plans to win the congressional vote away from Allende. It stated: "The anti-Allende effort more than likely will require some outside financial support. The degree of this assistance will be known better around October 1. We have pledged our support if needed." Discussing a meeting with a Chilean politician, they said he "did not mention money or any other needs. At the end when it was mentioned, we were, as always, ready to contribute with what was necessary. He said we would be advised."

Moves to engineer the destruction of Chile's economy were discussed and weighed by the ITT manipulators. As one ITT document put it:

Some business sectors are encouraging economic collapse, hoping this eventually will necessitate a military take-over, or strengthen Alessandri in the congressional run-off. Undercover efforts are being made to bring about the bankruptcy of one or two of the major savings and loan associations. This is expected to trigger a run on banks and the closure of some factories resulting in more unemployment.

The pressures resulting from economic chaos could force a major segment of the Christian Democratic party to reconsider their stand in relation to Allende in the congressional run-off vote. It would become apparent there is no confidence among the business community in Allende's future policies and that the over-all health of the nation is at stake.

More important, massive unemployment and unrest might produce enough violence to force the military to move. The success of this maneuver rests in large measure on the reaction of the extreme and violent (Castroite-Marxist) left in Allende's camp. So far he has been able to keep these elements controlled . . .

We do not know whether the idea of impoverishing Chile began with the businessmen or the CIA, but ITT's Chile papers indicate that such a move was under serious consideration during the frequent meetings between the ITT and the CIA. In a September 29 cable to Geneen, who was in Brussels, ITT Vice President Edward J. Gerrity told of a meeting with "the same man you met with Merriam some weeks ago." (The visitor was identified in a subsequent Gerrity memo as the CIA's Broe.) Gerrity told Geneen that Broe's plan, "with which I do not necessarily agree," contained these elements:

1. Banks should not renew credits or should delay in doing so.
2. Companies should drag their feet in sending money, in making deliveries, in shipping spare parts, etc.
3. Savings and loan companies there are in trouble. If pressure were applied they would have to shut their doors, thereby creating strong pressure.
4. We should withdraw all technical help and should not provide any technical assistance in the future. Companies in a position to do so should shut their doors.
5. A list of companies was provided and it was suggested that we should contact them as indicated. I was told that of all the companies involved, ours alone had been responsive and understood the problem. The visitor added that money was no problem.

Gerrity wrote to Merriam the next day that Geneen "agrees with me that Broe's suggestions are not workable." Yet ITT, while dubious about the CIA's schemes, was eager to work with the CIA against Allende. Gerrity said Geneen "suggests that we be very discreet in handling Broe."

ITT's links with CIA were unusually strong. John McCone, a former director of the agency, was an ITT director. Merriam wrote McCone on October 9, described a luncheon conversation "with our contact at the McLean agency [CIA]," and said the man, apparently Broe, was "very, very pessimistic about defeating Allende when the congressional vote takes place October 24. Approaches continue to be made to select members of the armed forces in an attempt to have them lead some sort of uprising—no success to date."

It is quite possible that the CIA, or at least Broe, initiated the operations against Chile's economy without authoriy from the White House. But it is highly unlikely that the plot proceeded without the knowledge of the President and Kissinger.

ITT documents show that Ambassador Korry began his anti-Allende campaign on his own and learned later that his plans meshed with those of Washington. The Hendrix-Berrellez report states: "Late Tuesday night [September 15] Ambassador Edward Korry finally received a message from the State Department giving him the green light to move in the name of President Nixon. The message gave him maximum authority to do all possible—short of a Dominican Republic-type action—to keep Allende from taking power."

The same document also reported: "Ambassador Korry, before getting the go-signal from Foggy Bottom, clearly put his head on the block with his extremely strong messages to State. He also, to give him due credit, started to maneuver with the CD [Christian Democratic], the Radical and National parties and other Chileans—without State authorization—immediately after the election results were known. He has never let up on Frei, to the point of telling him to 'put his pants on.' " Korry, the report strongly suggests, was more candid about his activities when talking to ITT's men than when communicating with Washington.

When Allende's confirmation as President seemed certain, Korry came to Washington for consultation in mid-October and gave Neal a remarkably detailed account of his efforts. Neal reported: "Korry said he has reduced the amount of U.S. aid 'already in the pipeline' as much as possible. He estimates the amount to be $30 million." Korry informed Neal he was having difficulty selling his policy of stopping all aid, but Neal was able to assure his ITT superiors of a cutback. "This 'cutback,' " wrote Neal, "will be denied by State, who will say, as it has in the past, 'there has been no shutdown of aid to Chile; the program is under review.' " The government would lie to the public, but not to ITT. Korry also urged Neal to have Geneen submit his ideas on handling Chile to the White House and suggested "any complaints or ideas should be made now rather than after October 24."

At other times ITT showed an arrogant attitude toward the government. After Alessandri saw he would lose and withdrew from the presidential race on October 19, Gerrity wrote to Geneen recommending a series of queries about U.S. policy: "What does the State Department estimate will happen to U.S. investments in Chile? In the event of expropriation, what will the U.S. do? Will it press for payment in dollars to the expropriated owners? Will it invoke Hickenlooper Amendment, and if it did would it matter? Will AID funds be cut off? What does State estimate the effect of Allende's takeover will be in the rest of Latin America?"

He wanted the answers in writing from the State Department, and added: "We propose that the outlined program be implemented with: Dr. Kissinger, Mr. Meyer and Mr. Irwin of State, with certain other persons to be determined and, ultimately, with Secretary Rogers and the President." Charles Meyer was Assistant Secretary of State for Inter-American Affairs; John Irwin was Undersecretary of State.

"When these visits are carried out," Gerrity continued, "we should demand that U.S. representatives of international banks take a strong stand against any loan to countries expropriating American companies or discriminating against foreign private capital. As part of the overall action, we should ask our friends in Congress to warn the administration that continued mistreatment of U.S. private capital will bring about a cutoff to U.S. taxpayers' funds to international banks."

In an October 21 letter to McCone, Gerrity enclosed an unsigned document entitled "U.S. At the Crossroads —A Needed Reappraisal of Our Latin American Policy." It set forth what ITT thought U.S. policy should be in dealing with Allende, including what President Nixon should instruct his ambassadors to say. Its main points were: Allende should be told that unless compensation for expropriated U.S. property was made quickly in dollars or convertible currency, loans from private and international banks would be stopped; each U.S. ambassador in the Western Hemisphere should be called home and told individually of the diplomatic "review" with Allende; all aid funds "committed to Chile should be placed in the under review status in order that entry of money into Chile is temporarily stopped with a view to a permanent cut-off if necessary"; diplomatic representation in "certain Latin American capitals" should be reduced, with "the post left in the hands of a chargé d'affaires."

This same document, with only slight changes, was part of the October 23 letter from Merriam to Kissinger. Four paragraphs were added to warn of the Communist menace, and possibly in deference to Korry the suggestion that the embassy be left without an ambassador was dropped. In its place there was a demand to "strengthen the professional quality of U.S. diplomatic representatives throughout Latin America," and a complaint that no one had been appointed to fill the position of Undersecretary for Inter-American Affairs, though the creation of the post had been announced a year earlier.

Perhaps the most outrageous of ITT's suggestions was passed from Merriam to Gerrity on October 22. It pointed out that a $2.9 billion appropriation for the Inter-American Bank had passed the House and was awaiting Senate action. Merriam said that ITT, with other powerful business interests, was planning "to approach Senators Scott and Mansfield to see if they will just 'forget' to take up the bill. We could prepare statements for them which would get a message to the other Latin American countries that Chile's action is affecting them, too, albeit indirectly."

It is only incidental to the story that Allende was

sworn in as Chile's president and, ironically, used our exposure of the ITT plot as justification for nationalizing the telephone company. We also turned our files over to Senator Frank Church (D-Idaho), whose Senate subcommittee properly scolded both the CIA and ITT for their bizarre plottings. What is more important is that ITT was able to meddle so deeply in the affairs of a sovereign nation, whatever its politics, and to enlist the U.S. government in the machinations. ITT's power was so great that it spawned an arrogance that respected neither boundaries nor propriety. When profits were on the line ITT would spend millions and pull every possible political string to have its way.

The real scandal, however, is not so much that ITT will go to any length to protect ITT's interests, but that the government is willing to subordinate the national interest to promote private business interests. The popular fantasy that big fortunes are disappearing is a fallacy. For the business buccaneers, the postwar spoils have been rich.

Prelude to Watergate

At the acrimonious height of the Senate investigation into the ITT settlement, I cast an ill-considered slur on the competence of certain White House aides. My scorn was of the professional kind, occasioned by the discovery that several arms of the White House had been investigating me and had come up with nothing. I called the effort "amateurish," adding that if anyone on my staff ever produced such poor work I would have to fire him. On reflection, I feel an apology is due—which requires a bit of explanation.

The *Washington Post* of March 18, 1972, opened up the incident:

> The White House, angered by the length and scope of the Judiciary Committee hearings concerning the International Telephone and Telegraph Corp., is directing a major effort to discredit columnist Jack Anderson and the ITT memorandum he published which got the hearings started.
>
> The effort includes feeding negative material about Anderson and other information to be used in the hearings to Republican members of the Senate and to the press.
>
> In its campaign to disprove the implications in the memorandum allegedly written by ITT lobbyist Dita D. Beard, the White House has also used the resources of the Republican National Committee, the Committee for the Reelection of the President and the Justice Department.

The article described efforts by the White House staff to influence Dita Beard to disown her memo and also their attempts to discover some suitable scandal involving myself. The *Post* went on to quote from an "in-

terim memorandum" written for the White House by its
investigators reporting on my personal and business life.
I was one of the founders of the Chinese Refugee Relief
Organization, the report revealed; my fellow founders
included Mrs. Claire Chennault, a prominent Republican and the widow of the organizer of the Flying Tigers;
I had a bank account at the D.C. National Bank where
the widow Chennault was on the board of directors; I
owned a small interest in the Empress Restaurant in
Washington and in a newspaper in Las Vegas. The incriminating picture was rounded out by a mysterious
claim that I maintained "a close association with the *operating arm* of the Democratic Party," an entity I had
thought to be nonexistent. The White House report was
dismissed by the *Post* as "dealing with already known
and generally uncontroversial details about Anderson."
Such entries, while they might be helpful in an application for credit at Thom McAn's, seemed to me unwor-
thy of sleuths operating at the presidential level.

What I did not take into account was the secret
doings that were then fragmenting the energies of the
compilers of my White House biography. These gentlemen—James McCord, G. Gordon Liddy, E. Howard
Hunt, John Dean, and various presidential dispatchers
and controls—were engaged in truly momentous events,
compared with which their investigation of me was just
a sideshow. For example, they were preparing blueprints
for the burglarizing of Watergate and the bugging of
George McGovern headquarters; they were perfecting
schemes to burglarize the offices of Daniel Ellsberg's
psychiatrist, to recruit call girls who would romance
Democratic party leaders and report back the pillow
talk, to forge documents framing President Kennedy for
the murder of President Diem, to fabricate a new version of Chappaquiddick. The operatives were occupied
not only with conceiving and planning these vaulting designs but in making formal presentations to the Attorney
General of the United States and various high aides to
the President—presentations replete with elaborate

charts so that busy Nixon proconsuls could get a quick grasp of the finer points of the felonies within their purview. Little wonder, then, that their attentions to me had a Maxwell Smart quality, whereas in fact they were the efforts of men spread too thin. Their fate stands as an illustration of how the natural venality and mendacity of the Nixon regime was tempered by administrative mismanagement, which overloaded the investigators in the field. So much to do to so many, and so few to do it.

But an organized attempt by the government of the United States to destroy the reputation of a reporter who had embarrassed it need not be airily dismissed because it failed in part, or because its results had a comic side. For we see in the episodes revealed in the *Washington Post* in March 1972 an illustration of the *modus operandi* of the Nixon Administration which would soon come into full bloom.

I was informed by Justice Department sources that my house was being staked out and I was being tailed. I was given the descriptions of the cars that were following me and the license-tag numbers. My kids had a lot of fun spotting these cars. They reported back that they could see men with binoculars, bringing to our neighborhood an exhilarating air of intrigue. Occasionally I would catch sight of my pursuers, usually following about three blocks behind. I do not know whether my doctor's office was broken into, my phones tapped, my mail intercepted, my files photostated, or what other Administration routines were invoked.

At length, our pursuers hit paydirt, locating a photograph showing my secretary, Opal Ginn, in a group of six that included Dita Beard! To men who would comb the top-secret archives of the State Department and forge state documents to make a dead President appear a murderer, the photo offered considerable opportunity. They concocted a yarn to the effect that Opal and Dita were long-time drinking companions who met frequently at the Sheraton-Carlton. The implication was that they were a pair of souses who, in their degeneracy, had formed a conspiracy to "get" the Administration. No respectable reporter would use such a story without checking it out with the identifiable principals. But Senator Marlow Cook felt no such restraints and was happy to peddle the canard, using a meeting of the Senate Judiciary Committee as his forum. When skeptical newsmen still refused to print the material, presidential press secretary Ron Ziegler taunted them for "not following up the leads suggested by Senator Cook."

As it turned out, the picture had been taken at a party honoring a Sheraton-Carlton waiter, Bill Burazer, at which the contretemps occurred between Dita and Opal with which I opened this book. When questioned about the picture by federal agents, Burazer described the circumstances, affirming that in his twenty-five years as a waiter at the Sheraton-Carlton lounge, it was the first time he had seen Opal and Dita together. Senator Cook was left hanging, and his usefulness was curtailed as public conduit for later releases about Watergate. Cook's place was taken by the Senate Republican Minority Leader Hugh Scott.

At about this time, presidential aide Charles Colson allowed that he would "walk over the body of my grandmother to get the President reelected." The remark got a good run in the press as illustrative of the no-nonsense dedication of the Nixon elite. By this time the signals had changed on Dita. No longer was she to be portrayed as an unstable booze hound suffering from megalomania and hallucinations. The new line was to co-opt Dita. She would be promised her salary and other financial benefits in perpetuity. She would be assured the payment of her legal and medical bills. All she had to do was to deny authorship of the incriminating memo and insist that it was a forgery.

As I write this, the Watergate volcano is still erupting with daily explosions. Enough has already spewed forth to show that the Watergate crimes and their prolonged cover-up were but an elaboration of the basic approach used during the ITT preliminaries. This approach, sprung on an unsuspecting audience conditioned to trust their highest officials, substantially succeeded in hiding much of the ITT scandal and the 1972 campaign finance grotesqueries. By the time of the Watergate cover-up the techniques of conspiracy, fraud and perjury had been systematized into an automatic Administration response.

The illegal use of the law-enforcement apparatus to discredit myself and my associates was duplicated in starker form when the White House ring burglarized the offices of Daniel Ellsberg's doctor in search of confidential medical records. The attacks and slurs made by the Administration on news reporting during the ITT case were rerun during Watergate by Nixon, Agnew, Mitchell, Ziegler and Company in the most calculated way, until events blew apart the Administration's façade.

In dozens of particulars, large and small, the tactics used by the Nixon men to wriggle out of Watergate were imitations, albeit refined by practice, of those used in ITT. This is significant, for it shows that the conduct of the presidency in Watergate was not the spontaneous, makeshift reaction of otherwise honorable men trapped in a dilemma, but rather a standard operating procedure developed and used with growing success until cautious confidence became heedless arrogance.

The first response of ITT after we published the Dita Beard memorandum was to shred all pertinent company documents and remove key government papers beyond the reach of Senate investigators. The immediate White House response to the arrest of the Watergate Seven was to feed hundreds of documents into the shredder.

While Gordon Liddy was at the shredder, Howard Hunt sneaked an additional eight cartons out of the White House. An incurable romantic who had authored forty-six obscure novels, he apparently recognized the literary value of the papers and could not endure the wanton shredding of such precious story material. He arranged for an associate, Roy Sheppard, to stash the cartons in his basement. Incidentally, I almost gained access to this Watergate trove through Sheppard's lawyer, Peter Wolfe, who was deeply troubled by his knowledge of the secrets hidden in his client's cellar. I pressured Wolfe, pleaded with him and, I felt sure, persuaded him to acquire the papers from his client. But Sheppard destroyed the incriminating documents, and the chance was lost to blow the Watergate scandal wide open before the 1972 election.

The initial response to the ITT exposures at the highest level by Harold Geneen and John Mitchell was to deny any knowledge whatever of the events involved; similarly, the first Watergate response of President Nixon, Mitchell, and the top White House aides was to make the same protestation. The technique, which was to run for ten months before it became "inoperative," had been fully rehearsed during the ITT siege. Even the cast of characters was the same: John Dean, Charles Colson, E. Howard Hunt, G. Gordon Liddy, and James McCord, not to mention other faceless White House aides. Dean was the stage manager for the ITT coverup, just as he was for the later Watergate cover-up, taking his instructions from H. R. Haldeman and John Ehrlichman, who remained behind the White House scenes. During the ITT hearings Dean would slip up to Capitol Hill and operate out of Vice President Spiro Agnew's office. Dean would summon witnesses into these august chambers and discuss the testimony they planned to give on the witness stand.

While the White House worked to discredit my column and connived to turn Dita Beard around, Ron Ziegler innocently assured the press that so far as he knew no one in the White House was working on the ITT matter at all. Indeed, President Nixon personally tested out his later Watergate press tactics during ITT. He perfected the technique of making his points in a statement and then refusing questions from the press.

The Administration device of holding its own factfinding investigation and proclaiming itself innocent also received a successful tryout during ITT. The Ramsden Report enabled Assistant Attorney General Richard McLaren to make a complete turnabout on the ITT litigation while washing his hands of all inconsistencies.

About the same time, *Life* magazine revealed that President Nixon's long-time friend and financial supporter, C. Arnholdt Smith, the San Diego tycoon, had been excluded from an investigation into campaign-finance scandal by the device of a "personal interview" rather than an official interrogation. This was conducted not by the authorized federal agents but by U.S. Attorney Richard Seward, who had been appointed by Nixon at the behest of Smith. When this scandal was revealed, it too was resolved through another internal probe of the Administration by itself, this one conducted by Assistant Attorney General Henry Petersen. The probing Petersen privately found wrongdoing, but publicly cleared Seward. Thus, by the time of Watergate, the use of the inside investigation for whitewash purposes had been fully tried out.

And so we got the White House Watergate investigations by John Dean and the Justice Department investigation by Henry Petersen, both of which found that only the previously arrested Watergate Seven were involved. Because of inherent public trust in presidential integrity, these insider travesties were believed and got President Nixon safely past Election Day.

In neither ITT nor Watergate, however, were the White House and the Justice Department content to indulge in ersatz probes for public consumption; they also used their power to hamstring bona fide investigations into ITT and Watergate. Important information was pirated and turned over to those being investigated, thus crippling the investigations at every turn. For instance, in an unwise attempt at cooperation with Authority, I turned over the original of the Dita Beard memo to the Senate Judiciary Committee so that it could authenticate the document. Senator James Eastland passed this key document to the Justice Department. L. Patrick Gray then delivered the memo to John Dean, who slipped it to ITT. Dubious experts were hired to challenge its authenticity.

Gray and Dean, therefore, were just following a routine when they trafficked in the transcripts of FBI interrogations on Watergate. This allowed the White House not only to forewarn all its staff about the evidence that was being gathered, but also to pressure anyone who showed any inclination to testify to the truth in the matter.

The concealment of vital information about the genesis of the ITT settlement—which was practiced day after day by John Mitchell, Richard Kleindienst, and Richard McLaren before the Senate Judiciary Committee —provided an early illustration of one of the basic tactics of the White House during the Watergate cover-up. All incriminating involvements were denied outright or secretly hidden from investigators until the truth was independently revealed, whereupon Ziegler would declare past statements inoperative and start the process all over again.

The President's personal defense on Watergate, i.e., that all the crimes were perpetrated by overzealous subordinates acting with good intentions but poor judgment, got a dress rehearsal during the ITT siege. Claims of noninvolvement from On High were accompanied by low-level leaks that those who got caught were actually zealots, aberrants, and Walter Mittys living out fantasies. In the ITT scenario, Dita Beard was the oddball; the document shredders were the overzealous ones, acting rashly out of their passion to preserve the Company from embarrassment and doing harmless but unwise things that Higher Authority would have vetoed had it only known. As we have seen, Dita Beard, the potentially damaging witness, was to be the scapegoat in the ITT fiasco.

At this writing, John Dean, today's potentially damaging witness, seems to have been selected for the Dita Beard role in the Watergate drama. A few weeks before he drew the short straw, Dean was the trusted legal confidant upon whose recommendations President Nixon was basing the most sweeping claims of executive power ever made by an American President; then suddenly he was transformed into a non-person by Ziegler ("He is in his office doing whatever he does") and labeled an "embezzler" and "liar" on the Senate floor by the ever-accommodating Hugh Scott. Thus another paragon is transmogrified into a scapegoat.

Until the scapegoat passes the point of no return, however, the door is held ajar for him. The tactic which brought the bewigged Hunt and the ITT-paid attorney David Fleming to Dita's bedside in Denver—a tactic that worked—was possibly behind the White House's Easter phone call to John Dean on the eve of his excommunication. Mr. Nixon's wishes for a happy Easter were relayed to Dean, who was reassured: "You are still the President's lawyer, John."

The same inducement that brought Dita Beard back into the fold was also offered later to the Watergate Seven. At this point in the cover-up, it was the White House strategy to keep the sordid details from being spread on the court record. In return for pleading guilty and keeping silent, they were paid living expenses and legal fees—a remarkable beneficence, coming as it did from the same people who were publicly berating the Waterbuggers as meddling idiots.

The four Miami members of the bugging crew, for example, had planned to put up a defense in court until Hunt met with them on the night of January 11, 1973, in the Arlington Towers, just across the Potomac from the Watergate. I waited secretly in a nearby room for a report from one of the participants. He told me that Hunt, in return for their silence, had promised to seek eventual executive clemency and to arrange $1,000-a-month payments to their families.

When John Mitchell was confronted by press accusations that these sub rosa cash deliveries amounted to hush money and to suborning of witnesses, he likened the practice to that of a corporation that pays the legal fees of employees who are indicted in the line of duty. He may have been thinking of Dita Beard.

There are many other examples of the evolutionary relationship between ITT and Watergate—how the post-exposure flights of Howard Hunt and Donald Segretti paralleled Dita's, how Colson's use of a staged lie detector test recalled ITT's purchase of the microchemical analyses, how the President's private lawyer, Herbert Kalmbach, set up the legal façades for both the ITT gift and the laundered Watergate funds—but let us conclude with the details of one further illustration.

If all else failed, the White House ring felt it could rely on naked power. The President could invoke executive privilege to protect his associates from investigative scrutiny. The dress rehearsal for the invocation of this massive gag rule came during the ITT probe in the instance of Peter Flanigan. Ultimately, the White House had to relent a bit and allow Flanigan to at least appear before the committee. But its gag rule effectively barred key questions from being asked or answered.

Fortified by the Flanigan success, when Watergate began to get sticky the President and his Attorney General made the grandiose claim that none of his aides, past or present—nay, none of the millions of federal employees —could be called before the Senate Watergate Committee. Thus, according to the presidential plan, Haldeman and Erlichman, Dean and Magruder, Colson and Krogh, Mitchell and Stans, and others were never to be questioned under oath or in front of the American public about the felonies committed in the President's cause. Meanwhile, private assurances had been passed from the White House to the indicted Watergate Seven that the President would grant them clemency when things quieted down if they kept their mouths shut.

Why, then, did Humpty Dumpty suddenly fall and crash into many pieces? The larger reason is that the American legal system is as yet a bit too complicated and cumbersome to be totally controlled by the White House, even by an authoritarian Administration that is unrestrained by loyalty to the basic American values of political freedom and due process of law.

Their arrest set in motion the criminal investigative process which, under the spotlight of aggressive journalists, is difficult to nullify. Yet the Administration managed to nullify it until another circumstance—the appearance on the bench of an honest judge—threatened disruption. Still, the cover-up squad almost succeeded in thwarting Judge John Sirica; he could not go beoynd prosecutors who would not prosecute the higher-ups, nor could he circumvent defendants who pleaded guilty and kept their silence. But Sirica had one recourse; on sentencing day, he used it. The imposition of twenty-year sentences, with leniency possible only for those who talked, brought the unsentenced McCord and Hunt to their knees. Had they retained their faith that Nixon would yet get them off, their secrets would have remained hidden; but under Sirica's threat, the heroes of CREEP (Committee for the Reelection of the President) had suddenly wrinkled into middle-aged men who could not face the prospect of spending their remaining vital years in prison. Once McCord and Hunt began to sing, the pressure on the higher-ups to save their own skins became irresistible, and a chorus of presidential aides could be heard, a cappella, all over Washington.

Meanwhile, another man of honor, Senator Sam Ervin, was breaking the remaining Administration bulwark against the truth—the claim of executive privilege. For more than a year, Erivn had been mulling over executive privilege—ever since Peter Flanigan had used it as a shield at the ITT hearings. Ervin had fought the claim in a limited way; the President had compromised by allowing Flanigan to appear but to choose his own questions. Flanigan's testimony, therefore, was an antiseptic fiasco for those interested in the whole truth. Ervin, thus, was forewarned about compromise on the issue.

When the claim of executive privilege was proclaimed again to block all testimony by presidential aides and confidents during the Senate Watergate inquiry, Ervin was waiting and ready. "What meat do these White House aides eat that they have grown so great?" he asked, and with many a parable, quip, and legal precedent, he backed the White House to the wall.

He threatened to have any presidential aide who refused to appear hailed before the entire Senate, sitting as a court of last resort, on a contempt of Congress charge. If contempt was voted, Ervin said he would have the Senate police force march down Pennsylvania Avenue, arrest the White House staffers, handcuff them, and take their honors into custody. The presidential family laughed, but it was a thin laugh. The Senate, which when properly led, will still fight for its power, rallied behind Ervin. In a matter of weeks, the President gave in.

A dozen aides now saw that the road of continued evasion could lead them to a choice between going to jail for perjury or going to jail for contempt. It was what their unofficial chaplain, the Reverend Billy Graham, is wont to call "the hour of decision."

But a few atypical circumstances do not explain the bringing low of the Administration. An imperceptible change of climate was also at work, affecting the Ervins and Siricas. Just as Flanigan's claim to be above the reach of the Senate had aroused Ervin's resistance and brought him to battle armed with the missiles of Shakespeare, Blackstone, and the Lord, so too the exposures, large and small, of a dozen dedicated newsmen over four years had, piece by piece, stripped away the armor of credibility from the White House barons, until one day it was gone.

Ultimately, the moment came when Nixon's invoking of God and patriotism, Mitchell's hauteur, Stans's evasion, Kleindienst's statistics on how many FBI agents were involved in the investigation, Haldeman's impenetrability, Ziegler's cryptic half-truths were seen as signs not of wounded innocence but of guilt. Suddenly, even Republican senators began to waver in their loyalty. For the men of "that extra dimension," who had so long basked in the sunshine of Key Biscayne and San Clemente, perdition was at hand. Honor to the Siricas and the Ervins. Honor, too, to the Woodwards and Bernsteins of the sparse investigative press. Its alarums, so often seemingly unheard and unheeded, registered better than we knew.

PUBLISHER'S NOTE

On August 1, 1973, the Senate Watergate Committee disclosed evidence which undermined the basic positions taken by the Justice Department and the White House during the ITT hearings. This evidence was summarized in a secret March 30, 1972, memo, to White House Chief of Staff H. R. Haldeman from Special Counsel Charles W. Colson, stating that the White House, the Justice Department and ITT had thus far managed to suppress documents that would show perjury in the testimony of Justice Department officials and that "directly involved the President" in the settlement. The suppressed files cited to Haldeman by Colson include the following:

• "A May 5, 1971, memo from Ehrlichman to the A.G. alluding to discussions between the President and the A.G. as to the 'agreed upon ends' in the resolution of the ITT case . . ." • An ITT internal memo which "states that John Ehrlichman had assured Geneen that the President had instructed the Justice Department with respect to the bigness policy . . . That revelation would lay this case on the President's doorstep." • A White House memo sent to Attorney General Mitchell "setting forth the $400,000 arrangement with ITT . . . This memo put the Attorney General on constructive notice at least of the ITT commitment at that time and before the settlement, facts which he has denied under oath." • A memo sent to Vice-President Agnew from ITT Vice-President Gerrity which "tends to contradict Mitchell's testimony because it outlines Mitchell's agreement to talk to McLaren following Mitchell's meeting with Geneen in August, 1970."

THE
EAGLETON
AFFAIR

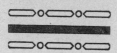

The Autopsy of a Dud

It has been my fortune recently to have figured in several of journalism's most celebrated coups—and in its most spectacular fiasco. In almost any other line of work—publishing, movie making, defense contracting, heart surgery, the saving of souls—such a record would be a cause not of chagrin but of exultation. But this rationalization is no balm for the wound. Investigative journalism must be somehow akin to shepherding, for it is the lamb that is lost, not the hundred that are safely shorn, which is most in my thoughts.

In the writing of this book, I would naturally prefer to relive the successes only, and for a time I trifled with the idea that I could quietly disown the black sheep by ignoring it. Nine out of ten times, I speculated, the reader is a child of the moment; surely by now he has forgotten my Eagleton misadventure, or, if he remembers the contretemps at all, mistakenly attributes it to Robert Novak or perhaps C. L. Sulzberger. But the tenth reader, knotheaded and implacable, will be out there studying my fingers, watching for me to palm the episode. In his eyes a book without Thomas Eagleton would be as suspect as a State of the Union message or the latest white paper issued by the New York Stock Exchange.

There is, of course, a larger issue—the stake we all have in public confidence in the basic integrity of the press. A mere mistake, however garish, is one thing; if honestly made, if promptly and openly corrected, it should not damage public confidence, for the public, knowing its own failings, requires the press to be not infallible but only honest. But an error negligently made,

wilfully persisted in, shielded against inquiry, unretract-
ed or retracted in a sneaky manner—this does diminish
confidence, a commodity that is of particular importance
today, when politicians and other special pleaders are
mounting a concerted effort to undermine trust in any
source of information that is not controlled by them.

Errors such as the Eagleton slip-up are grist for the
mills of those who seek to discredit the press as arbiter
of their claims and monitor of their official conduct.
When a reporter pulls a whopper, he has an obligation
to his own credibility and to that of the press to explain
it if he can. By doing so, the erring reporter distinguish-
es the press from, say, the Presidency, which will routinely lie about its responsibility for a Watergate, or the
Army, which will programmatically cover up for its
brass in a My Lai. He can thus hope to atone for his sin
and leave the credibility of the press as strong as he
found it.

But it is proper practice to retrace the evolution of a
story that was ultimately retracted, thus reviving anew
its allegations, if only to reject them again? This is one
of those questions to which there is no satisfying answer.
Normally, it would be a firm "no"; this was my initial
answer when first pressed by the publisher to do an
Eagleton chapter. But events have shown the Eagleton–McGovern tragedy to be one of those disorient-
ing news explosions that shatter conventional rules.
By seeking to vault within a heartbeat of the Presidency
while concealing a background of psychiatric disorders,
Senator Eagleton propelled himself into a historical rhu-
barb which robs him of the rights to privacy. And by
mismanaging the crisis and making a shambles of what
may emerge as one of the pivotal presidential campaigns
of American history, Eagleton–McGovern have created
an upside-down frame of reference as to the relevance
of information and the ethics of inquiry.

Political scholars have only begun to sift through the
debris. The psycho-historians are let loose, this time on
a live subject. Media critics are wading in. Thousands of
persons with records of emotional illness challenge the

rejection of Eagleton as a reflection on themselves and demand that the episode be analyzed more rationally. Constitutional tinkerers debate changes in the vice presidential selection process. For all these reasons, every factor which might shed light on those tortured days of July 1972 is mercilessly—and legitimately—pursued by journalists, historians, politicians, and students.

All participants, however reticent or peripheral, are sucked into the maelstrom and must thrash about in its currents. Aides to McGovern and Eagleton, at first sworn to silence, now feel compelled to leak out their versions in order to defend their own roles or bolster the sagging veracity of the principals. Confidential advice given to McGovern and Eagleton in the heat of the crisis is now broadcast. A former Attorney General noted for his propriety discusses the contents of FBI reports made on Eagleton back in the 1960's. Journalists feel called upon to make public why they published, or declined to publish, early reports of Eagleton's medical record.

I, too, have been caught in the rear-view mirror. Eagleton's press secretary recently told the media review, *More,* that my accusations revived the dump-Eagleton agitation just as it was subsiding, thus attributing to it a rather awesome historic role. Wherever I appear before audiences or on television interviews, I am questioned about the matter and run the hazard of an oversimplified or ill-chosen answer that such catch-as-catch-can encounters entail. A stream of articles and books even now begins to appear, and judging from those already published, many will address my role; this adds to the reasons why that role should be authentically presented.

I conclude that these circumstances justify and in a sense require the exhumation of matters that should otherwise remain interred. In doing so, I ought to set a tone proper to the recapitulation of an exposé that in the end aborted. And so to establish that tone at the outset, let me begin a that unhappy moment when my original story ended. The scene is a corridor on the sixth floor of the New Senate Office Building. I am standing beside a benign-looking Tom Eagleton, facing a battery of cameras, microphones, and reporters. I am reading the following statement: "I have exhausted my investigative activities . . . I have come out here to retract the story in toto . . . I owe [the Senator] a great and humble apology."

The events which led to that scene began more than four years earlier.

Early Whispers

In the spring of 1968 I was approached by an old friend seeking advice. True Davis had been President Kennedy's ambassador to Switzerland, President Johnson's Assistant Secretary of the Treasury and was currently a director of twenty-nine corporations. Tall, with clipped mustache, resonant voice and winning manner, Davis is the type society columnists and other professional romantics call handsome and charming. His forte is business; he was president of Norelco. But at the time, he was wading in the unfamiliar waters of electoral politics. He had declared for the Democratic Senate nomination in Missouri and was locked in a bruising three-way primary campaign against incumbent Senator Edward Long and thirty-eight-year-old Lieutenant Governor Thomas Eagleton.

True Davis and I went back a long way together. We could deal with each other candidly and in confidence, and it was in such a context that he called on me. He said that his strongest opponent was turning out to be not Senator Long, as had been expected, but young Eagleton, an attractive, articulate, sympathetic figure, and a formidable campaigner. The word among Missouri insiders, Davis said, was that Eagleton had a serious personal vulnerability. Davis wanted my opinion as to whether it could be successfully exploited, and if it could be, whether it ought to be. The story was widespread, Davis continued, that Eagleton had a drinking problem. Davis's campaign staff, which included old Eagleton allies, had ascertained that Eagleton became erratic under the stress of a campaign to the extent that

177

he had been secretly hospitalized no less than three times. This they laid to alcoholism. Some of Davis's advisers were of the opinion that Eagleton would never make it to primary day, since there was to be a grueling five-month campaign. They also speculated that Eagleton might hold together through the primary and win, only to collapse in the uphill battle that would follow against a united Republican party, thus forfeiting a Democratic Senate seat to the opposition. Davis had with him a collection of photostats, according to his own later recollection, which he identified as copies of arrest citations for drunk or reckless driving served on Eagleton over a period of years. The photostats had been slipped to Davis at a political rally by a man in civilian clothes who identified himself as a state trooper. True asked me what, if anything, I thought he ought to do about it.

My attitude toward the private follies of public officials is that they are not fair game unless they can be tied to malfunction in office, or unless the miscreant is so pious for public consumption, or so lacking in compassion for the foibles of his fellows, that a sharp needle needs to be jabbed into his gas balloon. I asked True if Eagleton had been a stable, hard-working public servant. Davis said yes, so far as he knew. Had Eagleton, as prosecutor and state Attorney General, been a Cato or a hypocrite? No.

My advice, then, even if we could assume the allegations to be true, was to drop the matter. And not just on ethical grounds. The great American public contains an incalculable number of reprobates and sentimentalists; to single out one candidate as a prodigal risks arousing to his support an army of kindred souls who might otherwise have seen no particular merit in the man. True agreed not to pursue the matter; in fact, I got the impression that he had been so persuaded all along and that my judgment only confirmed his own.

Contrary to the speculations, Eagleton was not overcome by drink under the strains of a double campaign but went on to beat both his primary rivals and to defeat a strong Republican challenger, Congressman Thomas Curtis, in the November election. In doing so, he is said to have waged a campaign that is memorable for its energy, endurance, and decency.

In Washington, Eagleton had impressed me as able, hard-working, and conscientious. For example, he had accepted assignment on the District of Columbia Committee, which acts as a sort of city council ruling over Washington. Most senators avoid service on this committee; they cannot easily parlay an investment of time and effort there into either of their main preoccupations: credit back home with the voters or rung-climbing within the Senate's power structure. Among those who do interest themselves in this committee and its House counterpart, all too often the motive is to play footsie with the local special-interest lobbies at the expense of the voteless citizenry. But Eagleton took up this undesirable assignment; and he took it up as a trust and plunged into the problems of the capital city in a dutiful manner. I honored him for his hard work as a member and, eventually, chairman of that committee.

For more than four years I had no occasion to recall that conversation with True Davis, until the 1972 Democratic National Convention met in Miami. From the outset of the convention, speculation buzzed about vice presidential possibilities, and prominent among them was the junior senator from Missouri. Scarcely had I checked into Miami's Hotel Fontainebleau than informants began contacting me with stories about Eagleton's alleged drinking problem. I recalled the bare outline of what True Davis had long ago told me, which gave this new crop of stories some credence; but I again decided not to investigate the matter. Conventions are awash in salacious rumors, many of them politically motivated, and I did not want to lend my column to any Stop Eagleton ploy. In the frenetic atmosphere of a national convention, when vice presidential candidates rise and fall for the most frivolous of reasons, an ill-timed exposé could do unwarranted damage.

And there was something else. A reporter must at

length resign himself to the gothic idiosyncrasies prevailing among men who are driven toward power and fame. The political tree is curiously infested with alcoholics, compulsive womanizers, narcissists, paranoids, megalomaniacs, and aberrants of the most picturesque persuasions. Perhaps the psycho-historians will one day be able to explain this phenomenon. I suspect its common root is inner insecurity, some sense of unworthiness and inadequacy, usually justified, which drives its victims to prove themselves through the meretricious vindication of public acclaim. But while we await a definite answer, let us not carelessly rush in to push aside the senator who occasionally executes le droit du seigneur upon an office secretary lest his place be taken by a neurotic of a more antisocial strain.

I dismissed, therefore, about a dozen tips, some of them highly placed, to look into Eagleton's personal past. Full of fatuous philosophizing, I fell into the error I most condemn in my fellow reporters—the making up of reasons for *not* investigating, for *not* reporting.

The Week That Was

What Tom Eagleton would later call "the week that was" blasted off on the mountain-crisp morning of July 25 at Sylvan Lake in the Black Hills of South Dakota —the McGovern vacation retreat where he was to have repaired the ravages of eighteen months of nonstop campaigning and gained strength for the climactic battle against President Nixon. No hint of an impending crisis charged the relaxed air of the Sylvan Lake Lodge as unsuspecting reporters ambled in for a routine press conference. The two-week-old Democratic ticket of McGovern and Eagleton entered unportentously in opennecked sportshirts. Eagleton stepped to the microphones, appealingly casual in a blue-and-white checked jacket, and jolted lolling reporters to attention when he said, "On three occasions in my life, I have voluntarily gone into hospitals as a result of nervous exhaustion and fatigue." His voice was under control, but his hands trembled and sweat beads glistened on his forehead as television lights and inquisitive eyes bored into him. He took pains to deny an accusation that had not been publicly made; his condition, he said, had nothing to do with alcohol—he had never had a drinking problem of any kind. "As a young man I drove myself too far," he explained. He had since learned to pace himself . . . "I make it a regular practice to be as idle as I can on Sundays."

When the questions began, however, a picture more politically ominous than fatigue and dyspepsia emerged.

Q. During these periods, did you receive any psychiatric help?
A. Yes, I did.
Q. Can you tell us what type of psychiatric treatment you received?
A. Counseling from a psychiatrist, electric shock.
Q. What were the purposes of the electric-shock treatment?
A. At that time it was part of the prescribed treatment for one who is suffering from nervous exhaustion and fatigue and manifestations of depression.

Eagleton had trapped himself and the unsuspecting McGovern in a nightmare from which there could be no awakening. All their writhings in trying to escape were so foredoomed that even reporters and politicians, scavengers of tragedy that they are, were numbed, momentarily at least, by the destruction irreversibly closing in. An engaging young man of refreshing talent and vast promise, pushed beyond his capacities from boyhood by a doting but overambitious father, had now been overtaken by a dead history that had already exacted unknowable agonies. And by Eagleton's side stood George McGovern, made vulnerable by a sympathetic nature; still elated over his political miracles of the winter and spring, seeming not yet to realize that he had been felled by a fate demoniacally fashioned not only to end his journey but to bemuse him into dancing the steps and singing the songs of the evasive, faithless, inconstant *Homo politicus* he so detested.

Confronted with a similar predicament in the 1952 campaign, Dwight Eisenhower, that cool manipulator of ambitious men, had simply detached himself and moved above the battle. Richard Nixon was put on his own, given a few days to extricate himself from the slush-fund scandal and prove he was an asset to the ticket; otherwise he was to be matter-of-factly dumped with no appreciable loss to Ike. But McGovern characteristically, if foolishly, rallied to Eagleton's defense from the outset. Already he felt the compulsion to huckster Eagleton's announcement as a voluntary confession, when in fact it had been forced by the imminence of a *Detroit Free Press* exposé that had been delayed by the false promise of McGovern aides to produce Eagleton for a crowning, exclusive interview.

"What you have already seen here today," McGovern was saying, "is a demonstration of the kind of candor and openness that you're going to get in this campaign . . . If I had known every detail that he discussed with me this morning . . . he would still have been my choice for the vice presidency."

Such obvious humbug changed my attitude and revived my normal skepticism. The fact was that Eagleton, however ill-used by fortune, had tricked McGovern. Here we had a seasoned Missouri politician (than whom there are none more seasoned) who, by his own admission, had been obsessed for years with visions of the presidency. As he drew ever closer to his goal—state attorney general, lieutenant governor, U.S. senator, vice presidential possibility—how many hundreds of times must he have anticipated, in feverish moments before dawn, the dread disclosure which, undisabling though it might be to other men, would be crippling to his one consuming ambition.

Yet here he was, contending in a "Golly, gee" tone that it just hadn't occurred to him to tell McGovern about the hospitalizations and the fits of depression and the electric-shock treatments—even when he was pointedly asked, in the unmisinterpretable language of politicians, Was there anything in his past that could be used to damage the McGovern candidacy? That this lapse by Eagleton was contrived, that his medical history was indeed much on his mind, he later revealed in a *Newsweek* interview.

"When we got to Miami Beach, Barbara and I discussed the possibility of my being chosen as McGovern's No. 2, and she said 'Tom, you realize that you're running the risk that if you go into a national campaign that there will be a public disclosure of your hospitalization.' And I replied: 'Yes, I realize that. It's quite probable in fact . . .' I would take a *calculated* risk that the story would not leak out, at least not in the form it ultimately did."

It was McGovern as well as himself whom he calcu-latedly risked. If Eagleton stayed on the ticket, doubts about his emotional stability were bound to be increasingly exploited. The word would spread that Eagleton, don't you know, could become President with his finger on the nuclear button if anything happened to Mc-Govern, yet couldn't qualify to guard the White House, let alone occupy it, etc., etc. By November a ticket liable to such an attack would become submerged in a sea of doubts. Yet, if Eagleton were now to be forced off the ticket after McGovern had endorsed him "1,000 per-cent," McGovern would be placed in the ugly role of one who, for political expediency, had sacrificed a friend in the hour of need.

The only way out of the dilemma was for Eagleton either to produce medical records that would clearly negate the issue or to resign, not under pressure, but on his own, preferably over the protests of true-blue Mc-Govern. But Eagleton would not reveal his medical records, even to McGovern; nor would he release his doctors for public questioning. And he had no intention of resigning. He left Sylvan Lake obviously determined to keep McGovern over the barrel while he created such a sympathetic commotion in his own behalf that it would hurt the ticket as much to drop him as to keep him. He resumed his campaign schedule, announced daily press conferences and began to elaborate such sympathy-evoking yarns as that he had concealed his medical history not for his own sake but for his son's, who was now cast in the role of the Gipper. "Terry is an impression-able boy at an impressionable age. And other kids can be terribly cruel about this kind of thing. I never, never would do anything to hurt or embarrass my boy . . . I've got to win. I've got to do it for Terry. I've got to make it for Terry."

As the week progressed the attractive and persuasive Eagleton began to appear to millions as the innocent victim of the debacle—instead of its architect—while in-decisive McGovern became the heavy.

The Elusive Photostats

Eagleton was driven by an ambition which had first
induced him to conceal his record from McGovern and
which now dissuaded him from accepting the consequences of its revelation. I found it impossible to get
documentation that would affirm or deny the truth of
Eagleton's version of his emotional condition and its history. Not only had the routine records of his hospitalization been inexplicably removed from the Barnes Hospital records files, but I later learned the doctors had been
forbidden to discuss the details even with McGovern.

But there was another way. I was drawn to his unequivocal denial that alcohol had ever been a problem for
him. Though I had twice dismissed the matter before,
the new circumstances reversed that judgment. Here, I
hoped, was a simple test of Eagleton's credibility that
could be resolved, clearly and in time to be serviceable.

Recalling fragments of my old conversation with True
Davis, I phoned him. He acknowledged that in 1968 we
had discussed an Eagleton drinking problem, but said
that he would rather not discuss it further. He had become friendly with Eagleton in the intervening years,
had supported him politically, and even had a son on
Eagleton's staff.

I then phoned a veteran Missouri correspondent who
offered some help if I would keep his name out of it. He
said he had heard the drunken-arrest stories and gave me
the names of three state policemen who might provide details. I also phoned a friend who had formerly been high
in Missouri government and had many contacts within
the state administration. He confided that state troopers

had told him the highway patrol had frequently picked up Eagleton. "Which state troopers?" I asked. The former official gave me the names of some patrolmen and a local magistrate. I now had several names and began to feel the exhilaration of the chase. Two of the most promising officers on my list, who were said to have personal knowledge, were on vacation and beyond reach. I spoke to one who claimed to remember a personal incident involving the stopping of Eagleton and had heard similar stories from other officers. But halfway into his account, he backed off and refused to be quoted, even on a no-attribution basis.

Another name on my list turned out to be a retired trooper. He was willing to talk, but as is so often the case, he had little of value to say. He could offer no personal experiences with Eagleton, but claimed to know several who had. What he did have to say was tainted by obvious hostility to Eagleton. He gave me names and offered to send documentation. But he never came through, except to write me a letter that was a mere diatribe.

The most damning report came from a trooper who, too, extracted a promise that his name would not be used; nor would he give me the names of any other policemen involved. (The fear public employees have of losing their jobs or suffering other reprisals is the most consistently frustrating obstacle an investigative reporter encounters.) But he was willing to tell me what he purportedly knew; he had helped collect and photostat Eagleton's traffic citations. His story was this. In 1968, he had worked under a captain who, he said, had become upset over Eagleton's traffic record. In deference to Eagleton's status first as attorney general and later as lieutenant governor, the troopers who stopped him on the highway usually would not ticket him. But over the years a few tough troopers wrote out tickets. My informant explained that one copy would go to the local magistrate, another to the capitol at Jefferson City. But a third copy would be retained by the arresting officer. Eagleton's friends, so the trooper's story went, usually managed to kill the first two copies but overlooked the copies held by individual troopers.

The captain, I was told, decided on a showdown with the superintendent over Eagleton. Maybe his motive was highway safety and police professionalism; maybe it was politics or even personal dislike. In any event, he had a plan of action. He reasoned that in the nature of things, a number of patrolmen would hang on to their copies, and he asked my trooper-informant to mosey around and collect as many as possible. The trooper said he collected about a dozen of these arrest citations, some alleging drunken driving, some careless driving, some speeding.

One day the captain confronted the superintendent. Afterward, the captain told my informant that he had been rebuffed and therefore would abandon any further efforts through official channels. But he was unwilling to let the matter drop entirely and directed my source to photostat the traffic citations. Three sets were delivered to Eagleton's political opponents: Democratic rivals True Davis and Senator Edward Long; and the Republican candidate, Representative Thomas Curtis.

I asked my informant to try to persuade his captain to talk to me confidentially; he agreed to try but called back later to say the captain would not talk to me under any circumstances. For the moment, I had gone as far as I could with the police. I now went to the alleged recipients of these photostats.

I reached True Davis first. I argued that I had pieced together the basics of the story without his help, that other reporters were right behind me, that the story was bound to be broken. Would he not now confirm in detail what he had told me four years before? He agreed on condition that his anonymity be respected (a condition he later lifted).

Davis said he had personally received the photostats at a campaign appearance in central Missouri during the primary race. He was imprecise as to the place—which was understandable in the context of a primary that embraced hundreds of towns and lasted five months. He said the photostats were handed to him in a plain brown envelope by a man in civilian clothes who identified himself as a state trooper. Davis said he examined the photostats personally and was convinced of their authenticity. There were ten or eleven; some were for speeding and reckless driving; three or four involved intoxication. He did not subject them to further checking, for it was at this point that he decided not to use them in the campaign.

He subsequently reminded me that, irony of ironies, he had shown the photostats to me during our 1968 conversation. Truthfully I could not recall seeing the photostats. Inspecting documents is almost a daily ritual for me; in order that I may remember information I consider important, my memory jettisons whatever at the time seems inconsequential.

Could Davis lay his hands on those photostats? No, he said. After his primary defeat, he had resolved never to run for office again, and as a hand-washing exercise he had ordered all his campaign files destroyed, including even his mailing lists of supporters and contributors —the ultimate renunciation of politics.

I next called ex-Senator Long, who said yes, an envelope containing photostats of arrest citations involving Eagleton had been presented to one of his aides. The aide had reported the delivery to Long, who said he was not interested in the photostats and therefore did not examine them himself. He said he did not know what had become of the photostats.

It was not until after I had broadcast the Eagleton story that my associate Mike Kiernan was able to check with Congressman Curtis. Eagleton's erstwhile Republican rival had a vague recollection of some traffic records but did not see them and could give us no information that was precise enough to be of use.

In the meantime I had called a source within the FBI. I knew that the bureau maintained dossiers on members of Congress. Could I get the Eagleton file? My source reported back that the Eagleton file already had been pulled and was in the hands of the Justice Department

high command. So I phoned a White House contact—
which merits a word of explanation. Shortly after President Nixon took office, one of his aides contacted me.
He said he had access to the President and could get to
him any time it was important; also he could, under
some circumstances, help me get certain information. In
due time, I tested this channel by asking for the records
of the investigation into Governor George Wallace's income tax returns. I got the records.

Time had blighted my relationship with the White
House as the stories I wrote became more embarrassing
to the President. Nevertheless, gall springs eternal in the
muckraker's breast, so I called my one-time confidant
and asked for the Eagleton dossier. He said he would
see what he could do. Meanwhile my associate Brit
Hume had placed calls to Eagleton's press secretary in
Washington and Los Angeles.

Thirty-four hours had now passed since the July 25th
Eagleton-McGovern press conference at Sylvan Lake.

The Fateful Broadcast

I arose on the following morning, July 27, anticipating that at any moment I would receive incontrovertible proof. As I drove toward the Washington studios of the Mutual Broadcasting Company to tape my morning radio broadcast, I mulled over the information I now had.

First, there were all the stories told me at the Miami Convention, many of them by substantial, believable people. Second, I had talked to two state patrolmen who claimed personal knowledge of drink-related arrests and another who had heard similar stories from other patrolmen. Third, I had an intricate account of the collection and distribution of arrest photostats, right from the horse's mouth. Fourth, two prominent public officials had confirmed to me that the photostats had indeed been delivered to them, in the manner stated to me by the trooper, and one of the two, True Davis, an astute businessman, diplomat, and financier who had risen in the world by being able to assess documents, had personally, though superficially, examined them and considered them authentic. Fifth, according to Davis, I had actually seen the photostats four years earlier, though, strain as I might, I could not remember. Sixth, we had located in Missouri police records three speeding arrests and one minor accident involving Eagleton; drinking was not charged in any of these incidents.

The story was not yet nailed down, of course, and could not be until I received and authenticated the photostats. But certainly the matching testimony of so many reputable informants, persons who had not come to me but whom I had painstakingly sought out, had some news value. To be sure, some of these informants could conceivably be lying to me and others could have been taken in by forged documents, but the information and the ascertainable motivations just didn't have that ring. I judged I would have the photostats momentarily. I had at least four chances to get them—two police officers, Senator Long, and, least likely but still possible, my White House source. Moreover, we were at work on other leads, any one of which might turn the trick. I was also acutely aware that dozens of reporters were in Missouri on the trail of Eagleton's past and that political leaders all around the state were telling them Eagleton drinking stories.

With two minutes to go before the tape rolled, I began looking over my radio script. It contained a routine story from Mike Kiernan about Eagleton. I crossed out a line or two and penciled in: "Eagleton has steadfastly denied any alcoholism, but we now have located photostats of half a dozen arrests for drunken and reckless driving."

It was the word "located" that rattled around discordantly in my head as I drove toward my office immediately after the taping. There is a defective monitor somewhere in our brain that too late taunts us with visions of what we ought to have said. I had "located" the photostats only in the sense that I had traced their passage through an elaborate journey and had been given to believe that at least one set should soon be in my hands. But "located" was more likely to be taken as a claim that I already had the photostats in hand. The word "arrests" should have been qualified with a reminder that arrests were not convictions. The tone of certainty my words conveyed should have been more properly one of conjecture. The attempt to improvise and condense a story of such complexity into one quick line was inexcusable. Under ordinary circumstances my interviews with several public officials of varying degrees of eminence formed a proper basis for some kind of a story, but a story of this kind—in a hypertense atmosphere, in a time frame in which every hour was crucial to the decision that would be made respecting Eagleton—should have been governed by maximum, not minimum, standards of reliability, and I had failed that standard. I had reliable sources, I thought, but sources whose names I could not use; I had believable testimony that the photostats existed, but I did not yet have the photostats.

Fortunately, there was a fail-safe device. One of the advantages of taping news shows in advance of broadcast time is that the tape can be killed or changed. My broadcast was not "moved" by the network each morning until 10:15 A.M. It was now only about 9:50 A.M. I had plenty of time.

But I reached my office only to find that the tape had been moved early because of the news value of my Eagleton item and was already being broadcast across the nation. I had propelled myself into the midst of a bad dream.

Backfire

It is all too common in government to cover an error by silence. When a bold statement turns out to have timid foundations, many an official has disappeared into an impenetrable silence. This escape into the void is impossible for those of us who cast light on others; we must also stand in the light ourselves. As I looked about our offices, watching telephones lighting up everywhere, I could already feel the heat. These callers no doubt wanted confirmation and elaboration. Any equivocation on my part, even a change of wording, would be boomed as "Anderson backs off." I had full confidence in my story and immediate expectation of final proof.

I was tempted to become "unavailable" until the photostats arrived, but this would have turned an impetuous overstatement into a willful perversity. I decided to put out immediately a clarification that would bring the radio broadcast into balance; we would talk frankly to all comers and I would henceforth give the press a running account of the development of my proof or lack of it. At worst, I should be able to persuade my sources to step forward and confirm the substance of the story. This was a sorry substitute for nailing down the facts in the first place, but I had a responsibility to put the story in proper perspective at once. And so I immediately issued the following statement:

We have traced—but have not seen—photostats of Senator Tom Eagleton's traffic records.

A former high official from Missouri, whose reliability is beyond question but who has asked us not to identify him, has confirmed that a Missouri state trooper turned over to him

193

photostats of six to eleven traffic citations. He cannot be sure of the exact number, he said, but the figure eleven sticks in his mind.

These citations, he said, ranged from drunken and reckless driving to speeding. All of them occurred in Missouri during the 1960's, to the best of his recollection.

This was put on the wire right on the heels of the radio broadcast. In subsequent interviews I also emphasized that traffic citations were not convictions. I carefully avoided referring to the troopers who had talked to me, knowing they feared for their jobs. A wrong word out of me, I knew, would frighten them away.

Senator Eagleton, by now in Honolulu, got both my broadcast and my clarification at approximately the same time. He immediately summoned a press conference and fired back a strong denial that took due notice of my clarification.

Apparently Mr. Anderson does not have the documents. He does not have them because the documents do not exist. I have never been arrested or charged with drunken or careless driving, drunken or reckless driving. Mr. Anderson's statement is, in blunt but direct English, a damnable lie.

Eagleton's head-on challenge sounded the more authentic because of my admission. The burden was on me to prove the charge, not on Eagleton to disprove it—which was as it should be.

The telephone calls now poured in—from wire services, networks, newspapers, citizens—overburdening our modest four-line switchboard. To all, we stressed that we had not seen any documents, that our story was based on sources who must remain anonymous but whom we regarded as competent, that citations were not convictions. On the following day, Friday, I agreed to a nationally televised confrontation with Eagleton on the C.B.S. Sunday interview show, *Face the Nation;* and I issued another statement which recapitulated our phone interviews:

For competitive reasons, we went out fast yesterday with a story that Senator Tom Eagleton has been cited for drunken and reckless driving. The story was based on the recollections of a competent source, who personally saw photostats of the traffic citations. We also discussed the story with other responsible sources who had been told of Eagleton's traffic violations . . .

I repeatedly emphasized yesterday that I saw no documentation myself and that the alleged incidents involved no convictions. Prior to using the story, my office tried to reach Eagleton for twenty-four hours for his comment, but he failed to return our calls. In retrospect, I believe I broadcast the story prematurely and should have waited until I could authenticate the traffic citations personally.

Nevertheless, I have faith in my sources and stand by the story. If this faith should ever turn out to be unwarranted, I will issue a full retraction and apology.

Some Eagleton aides have said in retrospect that the Senator was weathering the electro-shock storm well when my allegations submerged him again and gave the "dump Eagleton" sentiment new impetus. There are some indications that my broadcast temporarily strengthened the hand of anti-Eagleton advisers to McGovern. But there is other evidence that Eagleton's position had already become untenable and that my attack and retreat were seen by the Eagleton forces as a sympathy-grabber for the senator, and as a peripheral vindication that could be exploited to reverse the tide. Before I catapulted myself into the controversy, McGovern's money-raisers had reported the Eagleton situation was a disaster; the mailing of two million fund-raising letters was called off; influential pro-McGovern newspapers were known to be preparing drop-Eagleton editorials; and McGovern himself had begun to waffle.

Following the old adage that in politics there is nothing better than to be the victim of an outrage, Eagleton went over from the inherently unrewarding defense of his emotional condition to a vigorous offense against an acknowledged public menace: "I am not going to be driven off this ticket by Jack Anderson . . . I am not going to let a lie drive me off the ticket. I have never been more determined in my life about an issue."

Absent suddenly was Eagleton's humble assurance that he wouldn't even have to be asked to resign if he so much as thought for an instant that McGovern might be uncomfortable with him. A greater issue had taken precedence; Eagleton had been wronged and must now be vindicated. Correspondents traveling with Eagleton began to report a new fire and momentum in his campaign to stay on the ticket. A Gallup poll taken during this fighting phase showed a two-to-one majority for Eagleton staying on the ticket. My master stroke for challenging Eagleton's veracity and clarifying the picture had only undermined my own veracity and muddied the situation.

Retract or Not to Retract?

A host of newspaper tub-thumpers, not known previously for journalistic enterprise or purity, now aroused themselves and began to charge me with irresponsibility and hastiness. Of more concern to me, friends and associates who had my welfare at heart urged me to go further than I had and issue an out-and-out retraction. They had various reasons: that Eagleton wouldn't have risked making such an unequivocal denial if there was a chance of getting tripped up; that anonymous sources were no proper basis for a story of such political importance; that even if the 1968 photostats did exist, they might be fakes.

I considered all these reasons—and in fact, had been preoccupied with them—but I rejected each of them as misinterpreting both the motivations of politicians and the role of the press. Eagleton's vehement counterattack could reflect a confidence born of being impeccably right, but it might also be the last desperate bluff of a gambler running in bad luck and trying to get back into the game. Already his claim never to have been arrested for careless driving had proven to be a play on words. Records of the Missouri Highway Patrol *did* show three arrests and fines for speeding, in 1962, 1954, and 1948, and a non-actionable 1963 accident in which he skidded off an icy road, ran into a road marker and damaged his car. (When Senator Eagleton later admitted to these incidents but claimed there were no others, the city attorney for St. Petersburg, Florida, recalling that Eagleton visited there occasionally, followed a hunch and checked local police records. He found a 1967 citation and fine for running a red light at a cross walk charged to Attorney Thomas F. Eagleton of St. Louis, Missouri.) Perhaps speeding at eighty-five miles per hour or ignoring red lights at cross walks does not technically constitute "careless" driving. Certainly, they did not visibly bear on the main charge at issue—drunken driving—but in my book their existence had already put a little puncture in his "damnable lie" response. And reports that might puncture it further were still coming in.

Nor did my reliance thus far on nonattributable sources seem to me a ground for retraction. It would, of course, have strengthened my position immeasurably if the three state policemen, Senator Long, Ambassador Davis, and the others had come forward to publicly attest to what they had told me. But their failure to do so did not of itself invalidate the story. The legitimacy of the anonymous source—known, tested, and trusted by the reporter but not identifiable to the public—is accepted throughout the world of journalism. Investigative reporting would dry up overnight if the inside volunteer of newsworthy information had to endure the embarrassments and reprisals that would follow his public surfacing; this realization is at the heart of the near-unanimous resistance by the press to government attempts to force disclosure of such sources. If unnamable sources were not valid, if they were not indispensable to the proper functioning of the press, reporters would not daily risk going to jail to protect the anonymity of their informants. It was my reference to photostats I did not actually have in hand and my unexpeced difficulty in obtaining them, that compromised my story—not the use of anonymous but in my judgment reliable sources.

I discounted altogether the idea that the photostats did not actually exist. Davis, whom I had known and trusted for years, had seen and examined them; the information of troopers who had handled them had matched up with the recollection of those who had received them. The existence of the photostats could not be doubted, but their authenticity could be—and if I could not verify that soon, I would have to retract.

Nor could I be persuaded by arguments that I was being conned by conspiratorial state troopers, or that the unwillingness of the anti-Eagleton Senate candidates to use them in 1968 showed these candidates had decided the documents were bogus.

There could be no motivation, now or in 1968, for state troopers to risk their careers in order to launch a fake smear. They, more than anyone else, would know that a false story of fixed arrests would be immediately shot down by their superiors, who would be as eager to protect their own maligned reputations as Eagleton's. Backed by a friendly Democratic state administration and a highway patrol eager to disprove the slur on itself, Eagleton would inevitably turn a smear attempt of this kind into a boomerang that would help him rather than hurt him. I could envision these troopers taking risks of exposure and official displeasure in order to bring to light a true story, but not a false one that was sure to defeat its purpose.

And the refusal of Eagleton's three 1968 opponents to use the scandal did not mean that they had checked it out and found it false. Politicians know that a personal attack upon an opposing candidate is a two-edged sword that can have the most unpredictable repercussions. Candidate A is afraid that if he unleashes a scandal on Candidate B it will (1) make A look like a bad sport and a mean fellow, (2) cause B to righteously unleash a counter-scandal involving A that he has been sitting on, afraid to use, and (3) result in C picking up the defectors from B, giving C enough votes to defeat A. Thus in the three-cornered Senate campaign in Connecticut in 1968 the reform Democrat, Reverend Joseph Duffy, refused to mention the scandals that had caused the Senate censure of an opponent, Senator Thomas Dodd, because he feared that most of the voters who were driven away from Dodd would go not to Duffy but to the Republican opponent, Lowell Weicker.

More to the point, in the very Missouri campaign we are concerned with, neither Davis nor Eagleton saw fit to mention a major scandal involving their opponent,

Senator Long, who had been revealed as the recipient of two thousand dollars a month for years from Teamsters Union president Jimmy Hoffa's lawyer, M. A. Shenker, while Long was raising a storm on Capitol Hill against the kind of electronic investigative practices that the Justice Department had used to convict Hoffa. Both Davis and Eagleton made a calculated decision that they would be better off not to use this issue at all. Thus the refusal of Long and Davis to exploit a lesser issue against Eagleton did not mean that they had investigated it and found it wanting. I knew from personal knowledge this was not true in Davis's case, and Long had told me he was just not interested in the drinking issue even though he believed it existed.

None of these arguments for retraction was convincing to me. Moreover, information was coming in from all sides that supported my expectation of getting the clinching proof at any hour. On the afternoon of my radio broadcast, Missouri's largest paper, the *St. Louis Post-Dispatch*, quoted "a former official of the Missouri State Highway Patrol" as saying, "he had stopped Eagleton three times himself before 1968" and that "troopers in Jefferson City and Kirkwood had stopped him on other occasions to and from St. Louis and Jefferson City. No arrests were made because of Eagleton's position in the state government." The source was not one of mine, but I hoped to somehow get to him.

The *Washington Post* had quoted an unidentified former Missouri state official as saying an unnamed highway patrolman approached him at a 1968 political rally with a sheaf of traffic citations allegedly issued to Eagleton. Was this source True Davis or Ed Long or Tom Curtis, or someone else? I had hopes of finding out.

Even as it headlined "Anderson Backs Off," the *Washington Star-Daily News* was saying, "In Missouri, political leaders during the past couple of days have readily repeated to the hordes of reporters, who are in the state checking on Eagleton's past, the long-standing rumors that he had a drinking problem."

I also had leads on drunken scenes involving Eagleton but was unable to verify them. But Michael Satchell of the *Washington Star-Daily News* now wrote a story that charged Eagleton with having been "drunk, boisterous and creating a disturbance" one morning in 1960 at the Tiger Hotel in Columbia, Missouri. The fracas was serious enough for the hotel management to call in the police, and Satchell backed up his story with quotes from the hotel manager, Louis Shelbourne, and Captain William Morgan of the Columbia Police Force, who ordered Eagleton to leave the hotel. Eagleton obeyed. No charges were filed; nothing was entered in the official record.

Other reporters, then, were now coming in with findings that supplemented our own. And influenced by the heightening pressure of events, sources were beginning to come out of hiding. Senator Long still held me to my pledge of anonymity, but he had already been identified by the *Washington Star-Daily News* as the original source of the Tiger Hotel incident, and his information had stood up. Moreover, True Davis, seeing me withering on the limb, had agreed to be interviewed by the *New York Times,* again on an anonymous basis, and though his testimony could corroborate only one aspect of my story and was inconclusive without that of the Missouri police officers, who still refused further interviews, it at least represented some progress. For all these reasons, it seemed to me likely that either our own investigative efforts, which were being pressed to the limit of our endurance, or those of the legion of reporters now fanning out across Missouri would at any moment turn up the investigative nugget that would crack the thing wide open.

By the same token, if all the factors now at work did not within a few days flush out either the photostats or reliable eyewitnesses who were willing to talk for the record, I would have to concede that conclusive proof was either unobtainable or nonexistent and issue a retraction. But to retract prematurely a story I had good reason to believe in, when its vindication seemed within my grasp, might only compound my error of prematurely breaking the story.

Most of my staff now disagreed with me. On Sunday morning I was to appear on *Face the Nation* with Senator Eagleton. Some of them thought I should not appear on national television while I was in the vulnerable position of being unable to prove my story but unwilling to abandon it. Other members felt I should use this dramatic national forum to issue a retraction. Brit Hume and Opal Ginn summarized this view. They were convinced, they said, that the original story was true, but felt that I lost all chances of ever proving it when I publicly aired it before fully nailing it down and drove the already timid troopers a mile underground. They urged that I should cut my losses and end the agony now by retracting, rather than persisting in an argument that I could not support by documentary evidence.

But I didn't agree. I could not see any incongruity in admitting partial error but refusing to admit total error.

The Confrontation

Such was my rationale on Sunday morning, the third day after the now famous radio broadcast, when I arrived at the CBS studios in Washington. Eagleton had borne the week's ordeal well. At no time had he cracked under what must have been an appalling strain. He had ably conducted a battle for public opinion which his supporters saw as gallant and his would-be dumpers conceded was effective. The polls showed a big majority in his favor. But McGovern, recognizing that any liability at all in a vice presidential candidate was insupportable, had dropped his endorsement in everything but the formal declaration, and the McGovern camp was already leaking out in a variety of ways that Eagleton would have to be dropped.

The program began, and at the first opportunity I said to Eagleton, "I violated my own rules. I did not authenticate whether or not these tickets were genuine. Using these sources, I went ahead with a story that I should not have gone ahead with, and that was unfair to you. And you have my apology."

Eagleton was gracious and made the perfunctory comments the situation seemed to him to call for: "It takes a real man to get on nationwide television to say he had made a mistake. I commend you for your courage."

The CBS moderator, George Herman, not being on my convoluted frequency, called my apology a "retraction," which put me in the position of either letting the "retraction" stand or reopening the dismal subject. I felt

I had no choice, so at my next opportunity, I broke in with: "Well, Senator, I would like nothing better than to dispose of this issue right here and now and I wish I could retract the story completely . . . I cannot in good conscience do that."

"You can't?" Eagleton asked.

I expressed the hope that I could meet privately with Eagleton to go over my documentation and settle the matter once and for all. Eagleton responded: "I'm going to cooperate, but I don't quite get the apology and then the no retraction business."

I left the studio resigned that I had come out as badly as Opal and Brit had predicted, and if I had harbored doubts on the matter the press reaction would have promptly dispelled them. But so be it. I would make a final effort to get my informants to come out of hiding, and we would press on in our search for new sources. On Tuesday morning I was to interview Eagleton. If I did not have conclusive proof by then, I would give up and retract—in as public and sweeping a manner as possible.

Sunday passed, and Monday, and the proof eluded me. I still could not reach the "vacationing" police officials who I had been told were the key witnesses. The patrolmen I had talked to had not come through with the photostats. Nor had Senator Long. In fact, Senator Long was now disavowing any knowledge of the subject. True Davis had appeared on CBS and acknowledged that he had told me of the photostats. But reporters, thinking he had peddled the story to hurt a former political rival, gave him a scalding. The trooper who had made the photostats, his captain, and the officer who had claimed to me to have personally stopped Eagleton remained adamant in their public silence. My White House contact returned to me with the scorn due one who had not requited its love: "Why should we bail Anderson out?" I had persisted as long as I decently could—longer, in the opinion of many— and so on Monday night I determined to make my retraction the following morning when I was scheduled to meet with Eagleton. Meanwhile, on that same Monday night, McGovern and Eagleton were jointly announcing Eagleton's withdrawal from the ticket.

Eagleton and I met at his Senate office while an assemblage of reporters and cameramen waited outside. It hadn't been a very good week for either of us. I had questions to ask, since I did not want Eagleton to think I would make a charge against him without a basis, so I went over some of my information with him. I thought I shook him up a couple of times when I quoted the words of patrolmen, but he has since assessed his attitude as incredulity that I was still hounding him. I accept his version; having failed in the matter as a sleuth, I have no stomach for reassaying it as a mind reader.

I told the senator that I was going to issue a full retraction and asked him in what form he would like it. He suggested that since a crowd of reporters and cameramen were outside the door, that would be a suitable forum. We went out to them together. Eagleton said, "Here's Mr. Anderson; he has something he would like to say."

I took a deep breath. "I have exhausted my investigative abilities," I said. "I did not give him a full retraction before because I had some additional questions. I am totally satisfied there is no evidence. I have come out here to retract the story in toto . . . I think the story did damage the Senator. I owe him a great and humble apology."

It was not the first mistake I have made. Being an optimist, I hope it will be the last. I have recounted it here in the hope that some who are down on the press will see how much effort and anguish it takes to produce a flop, and find in this failure not a confirmation of their general distrust, but rather a better understanding of the news business and, hopefully, new faith that a free press, in its stumbling way, is the best safeguard for ultimate truth.

THE FBI STORY

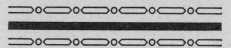

Law and Order

Among the paladins of justice chosen by President Nixon to enforce the federal canons, law and order were honored more in the preachment than the practice. The term was introduced to politics by Richard Kliendienst, who suggested "law and order" as a campaign cry for Barry Goldwater in 1964. John Mitchell picked it up in 1968 and made it the main theme of Richard Nixon's campaign. The happy victor, thereafter, put Mitchell and Kleindienst in charge of law and order at the Justice Department.

Their new positions brought them national attention and adulation, which they accepted as their rightful due. When men referred to them as the "Honorable——" they thought it was a true adjective, not an honorific. They began to believe they were different from the rest of us, as if their new eminence had somehow lifted them above other Americans and had made them more worthy and less subject to the laws they required others to obey. Insecure in the possession of rank, they also over-indulged in its perquisites and privileges. They put much store in limousines and chauffeurs and the trappings of office. One of their number, L. Patrick Gray III, who was shifted from Assistant Attorney General to temporary FBI Director, took to flying about the country in Air Force planes and staying at fancy hotels.

From the first, they were more enthusiastic about enforcing the laws against malefaction than malfeasance. They were quick, for example, to prosecute overzealous protesters who, in the name of peace, violated the peace, but slow to enforce the laws against perjury when their own people found it expedient to fib. During the ITT hearings, for example, Mitchell told demonstrable whoppers about his part in the antitrust settlement and his knowledge of the Republican convention arrangements. Kleindienst also lied, although not under oath, when he claimed that the ITT settlement had been "handled and negotiated exclusively" by the antitrust chief.

Another member of the law-and-order team, Assistant Attorney General Shiro Kashiwa, lied to Congress about White House intervention in a landmark antipollution case. After a federal judge ordered Armco Steel Company to stop dumping toxic wastes into the Houston ship channel, the Justice Department negotiated a settlement more favorable to Armco. Kashiwa testified that he had no dealings with the White House. This is contradicted, however, by a memo from the Justice Department's confidential files describing several White House phone calls. Presidential aides John Glancy and George Crawford, according to the memo, "said that the President does not want plants closed down and more unemployment created . . . [They] said that something would have to be worked out whereby we join with Armco in requesting the judge to stay the execution of his judgment."

Whenever the giants of commerce bumped up against the law, it seems, Mitchell, Kleindienst & Co. were more eager to negotiate than to prosecute. Kleindienst, for instance, blocked the Justice Department from going to court to stop Warner-Lambert from merging with Parke, Davis and Company. Elmer Bobst, the venerable old granddad of Warner-Lambert, made no secret of the fact that the company had gone through the White House to get the injunction called off. Bobst has said he regards the President as a son; Nixon has maintained he looks upon Bobst as a father.

Mitchell also ordered a case settled against five big drug firms—Pfizer, American Cyanamid, Bristol-Meyers, Squibb, and Upjohn—which had been accused of "unlawful conspiracies" in marketing the antibiotic tetracycline. The proposed settlement was brought before Judge Miles Lord, the earnest St. Paul, Minnesota, jurist who had been hearing the case. Prosecution would be dropped, the Justice Department proposed, in return for a $14.3 million payment to the Treasury. The overcharged customers would get nothing. Judge Lord, hardly believing his ears, stammered, "It stings me just a little bit when the rug is pulled out . . ."

To help them uphold law and order, Mitchell and Kleindienst appointed as head of the Criminal Division a crackerbarrel crime buster from Texas named Will Wilson. On March 12, 1971, we linked him to another Texan, appropriately named Frank Sharp, who turned out to be the slickest stock promoter since Billy Sol Estes. He even persuaded the Jesuit fathers into making him the first Protestant patron of the Ancient New Orleans Province of the Society of Jesus, and then he left the reverend gentlemen holding the bag for $6 million. The Securities and Exchange Commission also charged Sharp with a massive stock-fraud "scheme and conspiracy," which enabled him and others to make a fast fortune.

Among the politicians whom Sharp showered with blessings was law-and-order man Will Wilson. Not only did Wilson serve as Sharp's principal attorney during the period of the alleged fraud, but after he was sworn in as Assistant Attorney General, he borrowed $25,000 from Sharp without putting up collateral. Wilson's net worth, meanwhile, had shot up from $680,000 to more than $1.5 million during his five-year association with Sharp. There was evidence, moreover, that Wilson acquired much of his new wealth through Sharp. Since the Criminal Division was supposed to prosecute Sharp, our stories caused such embarrassment that Wilson hastily terminated his career in law enforcement and returned to Texas.

But if the powerful were pampered, Mitchell and Kleindienst did not believe in permissiveness for the plebeians. The pair drafted a crime bill for Washington, D.C., and offered it as a model for the rest of the nation. It provided for reforms that were urgently needed, measures that would upgrade court and police functions. The bill was sent to Congress, however, with provisions for breaking down the doors of some crime suspects without first knocking and for holding selective prisoners without bail up to sixty days.

The Mitchell-Kleindienst regime, nevertheless, did not reduce crime in the nation's capital. People continued to be murdered for pocket change. Muggings were so frequent that they became a bore to all but the pedestrian with the knife at his throat. Banks were knocked over as if John Dillinger were still on the loose. On a trip to the war zone in Vietnam, I compared the crime reports and found the streets of Saigon were safer than the streets of Washington.

On May 3, 1971, Mitchell and Kleindienst directed a one-sided war against a determined horde of antiwar demonstrators who came to the capital announcing they would shut down the government. The Mitchell-Kleindienst tactics violated the Constitution, but they worked for the moment. Shaggy hair was enough provocation to bring arrest. More than twelve thousand handcuffed and sometimes bleeding demonstrators were herded into the open exercise yard at the Washington jail, then into a fenced football field near the jailhouse, and then into the Washington Coliseum. Children in their early teens were thrown in helter-skelter with hardened veteran militants, thereby increasing their education in the ways of the world.

Mitchell called the arrests a great victory. The hardcore revolutionaries also considered the arrests a great victory. The revolutionaries, however, took the longer view. They were less interested in shutting down the government for one day than in overthrowing it permanently. Their real objective in staging the demonstration, according to secret FBI reports we have read, was to provoke overreaction by the government. The activists dearly wanted the government to round up and beat up thousands of youths in violation of their constitutional rights.

It was almost as if Mitchell and Kleindienst had followed a script that the revolutionaries had written for them. The revolutionary movement needed new martyrs and new motivation for the hordes, who had become dulled by drugs and bored by the harangues of the militants. Mitchell and Kleindienst provided both the martyrs and the motivation, thereby giving the movement new life.

The prosecution of the Berrigan brothers, Daniel and Philip, produced two even more charismatic martyrs. However, they owed their exalted status perhaps more to J. Edgar Hoover, the late FBI chief, than to the prosecutors at the Justice Department. In Hoover's view, the two antiwar priests were "troublemakers." This was reason enough for him to tell two members of a Senate Appropriations subcommittee on November 27, 1971, of an "incipient plot on the part of an anarchist group on the east coast, the so-called East Coast Conspiracy to Save Lives. . . . The principal leaders of this group are Philip and Daniel Berrigan . . . This group plans to blow up underground electrical conduits and steam pipes serving the Washington, D.C., area in order to disrupt federal government operations. The plotters are also concocting a scheme to kidnap a highly-placed government official. The name of a White House staff member has been mentioned as a possible victim."

Hoover always had a habit of shaking up things when he went up to the Capitol to ask for more money for the FBI. Congress was always duly impressed and voted him the funds he needed to safeguard the nation. On this day they listened in such stunned reverence that they didn't even ask him to identify the supposed victim of the kidnap plot. The name of Henry Kissinger had to be quietly leaked to the press.

It did not matter to Hoover that the Berrigans had not been convicted or even officially charged with their plot. He knew they were troublemakers; the FBI had been watching their antiwar activities for a long time. As early as July 1967, ten months before the first Berrigan raid on draft-board records, the FBI was collecting information. An informant inside the Jesuit order, according to the FBI's confidential file on the Berrigans, reported that Father Daniel had "been invited to join the staff of Cornell United Religious Work . . . This source, who is a member of the Society of Jesus, as is Berrigan, stated that subject, although an accomplished poet, had developed a reputation as an outspoken critic of U.S. foreign policy, particularly with respect to Viet Nam, and that he had become more or less 'a thorn in the side' of the Jesuit order."

Other informants, newspaper clippings and, occasionally, legwork by FBI agents produced an image of Berrigan that Hoover would see as "anarchist." By October 16, 1967, agents came to the campus to listen to Daniel Berrigan address an anti-draft rally. Five days later he was in Washington for the first of the great peace demonstrations. The day was only twenty minutes old when the priest was arrested for refusing to move when ordered by a policeman on the Mall. More than six hundred and seventy-five other demonstrators were booked before the day ended.

A month later, informant "AL T-5" told how the priest participated in a sit-in when marine recruiters came to Cornell. On January 31, 1968, informant AL-T-1 said Berrigan was on his way to Hanoi with Boston University Professor Howard Zinn to accept the release of three American prisoners of war. The file noted that AL T-2 claimed he knew Zinn, if not Berrigan, in the Communist party between 1949 and 1953. In Hanoi, Berrigan met with another certified Communist, Premier Pham Van Dong. The antiwar pair were given custody of the prisoners but lost them to the U.S. government in Laos on the way home.

Berrigan's file grew fatter when he and his brother were part of a group of antiwar Catholics who poured blood on draft records in Catonsville, Maryland, in October 1968. They were both given severe jail sentences, but they made the FBI look foolish by refusing to report for their incarceration. Daniel eluded Hoover's dragnet for four months, popping up from time to time at religious services to preach against the war.

On April 17, 1970—a week after he refused to go to jail—Berrigan appeared at a service at Cornell before fifteen thousand students. Two FBI men showed up to arrest him. "I don't have any real yen to be put in the federal happy acres," the priest told the students. "When you think I should, I will." The agents were still mingling when Berrigan slipped away. It is noteworthy that the FBI files on Berrigan used the Cornell student newspaper for its source of information on the activities —not the report of the flatfooted G-men. Berrigan was ultimately captured by a squad of agents and led off to join his brother in prison.

Even behind bars, however, the Berrigans were not safe from FBI informers. Armand DeLorenzo, a bad-check artist described in the FBI files as having been "psychiatrically diagnosed as suffering from antisocial personality with final diagnosis of 'sociopathic personality, antisocial reactions with paranoid trends,' " reported on his conversations with the imprisoned priests. He had just begun a work program in a hospital outside the prison when, he said, Philip asked him to help bring "unauthorized material" into the prison.

A paragraph from the FBI report on its interview with Lorenzo is more revealing about the bureau than it is about the Berrigans. It states:

During his association with the Berrigans, especially Philip, DeLorenzo was impressed with their total absorption in and dedication to their ideals, which are, basically, to radically change the nature and structure of the government. Berrigans advocate that the present system is a degrading one, and that the FCI (Federal Correctional Institution) is a microcosm of the national situation, with Negro inmates holding menial, house-orderly/porter-type jobs, Puerto Rican inmates working in industries, and Caucasian inmates holding jobs of higher prestige, e.g., clerical jobs.

The agent also thought it worth reporting that DeLorenzo, the sociopathic paranoid, "is of the opinion that they, Philip and Daniel, especially Philip, would have an utter disregard for their own safety and well-being and that of any associates and/or bystanders, should the occasion arise wherein they could further their goals or demonstrate their objectives within, or outside, the FCI."

Another prisoner also reported to the FBI on the Berrigans' activities in prison. He was Albert E. Mc-Gillicuddy, serving five years for selling illegal drugs. Three days after Christmas, he told an agent that in late November or early December 1970 Daniel had asked him to draw the floor plan of the prison's industries building, with "particular attention as to the location of the missile harnesses." Danbury Prison, like three others, manufactures some electronic components for missiles. "Daniel stated that possibly they could do something here [at the FCI] to slow down the war effort and save some lives." This, too, went into the now bulging files.

On July 12, 1971, Hoover wrote to White House major-domo H. R. Haldeman and Attorney General John Mitchell warning of "proposed plans of antiwar elements to embarrass the United States government." Composer Leonard Bernstein, Hoover correctly reported, was composing a mass to be performed at the dedication of the Kennedy Center for the Performing Arts on the banks of the Potomac. He said Daniel Berrigan had been asked to write the Latin verse to be sung to Bernstein's music. "The source advised the words will follow an antiwar theme," he said. "Important Government officials, perhaps even the President, are expected to attend this ceremony and it is anticipated they will applaud the composition without recognizing the true meaning of the words. The source said the newspapers would be given the story the following day that the President and other high-ranking government officials applauded an anti-government song."

The FBI file does not carry an important footnote: Berrigan did not write the lyrics, which did not contain any coded peace messages other than those words of peace always in the mass. Possibly because of Hoover's hysterics, President Nixon missed what the audience and the critics thought was a superb performance.

It was earlier, on September 4, 1970, that Hoover had the FBI's White House liaison officer dramatically deliver a letter by hand to Kissinger warning him that he might be a possible target for a kidnap plot. Although both the urgency of the letter and its method of conveyance indicated a great crisis, the episode appears to have been an exercise in showmanship. For the FBI was told of the plot on August 21. Hoover mulled it over for two weeks before flashing an alert.

He had more than enough time to prepare his evidence and present it to a grand jury. Instead, he made charges without substantiation before a Senate hearing. Naturally, his accusation that the Catholic conspirators had plotted to kidnap Henry Kissinger and to blow up steam tunnels in Washington made headlines. The Justice Department had to either uphold or repudiate him. The Department chose to uphold him and went ahead with the prosecution, albeit with full knowledge that the evidence was insufficient to get a conviction. For the confidential files show that the FBI had failed to prove its case. The Secret Service, which is responsible for protecting the people at the White House, was also brought in. Its conclusions were even more blunt. "The plan to destroy steam lines in Washington, DC, has been investigated by the FBI and this Service," states a secret memo. "No information has been developed to confirm that plot."

This, however, did not deter the Justice Department, which put Hoover's sensibilities ahead of the rights of the accused. Our sources inside the Justice Department say Mitchell and Kleindienst took the gamble that once the alleged conspirators were hauled into court, a jury might convict them out of prejudice if not evidence. As it happened, the grand jury refused to indict Daniel Berrigan for anything. The jury that heard the conspiracy charges brought against Philip Berrigan and five others refused to convict them. Philip and a nun, Sister Elizabeth McAlister, were found guilty of the something less than sensational crime of smuggling letters past the walls of Danbury Prison. Instead of suppressing the political radicals, the trial gave them a national forum and made heroes of them. The whole circus, incidentally, cost the taxpayers a shocking amount.

Such are the abuses of power—the transgressions of morality and the law—that have been committed in the name of law and order. The symbols of power, meanwhile, tended to make Mr. Nixon's paladins of justice forget they were merely employees of the American people.

Imprisonment of the Press

At ten-fifteen on the morning of January 31, 1973, my associate Les Whitten was accosted on a Washington street by several men. They called him by name, identified themselves as FBI agents and announced they were placing him under arrest. Ever the reporter, Whitten took out pencil and notepaper and began taking notes, whereupon these were taken away and he was bound with handcuffs, loaded into an unmarked FBI car and lugged off to jail. He was locked in a cell for five hours, then brought before a magistrate and charged with "receiving and possessing stolen property for the purpose of converting it to his own use," punishable by up to ten years in prison and a $10,000 fine. He was released, without bail, to await grand jury indictment. Two days later, the U.S. government subpoenaed the telephone company for its records on all long-distance calls made to or from not only Whitten's telephone but mine as well for the previous six months. This was not known to me at the time, but immediately thereafter I began to hear from various sources in places as remote as Arizona and Guam that FBI agents were poking around asking questions about them.

This sort of audacity was not like the usual behavior of the FBI, which has been too sensitive about its press relations to throw reporters in jail and expropriate columnists' telephone records without some inspiration from On High. I searched persistently for the man behind the move and identified him on February 7 as H. R. Haldeman, then still secure as President Nixon's chief of staff. Haldeman had passed the word to the

Justice Department, I reported, "to try to make a case against us." Not until the Senate Watergate hearings, however, did I discover my name was on a long list of White House "enemies" who had been marked for federal harassment.

On February 14, in a rare rebuke to the Justice Department, the grand jury refused to indict Les Whitten and the two American Indians arrested with him, Henry Adams and Anita Collins. It concluded that far from receiving and possessing stolen property (three boxes of government documents) for the purpose of converting it to their own use, Adams and Collins had recovered the documents as a public service and were in the act of returning them to the government when arrested, while Whitten was merely covering the news event as a reporter. The charges were dropped.

Two weeks later, on February 28, Acting FBI Director L. Patrick Gray presented to the Senate Judiciary Committee the government's version of the arrest. According to the unabashed Gray, the FBI had acted on reliable information that Whitten, as my agent, was attempting to purchase the stolen documents; that elaborate plans had been made to accomplish the illegal purchase; and that the alibi of recovering and returning stolen property was concocted as a cover story in case the police should arrive upon the scene. Gray further maintained that the subpoenaing of my phone lists was routine investigative practice and that the information thus obtained had been used only to inquire into the matter of the purloined Indian papers. Nothing in Gray's testimony conceded that the arrests were improper or that the telephone subpoena was unconstitutional.

There is a profound lesson in this small incident. It is important, therefore, to contrast step by step the government's version of events with the facts accepted by the grand jury. If the government can falsely arrest two blameless citizens in order to frame a reporter, and then, even after its arrests have been repudiated by a grand jury and the charges dismissed, solemnly misinform the United States Senate about the matter, then who can confidently say we are not witnessing the bid for power of an incipient totalitarianism which arrogantly seeks—through the intimidation of critics, inversion of the truth, harassment of news sources and imprisonment of un-cooperative reporters—to destroy the one freedom upon which all our other freedoms depend: the freedom of the press?

The Great Document Heist

During the first week of November 1972, there occurred the most spectacular Indian uprising since the days of General George Armstrong Custer. A coalition of Indian groups arrived in Washington to protest innumerable and timeless grievances. They first occupied, then vandalized, then looted the building housing the Bureau of Indian Affairs.

On the seventh day of the occupation, a truce was negotiated with the government by Indian representative Henry Adams; Uncle Sam agreed to put up $66,650 for travel expenses back home; the Indians prepared to evacuate. But they were not to leave empty-handed. They had discovered on the fourth floor hundreds of file cabinets which contained documentary evidence of the bungling, neglect, and betrayal that have characterized the white man's conduct toward the Indian.

Angrily they bundled some of the documents in cardboard boxes and loaded them on a truck in the dead of night; they wrapped others in sleeping bags and packed them in car trunks, and spirited still other stacks aboard a chartered bus. After all this was done, the police, with motorcycles roaring, moved the forty-car Indian caravan through the city of Washington. As they whistled traffic to a stop to make way for the Indians, the police had no idea they were unwitting accomplices in the biggest documents heist in history. Not until the Broken Treaties Papers, as the Indians named them, were safely out of town did the authorities discover that about a ton of documents, paintings, artifacts, and office equipment were missing. The FBI rushed in to close the barn door; it organized a nation-wide dragnet to retrieve the stolen goods.

Agents began watching the caravan as it rumbled through Cleveland. The Indians became aware of the surveillance, and some of the cars began to peel off. In St. Paul the FBI made its move. Reinforced by police scout cars and paddy wagons, the G-men swooped down on a green van identified by an undercover Indian informant as the hiding place of the bulk of the documents. But the loot recovered consisted of one BIA typewriter, an Indian School application and a note pad. In one way or another, hundreds of thousands of documents slipped through the FBI dragnet. A government raid in Oklahoma recovered a few unimportant papers and brought some indictments that later had to be quashed, but 99.9 percent of the documents vanished without a trace.

We maintain a continuing interest in official papers that have gotten out from under lock and key. In a clean government, run openly and honestly, any citizen could inspect government files to see how his business is handled by his employees. That right, in fact, is guaranteed by law. But the government, to protect itself, makes this legitimate pursuit a futile chore and seeks even to make it a crime. Anyway, we started to search for the documents, and we had some advantages. Unlike the FBI, we could demonstrate a record of concern about the victimization of Indians.

Other reporters were on the trail, too. We were later told by the Indians that some offered money for the story. We do not pay for information; we prefer informants who want to right wrongs. We do not necessarily accept the government's claim that it is a crime for anyone but the government to buy purloined information, but we refuse to pay for documents for three other reasons: (1) penuriousness—we operate on a tight budget; (2) distaste for paid informers, who are a sleazy lot; and (3) purchased information is often unreliable. The FBI informer who led agents to the empty green van, for instance, was about as reliable as the one who misled poor Pat Gray about Whitten.

Consider Gray's testimony before the Senate Judiciary Committee; "I learned on 1/24/73, from information contained in a teletype from our Washington office, that a Metropolitan Police Department officer, working in an undercover capacity, had advised his superiors that he had learned that Anita Collins and Hank Adams had been conferring with Jack Anderson to buy documents stolen from the Bureau of Indian Affairs."

The truth, sworn by several people and uncontroverted by anyone, is that I never met or talked with Anita Collins or Hank Adams until after their arrest, that I never conferred with anyone about paying for the Broken Treaties Papers, and that no money was paid except for such things as airline tickets and car rentals needed to locate the stolen documents. We offered the Indians only our record for championing the underprivileged. The Indians spurned the money offered by others, and voted to show us the Broken Treaties Papers.

Les Whitten was instructed to fly to Phoenix for the first tryst. At the airport, Indian security men one jump ahead of the FBI told him to wait on a corner away from the terminal building. They hustled him by a devious route to a motel where some of the Indian leaders were assembled. The Indians wouldn't talk about the papers in the motel or even inside their cars for fear of FBI bugging, so furtive meetings were arranged at a bowling alley and a coffee house and on a parking lot.

Next day, Whitten, accompanied by two of the Indians, flew to Minneapolis. He was met by one of the leading Indian militants, who questioned him closely. At last Whitten was given four documents and questioned again about their meaning to find out what he knew about Indian matters. Then for twelve hours he was left alone.

The following morning, many thousands of documents were delivered to him. The door of his room was bolted and a tough Indian security man planted himself in a chair pushed against the door. As Whitten waded through the papers Indian experts helped him with the unfamiliar tribes and names.

Day after day we published stories pieced together from these documents—columns which told of Indian murders that went uninvestigated; of white trading posts that swindled the Indians with impunity; of Indian land leased out by the government to corporations and left strewn with timber wastes, its earth torn up, its waters polluted with mining poisons; of how the government, instead of giving special protection to tribal lands, removed them from the ordinary safeguards of the National Environmental Protection Act; of treaties which had guaranteed millions of acres of land but which delivered only thousands; of protected white interests at this moment illegally draining off the life-giving water of tribes in various parts of the country—the Papagos of South Dakota, the San Carlos Apaches, the Prima Maricopas, the Rincon and La Jolla Indians of the San Luis Rey Watershed, the Lummis, the Spokane Tribe, the Indians of Pyramid Lake—all alike despoiled of their water under the eyes of a government which systematically welshes on its commitments.

And while publishing these ugly stories which grew out of Les Whitten's collaboration with scattered Indian fugitives, I occassionally yielded to the temptation to make sport of the tribulations of the FBI, whose agents were tripping over their nightsticks in a dozen states, and had gotten no closer to the Indian documents than the quotations they read in our column. The FBI, apparently, took our jibes in ill humor.

The Frame-Up

Among the leaders of the raid on the BIA building, there was one who had played no part in the vandalism and the looting. I suppose it was inevitable, bureaucracies being what they are, that this one should be selected by the FBI and the Washington police as their principal target. He was the easiest to find. Henry Adams, an Assiniboin Sioux, who answers to the non-Sioux nickname of "Hank," has a quiet dignity not at once apparent in his rumpled, careless appearance. He could fade into a casual crowd as easily as his forebears faded into the rolling prairie. He speaks as softly, too, as the Sioux once trod. Not long ago, Adams was shot through the gut by white vigilantes trespassing on Indian land. But there is no vengeance in his attitude. It is more his nature to smoke the peace pipe than to shout war cries. His gentle manner, nonetheless, was but the moss on a character of granite. There is a nobility in his character that is missing in his features.

As chief negotiator between the Indians and the government, Adams helped work out a truce. He had remained aloof from the looting at BIA both because he opposed it in principle and because his Indian compatriots had deliberately kept their negotiator out of harm's way. To Adams the spectacle of marauding and pillaging put on by the Indians obscured the valid complaints that had brought them to Washington. The violence had caused the government to break off negotiations that he thought were likely to bear fruit for the Indians. Moreover, the stolen records contained vital documents that were important to the protection of Indian rights and claims.

Now that the events of November were behind, Adams wanted to return the stolen materials as a demonstration of Indian good faith so that he could reopen the suspended negotiations with the White House on Indian grievances. In this role as agent for the recovery of stolen goods, Adams entered into contacts with scattered Indian groups and with several government officials, all of whom urged him on. He also held well-publicized press conferences, at which he urged Indians to cooperate, made progress reports, and promulgated his schedule for the return of all documents. By December 11 he had participated in returning four separate shipments to the government.

Therefore, when the government decided to build a case against Hank Adams as a thief rather than a restorer of stolen property, it had to rewrite and fabricate a lot of history. To clarify the situation I shall itemize the events as they actually took place.

Early in November, Bradley H. Patterson, a White House aide, announced to reporters that Adams had requested a meeting with the White House and the Justice Department to arrange a system to return the documents. Patterson was quoted by the *New York Times* as saying he said to Adams, "Hank, if you know where any of those documents and other things are, or if you have any yourself, I encourage you to return them to the Washington field office of the FBI."

• Adams played an important role in the return to the government of thirty-one paintings that had been removed from the Bureau of Indian Affairs Building.

• On November 22, 1972, Adams wrote a letter to President Nixon in which he said that he had "acted through all forms available to me for the protection of such materials"—meaning the documents and other items taken from the building—"during all the days of this month."

• On approximately December 1, 1972, Adams sent

a large envelope to the FBI which contained important identifying information on the paintings that had been returned to the government—price tags, picture titles, names of artists, and other data. There was a credible witness to the sending of this envelope; Adams had it mailed by reporter Paul Houston of the *Los Angeles Times*.

● In early December, Agent Dennis Hyten of the FBI went to Adams's residence on invitation and accepted the return of several documents.

● On or about December 7, Adams informed Agent Hyten that he had recovered some additional materials and would like to deliver them to Hyten. Hyten said he could not accept delivery on that day but asked Adams to keep the items at his apartment until Hyten could come by to pick them up. On December 11, Hyten called at Adams's apartment and accepted the return of some Navajo drawings, some documents, and a few pieces of office equipment; he gave Adams an itemized receipt, in accordance with FBI regulations concerning the recovery of stolen property.

● On December 9, Adams held a press conference. The *New York Times* reported: "Mr. Adams said that all the stolen documents would be returned to the Bureau as fast as humanly possible after they have been copied and indexed and sent to the individual tribes concerned, so they can educate themselves."

● On December 11, our column published a message that Indian leaders had given us for President Nixon: "Tell the President that Indians do not want the documents any longer than it takes to duplicate and index them so that every tribe in America can educate itself to the double-dealing of the Federal government and find ways to forestall it."

● On January 12, 1972, the *New York Times,* under a four-column head, "An Indian Leader Pledges Return of U.S. Property," detailed Adams's plan for getting the documents back to the government.

● Adams had two principal helpers in his recovery

operation: Anita Collins, a Payute-Shoshone Indian girl of twenty-eight who was news editor of *American Indian Movement,* and John Arellano, a self-styled Pueblo-Apache, whom Adams had met during the days of the caravan. Arellano was particularly helpful because he owned a red Volkswagen camper which he frequently put at the disposal of Adams, who had no car. Each day during late January, Arellano and Miss Collins would go to the BIA building to make long-distance phone calls aimed at locating and recovering stashes of documents. Unknown to Adams, Arellano was not an Indian, but an Italian—with the high cheekbones of an Indian—and an undercover informer for the Washington police and the FBI.

● On January 18 an American Broadcasting Company film crew set itself up at Adams's apartment. Among those present was John Arellano. The film shows Arellano listening as Adams makes the following statement: "We have some information on the nature of the documents taken and know that these documents will be returned in a short period of time. And then the government will continue to lie. They'll say, you know, they weren't returned, or some were missing."

● On January 30, Adams sent Anita Collins and Arellano to the bus depot to pick up the largest shipment of documents yet to come into his hands; on the previous day he had informed Jane Wales of the *Congressional Quarterly* that he hoped to have all the documents returned to the government by February 10. The *Congressional Quarterly* published this information on the morning of January 31.

● On January 29 or 30, Adams made an appointment with Dennis Creedon, a counsel for the House Appropriations Subcommittee on Indian Affairs, for ten o'clock on January 31 at Creedon's office, which was on the third floor of the BIA building. Adams planned to deliver the newly arrived documents to the BIA and have Hyten pick them up there.

This was the information available to the FBI from

public and undercover sources when it sought to indict Henry Adams and, afterward, when Gray prepared his testimony for the Senate Judiciary Committee. From this vast array of data, Gray saw fit to present to the Committee only one item as indicative of Adams's intent. "Mr. Adams had said to a Bureau of Indian Affairs official, Mr. Oxendine," testified the temporary FBI chief, "just in passing with regard to the return of the documents, 'Maybe they will be returned, maybe they won't; I don't know,' something to that effect, I know. No commitment was made and Mr. Oxendine was asked by our investigators point blank whether or not any commitment had been made to return any documents and his testimony or his statements to our interviewers was 'no.' "

To those of us unfamiliar with the disciplines of the world's finest law-enforcement organization, Tom Oxendine's ambiguous statement would seem a rather thin straw on which to hand criminal intent, an insubstantial mite to place on the scales against the solid mass of evidence about Adams's known plans and deeds. It was not even clear in that quotation whether Adams was talking about his own intent or an inability to judge whether Indians out in the field would return documents to him. Only an organization determined to produce evidence, whether it exists or not, could make such use of "maybe"s.

But as it turned out, it is doubtful whether Oxendine ever made such a statement at all, for a source without an ax to grind quotes Oxendine as having said the opposite. Here is Oxendine's account of the same conversation given to the highly respected reporter, Fred Barnes of the *Washington Star-Daily News* and published in that paper: "Tom Oxendine, the director of the Bureau's Office of Communications, said he had a brief conversation with Adams on January 24 at the BIA building. At that time, Adams indicated to him that plans to return the material, taken from BIA during the Trail of Broken Treaties protest in November, were being carried out, Oxendine said."

On the night of January 30 Hank Adams went to bed thinking he was about to take the most important step toward his goal of returning the stolen properties and reopening the negotiations. He was unaware that all his efforts to serve both the government and his people were being warped into evidence of criminal acts or that the friend he was counting on to help him return the documents on the morrow would come as the leader of an arrest party.

The FBI Strikes

Here is how L. Patrick Gray described the plot to the Senate Judiciary Committee: "The Metropolitan Police Department advised us that this informant had information to the effect that this, these documents, were in a certain location in North Carolina, that these documents were initially going to be delivered at North Carolina to representatives of this column for a sum of money, and then later we were informed that no, the documents were going to be shipped to Washington and would come in through a bus, a commercial bus, and that the documents were going to be picked up at the bus station . . . They picked up the documents, they returned them to Hank Adams' home . . . that area, of course, was under surveillance and our agents were watching it. We also had information that the next, that evening or the following day, the transfer for money was to be made and when an individual showed up we waited until these documents were brought out of the house and the people actually had them in their possession before we moved in to make the arrest. It was, in our judgment, a valid arrest."

Unaware of the imaginary feats and dire plans being attributed to him by the government, Les Whitten awoke early on the morning of his criminal rendezvous. Had he known of the elaborate FBI scenario, he probably would not have been disturbed; it was too preposterous for belief. He knew there had never been any plan for us to pick up and pay for any documents—which came, incidentally, from South Dakota, not North Carolina. Our antipathy to paying for information has been a source of resentment among information merchants to whom the FBI is privy.

At about 8:45 the telephone rang at Whitten's home in Silver Spring, Maryland. It was Hank Adams calling to let Whitten know that a cache of documents was to be returned to the government in about an hour. "There's nothing newsworthy in them," Adams said. But Whitten discerned that the return itself would be newsworthy. For almost three months the forces of the United States had been scouring the continent in vain for BIA documents; now one modest Indian citizen, alternately encouraged and derided by the government, operating in a goldfish bowl through public appeals to the Indians and open announcements to the public of his plans for the return, was about to drive up to the Bureau of Indian Affairs in a red Volkswagen camper and deliver thousands of documents. This seemed to Whitten a "man bites dog" story on a grand scale and so he asked to go along with Adams to the BIA to cover the return and write an exclusive story on it. Adams agreed.

Whitten hurriedly dressed and left his home. For one who was supposed to be on his way to a clandestine criminal heist of contraband, he was behaving in a rather unaccountable manner. He drove off blithely toward Adams's apartment in a conspicuous yellow-orange Vega hatchback, the model with the wraparound glass. On arrival, he parked his car in a no-parking area in front of the apartment building, checked his coat pocket for his pencil and reporter's notebook, and bounded through the front door of Adams's apartment building. He already had a lead composed in his head "Hank Adams, derided by the White House for his efforts, has quietly returned the largest stash of stolen documents to the federal government."

Whitten was admitted by Adams at about 9:55. Arellano had not yet showed up with his camper, and Whitten offered the use of his Vega. Seeing he would be late for his appointment at the BIA, Adams phoned Dennis Creedon to assure him he was "on his way." Whitten looked cursorily through the documents; they were old

Indian land decisions and the like, of no news value as Adams had said, but of considerable importance to the Indians.

The documents were to go to FBI agent Dennis Hyten, who had picked up material at Adams's apartment on two previous occasions, so Adams and Whitten now wrote Hyten's name and phone number at the bureau on the top of each of the three cartons of documents. For the return to Hyten was not to be direct but via the Bureau of Indian Affairs, and Adams wanted to make sure the boxes were readily identifiable when Hyten arrived to pick them up.

Adams had a number of solid reasons for taking this circuitous route. In the first place, he wanted a credible witness to the fact that the documents had indeed been returned, so that it would not be a matter of the word of an Indian against that of the United States of America. Secondly, Adams wanted Creedon to get a look at the documents before the FBI got them, because the House Appropriations Subcommittee on Indian Affairs, for which Creedon was an investigator, was probing the question of the missing property. Knowing the Justice Department's penchant for making its "investigative files" unavailable to congressional committees, Adams wanted the committee to have a chance to look through them, or at least to be aware of their existence, before they disappeared. And finally, there was a certain symbolism in making this return to the place from which the documents had originally been taken. Adams's delivery plan was wiser than he knew; had he not involved a third party in his arrangements, had he left himself at the mercy of the veracity of the Federal Bureau of Investigation, he might now be in jail.

With the phone call to Creedon concluded and the cartons marked, Adams was ready to leave. Whitten offered to help him carry the fifty-pound boxes down to the street. He knew about the shooting of Adams by white vigilantes two years earlier and a recent automobile crash in which Adams had sustained chest damage.

Whitten, therefore, lugged two of the three boxes into the elvator and helped get them to the street.

He was about to begin to load the boxes into his Vega when the federal agents sprang forward. Other agents rushed to the door of the apartment house to arrest Adams. Had Arellano showed up as expected, Whitten would have had no occasion to be standing at his car holding a box of documents—the proof of his participation in a "criminal" act.

But Arellano was not idle that morning. Clad in his familiar parka and stocking cap, he now led three federal agents into the apartment building where Anita Collins lived. He knocked on her door. When she opened it, he stepped aside and three federal agents—short-haired, in neat suits and trenchcoats—stepped forward. "Anita Collins? FBI. You are under arrest." Anita has since described Arellano's shamefacedness. "I could see his little head poking out from behind them. Johnny said, 'Nita, I hate to tell you this, but I'm a cop.'"

Leaving nothing to chance, the intrepid agents slapped handcuffs on Anita and led her away.

Come On, Now!

Even as the defendants were sitting in jail awaiting to learn the nature of the charges against them, the news of their arrest was receiving prominent attention. For instance, the *New York Post* shunted aside the announcement of a Henry Kissinger trip to Hanoi in favor of a banner front-page headline: "U.S. Arrests Aide of Jack Anderson." I cite this, not out of any particular pride in notoriety, but to show that the FBI henceforth had to know that its actions were under a national spotlight. Its moves, therefore, can be regarded as deliberate and calculated, rather than the untypical, slipshod antics that might attend an obscure investigation.

At the time of their arrest, the defendants stated their innocence and pointed out that the documents were being returned to the government. On the following day, two FBI agents called on Dennis Creedon. He confirmed to them that Adams indeed had an appointment with him at the BIA, set for ten o'clock on the morning of the arrest. Creedon had notified ahead of time the security guard at the Bureau of Indian Affairs that Adams was coming in and that he was cleared for admission. The security guard was conspicuously aware of the Adams appointment, for at 2 P.M. on the day of the arrest an officer came up to Creedon with a message: if he was still expecting Hank Adams, he wouldn't be showing up; the guard had heard on the radio that Adams had been arrested. On the following day the *Washington Post* printed this account of its interview with Creedon's superior, C. R. Anderson, director of the House Appropriations Committee Surveys and Investigative Staff:

"Creedon's boss . . . confirmed yesterday that Mr. Adams had a 10 A.M. appointment with Creedon at the Bureau of Indian Affairs Building. The House Committee is using a third-floor office at the B.I.A. . . ." C. R. Anderson also confirmed to us that Creedon had told him Adams called about thirty minutes before the arrest to say he was "on the way." This was the call that Whitten heard Adams make.

How, then, shall we explain that a month after these events Director Gray could tell the Senate Judiciary Committee: "We have checked with everyone at the Bureau of Indian Affairs that we could check with, and not one of them said that they had any such appointment with Mr. Adams"?

Is it possible that the FBI agents who questioned Creedon did not turn in a report of their interrogation; or that the FBI did not make the inescapably obvious check with the security guard, who had to be alerted for the Adams appointment; or that it did not check with staff director C. R. Anderson after he was prominently quoted on the matter in the press? Only two answers are possible: a systematic incompetence not characteristic of the FBI particularly in sensitive cases; or a deliberate policy of suppression and misrepresentation.

Telephone Tracing

Nothing is more important to an investigative reporter than the confidence of his sources that they will not be exposed. If upon the slightest pretext the government can secure from the phone company the call numbers of those in telephone touch with a reporter, then he must either give up one of his chief investigative tools, the telephone, or spend his life running from phone booth to phone booth, his pockets bulging with coins. The seizing of my phone records by the government was therefore a most serious matter.

The time sequence is significant. On February 1 FBI agents took testimony from Dennis Creedon which confirmed Adams's appointment with him. This clearly left them with no case, even if they thought they had one at the time of the arrest. Yet the following day, the FBI commandeered from the telephone company the records of my long-distance phone calls.

Patrick Gray later was to explain to inquiring senators: "This was an, actually an, action initiated by the Assistant United States Attorney in charge of the grand jury, and these subpoenas [for our telephone toll records] were prepared in his office . . . No attempt was being made to inquire into anyone's sources. Attempts were being made to locate the documents that still remained out of the hands of the Bureau of Indian Affairs, and of the toll calls, 96 were selected as the most probably because of their location."

There are several discrepancies in this explanation. For one thing, the date of the occupation of the BIA building was November 2, 1972; yet the government subpoenaed my telephone records as far back as July 1972, four months before a single Indian document was taken.

Then, shortly after the FBI obtained these records, I began to hear from sources around the country and abroad who said FBI agents were suddenly making inquiries about them. And these sources weren't Indians. One was Robert Updike, an assistant prosecutor in Phoenix, Arizona, whom I had called in tracking down the story of the attempted suppression of a drunken-driving charge against Senator Paul Fannin of Arizona. Others were the members of B-52 crews stationed in Guam who had given me information that because of faulty tactical planning they were flying identical bombing routes over Hanoi each day, with the result that planes were being shot down unnecessarily by waiting North Vietnamese gunners. Guam did not seem to me to be a likely place for FBI agents to be poking around for missing Indian documents. I have not heard that any absconding Indians have been flushed out of my telephone logs, but I do know that a number of news sources have been intimidated.

Showdown in the Senate

As it turned out, of course, the government came out
of the great Indian-arrest saga with egg all over its face.
It suffered the humiliation of having a widely publicized
action peremptorily thrown out by a grand jury. It
brought upon itself a plethora of adverse newspaper editorials, many from normally friendly papers. It further
destroyed the government's credibility with the Indians
and blew all chance of getting back the documents it
had spent so much time and money tracking down. The
respected Indian author Vine Deloria, Jr., said that Indians all over America knew Adams was trying to get
the documents back as a means of showing good faith.
His arrest put an end to Indian cooperation.

Could all this be attributed to pure blundering, or was
there an ulterior motive? We have already considered
the mountain of information the FBI had to ignore in
order to arrest Hank Adams and drag him before a
grand jury—all the evidence of Adams's past cooperation, his four returns of government property, the cooperative relationships he had established with various
government officials.

We have shown that the government had to suspend
common sense in order to pursue the case. When the
FBI got the documents back to headquarters and saw
they contained ancient Indian land decisions that could
have been of no news value, and when they faced the
fact that they had come up with no proof of payment
whatever, then what but a larger motive than law enforcement could have prompted them to proceed?

The manner of the arrest, itself, nullified its alleged

purpose. Whitten was supposed to be picking up contraband, pursuant to a deal made between the Indians and me, in order that we might "convert" it to our own use. Had the FBI believed its own complaint, the agents would have followed Whitten in his little yellow-orange Vega, would have observed him entering our offices on K Street and would have nailed him in the act of delivering the documents to me. Why did they abort their investigation and, by premature arrest, prevent Whitten and me from having an opportunity to consummate our crime?

My answer is: the government knew that no crime was contemplated and that the documents were being returned. The arrest had to be made, therefore, before the documents could be delivered back to the authorities. It also seems significant that the FBI left the documents in Adams's possession all night and waited for Whitten's appearance on the scene before moving in. I think there were two motives for these false arrests— one a petty matter of FBI pride, the other a more serious issue affecting the survival of democracy. If Adams had returned a major shipment of documents to the BIA building, after the FBI had futilely searched up and down the country for them, the bureau would have been humilated. But what is worse is that H.R. Haldeman in the White House saw this as another opportunity to intimidate the press. So what if the case is ultimately thrown out of court? In the meantime, they have arrested a troublesome reporter, clapped him in jail, threatened him with ten years in prison, flushed out some of his sources, and in doing so, reminded other troublesome reporters that the same thing could happen to them.

Haldeman had already won his victory the moment the headlines hit the streets announcing the arrest of another reporter. It was a victory that will bear fruit every day, whenever any reporter holds back for fear of getting into trouble, whenever a source fears to come forward lest he be exposed, whenever an editor "goes easy" for fear of government retaliation, whenever a publisher tones down the news for fear that a lucrative television franchise his paper owns might be taken away by a federal agency, whenever a citizen anywhere can be influenced to think of reporters as lawbreakers, the kind of people who have to be arrested.

There are people in the government today who are bloated as never before with power and the notion of their own importance, and who have come to believe that the government owns the news. The *Washington Star-Daily News* quoted a government source as saying, "Had Whitten gone to Adams' apartment and extracted information from the original documents for publication, he would have been technically liable to prosecution. In other words, Whitten didn't have to carry out the documents, or pay for them, all he had to do was look at them and print news from them to have violated the law."

This assertion of omnipotence was not missed by the Reporters' Committee for Freedom of the Press, whose membership includes representatives of the major newspapers and broadcast outlets. It said that the arrest of Les Whitten was "based on the outrageous proposition that information about government activities is property, like an automobile, which can be owned by the government. . . . Government information belongs to the public. It is not owned by the Defense Department, or the President, or the Bureau of Indian Affairs."

The proper answer to corruption, arrogance, power grabs, and delusions of grandeur on the part of the government is exposure, deflation, and ridicule by the free press. The nation-wide press reaction to the Whitten incident, and a dozen similar usurpations, encourages me to believe that the press is rising to the battle.

There is a footnote to the Les Whitten episode. Because one of my reporters had been arrested on the streets by the FBI, I stepped out from behind my typewriter for the first time since taking over the column and helped to line up the Senate opposition to Patrick Gray. I wrote a column on February 21, 1973, attacking Gray.

"We hope the Senate," I wrote, "will refuse to confirm him." Throughout his confirmation hearings, I worked behind the scenes, planning strategy and making calls to senators. Gray's confirmation hearing was heavy with helpful liabilities, of course, but to the extent that this prominent false arrest added to the considerations that forced Gray's withdrawal, it was a vindication for Whitten and a victory for press freedom.

Someone Is Watching

The FBI's crime statistics are the official yardstick of just how much evil lurks in the hearts of men. The arithmetic does not reflect favorably on the FBI, which appears powerless to cope with the rising crime rate. The G-men, however, show no embarrassment over the increase. The more crime that is committed, the more money they require to fight it. So at appropriations time, they point to the grim statistics not as evidence of their incompetence but as justification for a bigger budget.

While he was in the White House, Lyndon Johnson gave the FBI an opporutnity to reduce crime. He noted that drug addiction was foremost among the causes for the soaring crime rate; men enslaved by drugs used the gun, the knife, and the yoke to get the money they needed to finance their habit. Johnson thought that since the FBI had more manpower than any other enforcement agency, it should be enlisted in the fight against drug abuse. He discussed his idea with J. Edgar Hoover. The late FBI director, whose bulldog visage had become a national symbol of the crusade against public enemies, Communist spies, and other forces of evil, was too formidable a public figure even for Presidents to challange. And Hoover had no intention of risking his reputation in so uncertain an imbroglio as the war against drugs. He politely declined the opportunity and continued to engage his agents in more statistically satisfying pursuits, such as tracing stolen automobiles and chasing bank robbers.

The revered Hoover not only lasted on top of the bureaucracy longer than any other American, but he also became the most powerful and feared bureaucrat in the history of the republic. He had his own standards for patriotism. He grew up in Washington when it was still a small Southern town, where segregation was the law as well as the custom. To Hoover the struggle for equal rights by blacks smacked of rebellion. His own power depended for half a century on the good will of the nation's elected leaders, whose favor he curried and whose policies he defended. In dissent he saw sedition. Hoover was an incurable curmudgeon, conservative in his ways, and narrow in his outlook, who fiercely believed the words, "My country, right or wrong." The argument of conscience against the war in Vietnam bordered, by his lights, on outright treason.

He used his enormous power as director of the FBI to uphold his viewpoints. His personal power ended with his death, and his rigid rules have been relaxed. Some of the old standards, as out-moded as the bureau's famous battles with the likes of John Dillinger and Kreepy Karpis, have been discarded. Hoover's point of view, however, largely continues to dominate the policies and actions of the FBI. The new FBI, with sideburns, patterned shirts, and narrow-brimmed hats, still devotes an incredible proportion of its manpower, its budget, and its priorities to spying on citizens who exercise the constitutional guarantees of free speech, assembly, and petition.

A huge and esthetically displeasing structure was already rising across the street from the Department of Justice at the time of Hoover's passing. It has now taken his name, and it is an appropriate monument to his memory. Its bulk overwhelms the parent agency much as he overwhelmed the Attorney General, who was his superior. Its interior is designed to accommodate the world's largest collection of papers, documents, photographs, and fingerprints; these are the files of the FBI.

The files are a repository for the black deeds of criminals—murderers, rapists, arsonists, thieves, blackmailers, panderers and the like. The files are also heavy with the names of Americans who have committed no crime other than to take stands that are contrary to the attitudes Hoover imposed on the FBI. There are actors and writers, teachers and students, athletes and physicians, preachers and atheists, whites and blacks (an incredible number of blacks). The political files do not match the criminal files in either number or volume, but their mass is substantial, and their existence is irrefutable proof that the FBI is, indeed, a political police force, deeply involved in thought control.

All the files are sacred property, supposedly hidden from the eyes of all save the FBI, although choice tidbits are sometimes officially bootlegged to influential politicians. We have had access to these forbidden files.

Even the thickest folders contain little wisdom and no wit. They provide typical police blotter information—name, height, weight, address; identification of parents, mates, and children; previous arrests, even for the most trivial offenses and even if the charges were later dropped or dismissed. The FBI folders serve also as repositories of rumors, chitchat, and vicious slander. Little of this information is generated by the FBI itself. Instead, a network of informers feeds the FBI's agents, and the whispers become the basis of turgid prose forwarded to Washington.

Newspaper and magazine articles are also dutifully clipped, pasted on special forms, and sent on to become part of the massive mountain of catalogued minutiae. Occasionally the Central Intelligence Agency, the Secret Service and the National Security Agency contribute items. Frequently the FBI violates the law by obtaining information from banks and telephone companies without subpoenas. This data, too, is shoveled into the files.

Read singly, the political files seem merely another dreary example of bureaucratic excess. Examined in larger lots, they provide an intriguing case-by-case study of just how far the government has intruded into the lives of Americans.

When actress Jane Fonda told a friend she wanted to overthrow "the establishment," an FBI informant was listening. She opposed the war.

When Dr. Benjamin Spock, whose book on child care has helped millions of Americans raise their children, planned a visit to Australia, the FBI had his itinerary. He advocated peace.

When Roy Innis called for a separate school board for Harlem, the FBI made another entry in his folder. He is a black leader.

When an obviously phony diatribe against Jews was circulated under the misspelled name of Muhammad Ali, it was included in the boxer's dossier, which the FBI labeled "Cassius Clay." He is a Black Muslim.

When the *Washington Post* reported that David Eaton was named senior minister for All Souls Unitarian Church, the news made its way into the FBI records. Eaton, too, is black.

Hoover was almost as famous in Washington for his sexual conservatism as he was for his hard-line views on law enforcement. The FBI is the only part of the bureaucracy whose employees are not protected by Civil Service rules. They can be fired or shifted or demoted at the Director's whim. In Hoover's day, many an agent, and probably even more file clerks, were banished from the bureau because someone said, or someone thought, they were engaging in sex without first having gotten a marriage license. Female employees were not allowed to wear slacks, nor were they allowed to stay overnight in the same residence with a lone male, not even their own fathers. Of course, Hoover tolerated no lady agents.

Like the rest of Hoover's traits, his Victorian morality became agency policy in all matters, and operatives spent a great deal of time observing and reporting on the sexual adventures of a wide variety of noncriminal Americans. Indeed, from the quantity and detail of information, we suspect there was as much voyeurism as sleuthing in the investigations.

The FBI follows the affairs, sexual and political, of film personalities, athletes, and other celebrities as avidly as the fan magazines, and the files can truly be said to be star-studded. Marlon Brando's pillow mumbles and Zero Mostel's leers are all recorded. Not even Cool

Hand Luke could escape; Paul Newman's name is there.
Rock Hudson did not get top billing, but there is an FBI
folder on him. The agent reporting on Jane Fonda's visit
to an Indian reservation to drum up support for the Indians who took over San Quentin noted suspiciously that
her hair was "disheveled." Life for Eartha Kitt, according to the FBI, is *c'est si bon.* Joe Namath's passes are
in the records.

Joe Louis, the former heavyweight champion,
aroused the sympathy of millions of admirers when he
suffered a mental disturbance several years ago. Many
Americans believe government agents are following
them, and Louis developed the same paranoia. He took
a punch at a man he thought was a federal agent in the
upstairs lounge of a 747 on a cross-country flight, and
told his victim to leave him alone. The victim, according
to Jolting Joe's FBI file, *was* a government agent, who
reported he had stayed at his post despite the blow.

Not even the pulp magazines would bother with some
of the gossip collected by the FBI. An actor who has figured in the fantasies of millions of American women is
apparently important also in the fantasies of some FBI
men. With the disclaimer that he "has not been the subject of an FBI investigation," the FBI nevertheless kept
a folder on him and slipped in this titillating report:

During 1965, a confidential informant reported that several
years ago while he was in New York he had an "affair" with
movie star ——. The informant states that from personal
knowledge he knew that [the actor] was a homosexual.

The belief was expressed that by "personal knowledge" the
informant meant he had personally indulged in homosexual
acts with [the actor] or had witnessed or received the information from individuals who had done so.

On another occasion, information was received by the Los
Angeles office of the FBI that it was common knowledge in the
motion picture industry that —— was suspected of having
homosexual tendencies. It is to be noted in May, 1961, a confidential source in New York also stated that —— definitely was
a homosexual.

Our files contain no additional pertinent information identifiable with ——. The fingerprint files . . . contain no arrest data
identifiable with [him].

A famous lady, noted as an entertainer on and off the stage, kept the FBI busy at home and the CIA intrigued on two continents as she bounced on the bed springs of almost anyone who asked. A typical item: "In October, 1966, information was received from a reliable source that [a woman] was suing her husband, principal owner of [a Las Vegas hotel], for divorce as a result of Mrs. —— catching her husband in bed with [the entertainer]." The entertainer was suspected of neither criminal nor espionage activity.

If the FBI has a file on you—and there is a chance it does—there are a number of ways the FBI gets information about you. Even if you haven't broken the law, it is quite possible the FBI will break it to learn about you. Agents may go to your bank and get a list of all the checks you have written, even though the law says they must have a subpoena to gain this information. They will photocopy your private papers, as they did Miss Fonda's while detaining her briefly on a phony drug charge. They will go to the telephone company, and, in spite of the legal requirement, again, for a subpoena, get a list of your long-distance calls.

Neighbors, friends, ex-spouses, building superintendents, and school officials may be approached for information about you. Dismayingly most of them become positively garrulous in the presence of FBI agents. The files of the federal government itself is a smorgasbord of information. Selective Service and military records, income tax returns, and social security files are wide open to the G-men.

They may even follow you around to bars. Consider the case of an athlete who is the idol of millions. "[He] has been observed intoxicated on several occasions and also reportedly had an affair with an airline stewardess who became pregnant as a result of this association," an agent wrote reproachfully. "It is alleged that an abortion was arranged for this girl by the wife of ——, the operator of a restaurant-bar in New York. It is understood that the abortion had to be postponed due to the arrest of ——'s wife on charges stemming from an abortion ring."

The FBI men had little interest in Muhammad Ali while he was Cassius Clay. It was his conversion to the Nation of Islam that aroused them. They recorded his public utterances and interviewed his ex-wife and members of the syndicate that once managed him. They also made the mistake that beginning sports writers learn to avoid: they believed much of the gossip that hangs in the air of boxing gyms like sour cigar smoke.

Sonji Clay, the boxer's ex-wife, was contacted by FBI men at her residence. They reported afterward: "She advised that from her personal association with Clay, she knows that the NOI [Nation of Islam] controls his boxing career and through Main Bout, Inc., of New York City, which is owned and operated by the NOI, limits Clay's income to 20 percent of his earnings and the remaining 80 percent is for the NOI. She advised that Clay would comply with any directive of the NOI in that he is an absolute blind follower of Elijah Muhammad [the Black Muslim leader]."

The most amazing facet of the file labeled "Cassius Clay" is the patience of the government servants who compiled it. The fighter's ability to talk is unchallenged; his ability to generate new ideas is on the record. Muhammad repeats himself over and over, to the point where even he himself is bored. But the FBI keeps listening. Sometimes, to break the monotony, Ali lies. The FBI still listens.

An informant was on the scene the day in 1969 when Muhammad dreamed up a championship fight between himself and his old sparring partner Jimmy Ellis. It was during the period when Ali was still awaiting a favorable ruling from the Supreme Court on his draft case, and those who run the boxing commissions had barred him from the ring.

As Ali explained with tongue in cheek, the big money for his fights was not in the arenas but from television. He suggested fighting Ellis in a TV studio, with no boxing commission between him and the paycheck. As reported to the FBI, and recorded in its files, broadcaster Howard Cosell would negotiate the deal and would be paid fifty thousand dollars for his services. Both the FBI files and the Ring Record Book show that no such fight was ever held. Our investigation shows that no such plan was ever considered. Cosell insists he never even heard about it. Only the FBI took it seriously.

The federal sleuths, snooping on black leader Ralph Abernathy, consulted "Mr. John A. Ritter, Credit Bureau of Greater Atlanta, Inc.," who gravely informed the FBI that Abernathy "was employed from 1951 to 1961 as pastor of the First Baptist Church . . . Montgomery, Alabama."

When Dr. Spock was speaking out against nuclear warfare in the mid-1960's, the FBI visited Case Western University, where he was teaching. The agents obtained "the personal file pertaining to Dr. Spock."

For information on black author James Baldwin, they called on "Joseph Brusco, [building] superintendent, 137 West 71st Street, New York City" to learn that "Baldwin had returned from his trip to Turkey." This choice item was stamped "Secret—No Foreign Dissemination."

Incredibly, the FBI eavesdropped on Jane Fonda while she was talking with Dick Cavett on coast-to-coast television. "I spent a lot of time in an ivory tower, kind of up there in Beverly Hills looking through the smog down there . . . ," she said. "One day, I dropped down there, and there were people, and I began to find out what was happening to the masses of people." Her remarks were taped by the FBI and placed in her file.

When she subsequently appeared on the David Frost show the agents got weary after recording the first part. A notation in the file explained: "The remainder of the show was devoted to questions from the audience concerning the Vietnam war. The subject [Miss Fonda] did not make any inflammatory remarks, during the question and answer period." (We copied her comments on nation-wide television from her FBI file, which was marked "Top Secret. No Foreign Dissemination. No

Dissemination Abroad. Controlled Dissemination. For Background Use Only.")

For some, having a file in the FBI has become a status symbol. Absolom Frederick Jordan, a Black United Front member in Washington, D.C., greeted FBI agents with a satisfied smile. It had taken them altogether too long, he complained, to get around to him. Their confidential report says: "Jordan stated he was somewhat hurt that the Federal Bureau of Investigation had not interviewed him. He remarked that practically all of his friends in the BUF had been contacted and he could not understand why he had not been interviewed."

BANGLADESH:
BIRTH BY FIRE

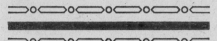

How to Start a War

Thirty years after Pearl Harbor, President Richard Nixon brought the United States to the edge of another world war. His actions were deliberate; he operated in secret; and he lied to the American people about his actions. While preaching peace, he risked war.

Throughout U.S. history, Presidents have distorted and twisted and perverted the constitutional right given only to Congress to send Americans into battle. Article 1, Section II, is clear. It is not diluted by qualifications or ambiguities. It says: "Congress shall have the power to declare war."

In the past half-century Congress has declared war once—against the Axis powers in December 1941. American Presidents, in this same period, have usurped the war-making authority on a number of occasions, some of them still hidden from the public. Harry Truman did not seek the permission of Congress before ordering 157,000 Americans to fight in the ugly and inconclusive war in Korea. Dwight Eisenhower acted without congressional approval when he sent battle-ready marines and paratroopers to Beirut in 1957 to shore up a beleaguered Lebanese government. Nor was Congress consulted when Eisenhower made the first military commitment to South Vietnam. John Kennedy by-passed Congress during the Cuban missile crisis when he ordered the naval blockade, which was an act of war. Lyndon Johnson's invasion of the Dominican Republic in 1965 was not approved by Congress. And Congress was not even informed of the secret war waged by the

Central Intelligence Agency in such places as Guatemala and Laos.

The President has such tight control over diplomatic and military activities, as well as what the public is told about them, that he can manipulate events and opinion to create public hostility and, step by step, to commit the nation to a point where war is inevitable.

In his memoirs Ulysses S. Grant wrote about the American acts of provocation before the outbreak of war with Mexico. "The presence of United States troops on the edge of the disputed territory furthest from Mexican settlements," he said, "was not sufficient to provoke hostilities. We were sent to provoke a fight, but it was essential Mexico should commence it. It was very doubtful whether Congress would declare war; but if Mexico should attack our troops, the Executive could announce, 'Whereas, war exists by acts of, etc.,' and prosecute the contest with vigor. Once initiated, there were but few public men who would have the courage to oppose it. Experience proved that the man who obstructs a war in which a nation is engaged, no matter whether right or wrong, occupies no enviable place in life or history. Better for him, individually, to advocate 'war, pestilence and famine,' than to act as obstructionist to a war already begun."

The covert military manipulations have continued into our own time. For instance, Lyndon Johnson posed as the peace candidate in 1964 while he secretly plotted to enlarge the Vietnam war. Like most Presidents before him, he thought he knew what was the best for the nation. He saw the "complete picture," which he felt could not be shown to the people. It was fitted together for him in the White House from the jigsaw pieces of intelligence that flooded into Washington by pouch and cable from all over the world.

The view of Southeast Asia that emerged from the intelligence reports and strategic analyses was one that stressed the Communist menace. Gravely, Johnson decided to draw the line in Vietnam so that some future

President would not have to draw the line in the Philippines or Hawaii. But he believed he needed a show of national solidarity, to convince the Communist leaders that they could not weaken American determination. The opportunity came when Communist patrol boats, looking for ships that had raided the North Vietnamese coast, attacked American destroyers in the Gulf of Tonkin. No one was hurt; no damage was done. A second dark-of-night "attack" probably never even occurred but was the deviation of faulty radar. With these dubious ingredients Johnson created a phony incident, which he used to inflame the nation.

Perhaps mindful of Grant's political lesson about those who obstruct a war, the Senate gave President Johnson a resolution he sought as a license to expand America's role in the Vietnam war. Neither the Senate nor the public learned the truth about the Gulf of Tonkin incident—nor about Johnson's war strategy—until it was too late. They had no real say about the sixty thousand Americans who would die in Vietnam, nor the $150 billion the war could cost, nor the damage that would be done to national prestige, nor the deep divisions that would be created at home.

Two years earlier, John Kennedy won a nuclear showdown with Nikita Khrushchev while the Pentagon lied about what was going on. The Soviets did not have enough intercontinental missiles to reach all the key U.S. targets in 1962, so Khrushchev began planting medium-range missiles in nearby Cuba. This brought more American bases and cities within annihilation range. Kennedy responded after agonizing deliberation by throwing a blockade around Cuba and preparing to stop Soviet missile shipments from entering Cuban waters. A blockade is, of course, an act of war.

As the confrontation approached in the Atlantic between Soviet ships en route to Cuba with missiles and American warships ordered to block their passage, President Kennedy had on his desk a national intelligence estimate warning that the risk of nuclear war was fifty-

fifty. Our military installations around the wourld were on red alert; our intercontinental missiles in their underground silos and our Polaris missiles under the sea were ready to fire; our B-52 bombers, their bomb bays pregnant with H-bombs, were in the air so they wouldn't need to waste time before taking off.

Inside the White House, President Kennedy plunged a thumbtack into a map of the Atlantic and ordered the Joint Chiefs to intercept the Soviet ships at that point. After the Soviet ships in disregard of the blockade reached the thumbtack, the President slowly withdrew the tack from the map, moved it back and pressed it in again. "Let's give them a little more time," he instructed the Joint Chiefs. "But when they reach this point, you'll have to stop them." As the missile-laden Soviet ships approached the second thumbtack, orders from Moscow crackled through the ether waves. In obedience, the ships turned around and headed back to Russia. Dean Rusk, then the Secretary of State, commented to subordinates: "We've been eyeball to eyeball, and I think the other fellow just blinked."

Throughout the crisis, government information was tightly controlled and carefully coordinated to give a false picture. Pentagon spokesmen denied that offensive weapons had been spotted in Cuba, that an alert had been ordered, that emergency measures had been set in motion against Cuba. Though not a word of this was true, Pentagon press chief Arthur Sylvester still insisted three months later: "There has been no distortion, no deception, and no manipulation of the news released by the Defense Department during the Cuban crisis."

Kennedy's handling of the Cuban confrontation made a deep impression on Richard Nixon. He spoke admiringly of the cold courage Kennedy had demonstrated when he faced an imminent nuclear holocaust. In December 1971 President Nixon had an opportunity to stage his own nuclear showdown in the Bay of Bengal.

While Pakistan and India fought over the dreary, humid, painfully impoverished piece of earth now called

Bangladesh, the United States, Russia, and China issued orders. Armies and navies with hydrogen-headed missiles responded. Deviously, the United States supplied the Pakistanis and dispatched a naval task force, led by the nuclear carrier *Enterprise*, to the Bay of Bengal. On orders from Washington, the ships operated under wartime conditions. It was more than just a training exercise.

The Ingredients of Violence

Vice President Spiro T. Agnew had his finger on the button, and a choir was singing about peace on earth. A small audience of townspeople and tourists had assembled on the Ellipse, the tree-ringed park between the White House and the Washington Monument, for the lighting of the national Christmas tree, part of a pseudo-religious promotion Washington businessmen call the Pageant of Peace.

On the other side of the world, Russia, China, and the United States had been maneuvering dangerously near the edge of world war. They had started choosing sides after the Indian army crossed into East Pakistan. The Chinese, who had been secretly sending supplies over the Himalayas to aid Pakistan, had troops poised to cross into India. The White House, which had put out misinformation about U.S. interests and intentions in the war, had dispatched a naval task force into the Bay of Bengal.

Top Soviet officials, meanwhile, assured Indian leaders that Chinese intervention would be offset by a Russian attack on China, and that any moves by the American task force would be opposed by the Russian fleet. In one bitter confrontation, a Russian officer warned his Chinese counterpart of the power of Russia's missiles. Using sophisticated electronic equipment as well as old-fashioned bribes, U.S. intelligence had gathered all these facts and had forwarded them to Washington.

Rather than being told of the dangers, Congress and he press were assured that America was following a policy of strict neutrality. President Nixon personally advised the top leaders of the Senate and House that his only interest was to bring peace. "We are neutral," he said to them. "We are not taking sides." Dr. Henry Kissinger, Nixon's foreign policy adviser, insisted to reporters that rumors of a U.S. bias against India were "inaccurate."

In secret, however, both Nixon and Kissinger were issuing instructions that could hardly be called neutral. Even before the shooting started between India and Pakistan, the President summoned representatives of the Washington Special Action Group into his office and directed them to seek ways to aid Pakistan. This high-powered group—called WSAG inside the White House —is the crisis-management team of the National Security Council. It is composed of representatives from the Joint Chiefs of Staff, the Departments of State and Defense, and the Central Intelligence Agency. Nixon and Kissinger created WSAG in 1969, when an American reconnaissance plane was shot down over North Korea, and they continued to use it in subsequent emergencies.

WSAG met frequently on the India-Pakistan crisis, and Kissinger, its chairman, constantly reminded the group of Nixon's determination to "tilt" in Pakistan's favor. He castigated diplomats who hesitated to violate the neutrality the United States had proclaimed and admonished WSAG's members to follow the President's wishes.

Kissinger's anti-India zeal troubled some subordinates. "Sometimes Kissinger acted like a wild man," a source on Kissinger's staff told me. "His animus toward India seemed irrational." My sources kept me informed as the developments became more ominous.

Every President is entitled to secrecy in matters of national security, but this privilege does not allow him to deliberately deceive the American people. When I was persuaded that America was being misled, I asked my sources for the documentary evidence that would also convince the public. I arranged to meet my sources in crowded places where the secret papers, in brown Manila envelopes, could be passed quickly and inconspicuously. My sources turned over a dozen key documents. They were so explosive that I had to be sure they were not taken out of context. I pressed for more documentation, until I wound up with hundreds of supporting documents.

With deepening concern, I studied the secret suggestions to send a U.S. task force into the combat zone. The sparks from a Russian-American naval confrontation in the Bay of Bengal, it seemed, could set off a nuclear powder keg. One of my sources alerted me, by a prearranged telephone signal, to meet me at a discount drugstore two blocks from the White House. He was anxious as he pretended to be picking over Christmas items at a drugstore counter next to me. The President had approved the plan to send a powerful flotilla into the Bay of Bengal, he whispered tersely. I walked out of the drugstore and wrote my first column on the secret American involvement.

To protect sources, I quoted cautiously from the secret documents at first. But the reaction inside the White House over these limited leaks was as angry as if I had quoted extensively from the documents. When Kissinger tried to dismiss my stories by saying he had been quoted out of context, I decided to provide the context. I still held back most of the papers, however, out of concern over legitimate security. I have now reviewed these unpublished papers for additional details that can now be revealed, to show how the Nixon Administration's foreign policy was conceived and executed and how the public was misled.

Briefly, this was the background. Nixon sought to correct an error of his early political career when he was a staunch friend of Chiang Kai-shek and an implacable foe of Communist China. His anti-Communist clamoring had helped to prevent the reconciliation that Mao-Tse-tung and Chou En-lai had sought with the United States, and the resulting enmity between China and America was a factor in precipitating two costly U.S. wars on the Asian continent. A quarter of a century too late, Nixon decided the Chinese-American hostility had been a ghastly mistake, and he set out to restore good relations with Peking.

This worthy quest led him into a close relationship with Pakistan's military dictator, Agha Mohammad Yahya Khan, who helped to open the doors in Peking. A warm friendship developed between the two leaders. Nixon was more than a little eager, too, to show common cause with China's ally on the Indian subcontinent.

His decision to aid Pakistan was a national tragedy, an abrogation of America's historic commitment to champion democracy throughout the world. The anti-India policy, moreover, was premeditated. As early as August 1971, four months before the outbreak of the war, Nixon told his foreign policy planners that he intended to back Yahya in his conflict with India.

Catastrophe and war and death have always been commonplace in Bengal, a piece of earth abused by man and nature. For centuries Hindus and Moslems have fought over the rights to the rich alluvial soil. Perhaps the Bengalis' war for freedom was inevitable. The seventy-five million people of Bengal—a land about as large as Louisiana, and with a somewhat similar river delta—were estranged by distance as well as culture and language from the government in the new capital of Islamabad.

Only a poet could have conceived of a political union between two such different bits of geography, separated in the middle by more than a thousand miles of the Indian subcontinent. The poet's name was Mohammad Iqbal. In 1930 he proposed a Moslem state independent of the domination of India's Hindus. Even in the days when Great Britain's colonial government siphoned off the wealth of India, the Hindu majority fared measurably better than the Moslem minority.

The word "Pakistan" itself was an invention, an acronym for four of India's Moslem regions—Punjab, Afghan, Kashmir and Sind. It was coined by Moslem students in England in 1935.

It was 1947 before the name had a place. With Indian independence, the Moslems voted for a separate state, and East and West Pakistan became a single nation. In the migration that followed, Moslems and Hindus clashed and hundreds of thousands were killed. The Bengalis in East Pakistan—more than half the nation's population—got short shrift from the beginning. Ignored in the letters spelling their country's name, they were also paid little heed in the processes of the new government. Pakistan's economy was ruled by the "22 Families," an oligarchy based in the west, who lived in the style of the British viceroys while most Pakistanis went hungry. Political power, too, was centered in the west, with the capital first in Karachi, then temporarily in Rawalpindi as a new capital was rising in Islamabad. While India was fashioning the world's largest democracy, Pakistan fell prey to dictatorship.

The Bengalis, however, did play a part in the life of the new nation. On 15 percent of the nation's land they produced more than half its foreign currency. Most of Bengal is a flat, almost marshy plain, bedeviled by oppressive humidity, monsoon rains, and cyclones. From June to October the clouds that move in from the Bay of Bengal build up into towering masses when they encounter the mountains on the east. With tiresome regularity the clouds give vent to pelting rains. For nearly half the year much of Bengal is under water.

It is a fertile place. The human birth rate is astonishing, and young and old work in the fields to bring forth other life. Eighty percent of the world's jute, a golden-flowered plant that provides the fiber for burlap and rope, is grown in Bengal. Even after twenty-four years of independence, Pakistan had managed to do little toward constructing an industry to process the jute, but the export of the fiber and her Bengal products brought Pakistan needed cash.

Little of the money found its way back into the Bengal economy. While the government built its gleaming new capital at Islamabad, and the 22 Families aped the British with their fancy prep schools, glittering parties, and exclusive clubs, life in East Pakistan was harsh and oppressive. Although commerce gave Dacca some appearance of a modern city, and the fishing port of Chittagong was transformed into a harbor for seagoing ships handling the jute trade, most of East Pakistan saw little progress. Only one of five East Pakistanis ever learned to read. For most, life was labor, and death came early.

The rains that enriched the fields also supported an ideal environment for cholera, smallpox, tuberculosis, and malaria. When the rains became violent, the floods brought more death. In 1966 a cyclone hit Cox's Bazar, a largely Buddhist town at East Pakistan's southeastern tip, and killed ten thousand. The disaster was regarded almost as a routine occurrence. In November 1970, the counterclockwise winds of another cycle swirled over the delta at the mouth of the Ganges River, killing more than two hundred and fifty thousand people. The survivors were also threatened. The rice crop, almost ready for harvest, had been ruined. Even in a land inured to catastrophe, famine was a horror beyond endurance.

Grief turned to anger, and anger to action. As peasants dug the corpses from the slime, they found their government only vaguely interested in helping them. In Islamabad, Yahya Khan, who ruled as President by virtue of the army's power, said there was not enough money in the nation's treasury to feed the Bengalis and help them rebuild. There were sufficient funds, however, for the government to continue construction of the palatial new buildings in the beautiful green valley of Islamabad.

In December 1970 Pakistanis went to the polls in the first free election for the National Assembly in the nation's history. With remarkable unanimity, the Bengalis cast their ballots for the Awami League, headed by the charismatic Sheikh Mujibur Rahman. Mujib's party won all but two of East Pakistan's 169 seats, and gained control of the new national parliament.

In West Pakistan, the leaders of the 22 Families were stunned. Their stranglehold on the nation was threatened for the first time by the new reform party, suddenly the largest of the nation's twenty political parties. Their enormous wealth threatened, the oligarchs huddled with

Yahya, and in March 1971 he announced the postponement of parliament's opening.

The Bengalis are a gentle but emotional people. Their riots had been a bane to the British and an annoyance to the Pakistanis. So again the angry Bengalis took to the streets, demanding the seating of a government that would, at last, be responsive.

While the Bengalis have always been peasants, the taller, lighter skinned Punjabis of the west were warriors for the British East India Company and, later, the British army. With independence, they assumed control of the Pakistani army.

On March 25, Punjab troops quickly and ruthlessly put down the uprising, shooting wildly, shelling homes, attacking student dormitories. On orders from Islamabad, they arrested Mujibur Rahman and shipped him to a prison in West Pakistan. Other Awami League members were arrested or killed.

The repression changed nothing. Young Bengalis armed themselves and fought back. The army then began a rampage of genocide seldom equaled in history. A million, perhaps two million—no one will ever know for sure—Bengalis were killed. Tens of thousands, possibly hundreds of thousands, of women and young girls were raped. Arson and pillage became the army's way of life. Defenseless refugees swarmed into India.

"The United States did not support or condone this military action," President Nixon said in his State of the World report to Congress on February 9, 1972. That is only partially true. The fact is that the United States did nothing to halt it, and dealt sternly with Foreign Service officers who sought to bring attention to the conditions in Bengal.

When the slaughter of the Bengalis began, Archer K. Blood, then U.S. Consul General in Dacca, the capital of East Pakistan, sent details to U.S. Ambassador Joseph Farland in Islamabad and to the State Department in Washington. He also forwarded a petition signed by most of his subordinates on the consulate staff, protesting America's apparent indifference.

Some members of the Dacca mission who had signed the petition were recalled. Wives of American diplomats, evacuated from Dacca to Islamabad as the terror increased, were told they only imagined the horrors they had witnessed and were offered tranquilizers.

Blood was summoned to Washington in June 1971, but planned to return to Dacca for the remaining eighteen months of his tour of duty. At the State Department he was told he was an alarmist, and was given a desk in the personnel office. Despite his humiliation, he was admired by many other Foreign Service officers who were aware of his courage and honesty in the face of top-level deception.

The Making of a War

General Agha Mohammad Yahya Khan was an anachronism—a strutting officer out of the Rudyard Kipling mold, dashing in battle, who drank too much and loved too many—a conniver who mastered the mechanics of intrigue without learning the art of politics.

He was a soldier by breeding. He was born into a military caste; his Persian ancestors conquered Delhi in the eighteenth century.

He was a soldier in bearing. He had a military mind and military manners. Wherever he went, however he dressed, he usually carried a swagger stick under his arm.

He was a soldier by education. He studied battle lore at military schools, including the British colonial military academy in India, where he stood tall on the drill field and led his classes.

He wore the uniform of a British officer during World War II. After the partition of the Indian subcontinent in 1947, he came home to head the new Pakistani army staff college. He gave his students a practical course in how to get ahead in the army. He was a brigadier at thirty-four, a general at forty, a commander in chief at forty-nine.

On his way upward, Yahya became a close friend of General Ayub Khan and was almost certainly on the inside of the coup that made Ayub president in 1958. It was this friendship as much as Yahya's ability that won him Pakistan's second highest military honor after the war with India over Kashmir in 1965.

Neither his training nor his heroics prepared him for civilian leadership, and he was sadly miscast when he succeeded Ayub as president in 1969. Yahya adopted a few reforms, and he pledged to institute democratic civilian government. Allowing Mujibur Rahman to win an election before jailing him was as close as Yahya came to keeping his promise.

He insulated himself from domestic turmoil—by distance and by isolation—at the Presidential Estate in Islamabad. He boasted that he killed a bottle of Scotch every morning without dulling either his administrative or sexual abilities. As his nation began to crumble he found comfort in the friendship of two widely dissimilar nations, Communist China and the United States.

Both great powers considered Pakistan a useful partner. The Chinese, always squabbling with India, were eager to have an ally on their southeast flank.

When Pakistan captured its third of Kashmir in 1947, it annexed a small common border with China's Sinkiang Province. An old caravan trail meandered over this frontier. In time this trail was widened and hardened to provide a modern, all-weather road. U.S. intelligence reported that motorized caravans roared over the mountains, carrying the tools of war to Pakistan.

In return for the weapons, the Chinese were given access to Pakistan's government. When Yahya selected Ali Bhutto as deputy prime minister and foreign affairs minister for his emergency civilian government, he was deliberately tapping the leader of Pakistan's pro-Peking party.

The Americans recruited Pakistan into the impotent Southeast Asia Treaty Organization. Like many other holdovers from the cold war, SEATO had an undeserved importance in U.S. defense planning.

With the changing East-West political tides, Yahya was able to execute the most profitable of all his intrigues. He acted as the power broker who brought the Chinese and Americans together. He helped Dr. Henry Kissinger, the White House adviser, through the bamboo curtain and provided a cover during the professor's secret visit to Peking. Yahya was even host at a small stag dinner party the night before Kissinger's departure.

Yahya's favors for Kissinger gave the dictator an epoxy-like bond with President Nixon, who has seldom hesitated to repay a political favor, no matter how high the interest.

As the price for Yahya's friendship, Nixon turned away from India, the world's largest democracy. It was a decision Nixon made easily. Like other American leaders, the President had been irritated by India's frequent carping about the international conduct of the United States. Further, Nixon harbored deep resentments against India's prime minister, Mrs. Indira Gandhi. She is a brilliant politician who, our sources say, outmaneuvered him in their private encounters in New Delhi and Washington. Nixon not only finds it difficult to regard women as statesmen, but resents being upstaged by foreign leaders who are more adroit than he is. Mrs. Gandhi annoyed him, both as a leader and as a woman.

Perhaps more important to Nixon was the balance-of-power concept espoused by Austria's Prince Metternich in the nineteenth century. This concept was revived a century later by President Nixon's Prince Metternich, Henry Kissinger. A change in the status of East Pakistan would alter the balance by removing that territory from the American bloc. Kissinger and Nixon felt they should not let this happen.

It was clear from the beginning that the American people would not tolerate American aid for Yahya's depredations in East Pakistan. When the slaughter of Bengalis began, Congress forced the White House to order an end to military shipments to Pakistan. Public sentiment in the United States favored the Bengalis. But when the fighting erupted between India and Pakistan, the great majority of Americans were even more committed to a policy of neutrality. To keep arms flowing to Yahya's murderous forces, therefore, Nixon was compelled to deceive Congress and the American public consciously and repeatedly.

As Nixon explained it in his State of the World message, oddly entitled "The Emerging Structure of Peace": "Immediately, in early April, we ceased issuing and renewing licenses for military shipments to Pakistan, we put a hold on arms that had been committed the year before, and we ceased new commitments for economic development loans. This shut off $35 million worth of arms. Less than $5 million worth of spare parts, already in the pipeline under earlier licenses, was shipped before the pipeline dried up completely by the beginning of November."

Yet, an investigation by Senator Edward M. Kennedy (D-Mass.) established in October 1971, that the United States offered weapons to Pakistan as late as June. Still more American arms were conveyed to Pakistan during the December war.

The first shots of the open hostilities between India and Pakistan are lost in the brown dust and green jungles of the battlefields, but it can be said with certainty that the war had its actual beginning on March 25, 1971, when Yahya ordered his army to begin its rule of terror. No nation is compelled to stand by passively while genocide is taking place on its frontiers. Further, the repression sent a flood of refugees into India. By the beginning of December, there were ten million survivors of East Pakistan huddled in the squalor and hunger of a thousand refugee camps. In a sense, this was an act of aggression against India, which is hard-pressed to feed its own hungry millions without the added burden of sheltering hordes made homeless by an unscrupulous despot.

A CIA report reveals that the revolution was raging furiously at the same time Yahya was proclaiming he had East Pakistan under control and the White House was insisting a political settlement was possible. In this one sector alone, the Mukti Bahini (the Bengali freedom fighters) had ten thousand men under arms, another five thousand in training, and "the youth camps [were] always full and several hundred recruits [were] usually awaiting admission." In this sector, the CIA report stated the rebels "have subdued and held areas within East Pakistan which the Mukti Bahini consider 'liberated areas.' . . . The principal 'liberated area' is well defended by about 4,000 men with rocket launchers, recoilless rifles, heavy and light machine guns, and two anti-aircraft guns. The Indian army provides artillery defense from the nearby Indian border . . . Because of intensive training, adequate leadership and a successful record of incursions into East Pakistan, near ly all operations since April 1971 in the sector have been carried out solely by the Mukti Bahini without the direct assistance of the Indian Border Security Force or the Indian army."

Beginning in late November there were border clashes between Pakistani and Indian soldiers, and Indian units crossed the border to attack Pakistani positions the Indians said were shelling their territory. Still, all the outward signs of peace were maintained by the two neighboring nations.

In the late afternoon of December 2 three American-made Sabre jets bearing the markings of the Pakistani air force strafed the Indian town of Agratala on East Pakistan's eastern border. It was the first air action by either side against civilian targets, but Indian and Pakistan still remained—formally at least—at peace.

At five-thirty the next afternoon, the Pakistani air force struck again, this time at eight Indian air force bases. The surprise was complete; at first the air-raid sirens were thought to be for a practice alert. The initial Indian reports listed only three bombed fields, but more were added as monitors picked up new reports from Pakistani broadcasts. Mrs. Gandhi was speaking to a crowd of five hundred thousand in Calcutta at the time of the attack, and did not learn of it until she left the rostrum.

The Washington Special Action Group met four hours after the attack began, and CIA Director Richard Helms admitted he was confused. "There are conflicting reports from both sides and the only common ground is the Pak attacks on Amritsar, Pathankat and Srinagar airports," he said.

Yahya had envisioned the attack as an Israeli-style master stroke, intended to neutralize India's air power. But other knowledgeable military experts were appalled by its clumsiness. The Pentagon knew the Indians had few planes stationed at the bases.

Admiral Thomas Moorer, chairman of' the Joint Chiefs of Staff, could find no logic in the Pakistani move. "The present pattern is puzzling in that the Paks have only struck at three small airfields which do not house significant numbers of Indian combat aircraft," he said. "The Pak attack is not credible. It has been made during late afternoon, which does not make sense. We do not seem to have sufficient facts on this yet."

Moorer and everyone else in the small, crowded room knew the facts were unimportant to the task assigned the WSAG members. Their job was not to establish truth but to find justification for the pro-Pakistan policy the President had endorsed four months earlier in his lecture to the group members.

The Dictator and the Diplomat

Yahya Khan had an extraordinary relationship with American Ambassador Joseph Farland; they met almost daily and sometimes shared a bottle of Scotch. From this contact, the Pakistani dictator was aware of Nixon's support even before American-made planes dropped the first bombs on India. Other ambassadors stationed in Islamabad complained that Yahya saw no foreign envoy other than Farland during November and December 1971.

When the war with India was still a distant possibility, Yahya and Farland talked about it. "He told me that Pakistan could not survive another war with India," Farland informed us. "This was apparent to even the most casual observer. I know he didn't expect victory, but I think he experienced a certain kind of relief at the outbreak that they were finally having another go at it."

Farland is short and solid, with a deep voice, graying hair, and a square jaw. He dresses precisely, and projects the image of the FBI agent he once was. He was also a lawyer, coal-mine operator and lobbyist, and a member of the research council and executive committee of Georgetown University's right-wing Center for Strategic and International Studies.

In 1957 President Eisenhower sent him to the Dominican Republic as ambassador, and he spent three years as intermediary with dictator Rafael Trujillo. Then the friendly Farland moved on to Panama, where he continued for almost all of John Kennedy's Administration.

When Farland arrived in Islamabad in the fall of 1969, he found the Pakistanis still bitter over America's refusal to support them in their 1965 war with India. Later, some Pakistanis portrayed him as a CIA agent, trying to subvert their nation and encourage the Bengalis to seek self-determination. It was only a short time, however, before the alcoholic dictator and the American ambassador were sipping Scotch together and sharing secrets. The Pakistanis who thought Farland had pro-Bengali sympathies were quite wrong. Farland was so close to Yahya that in recounting the horrors of the November 1970 cyclone to us, the ambassador betrayed an anti-Bengali bias:

The body count from the disaster was exaggerated for political reasons by the Bengalis. They have always looked at themselves as second-class citizens in Pakistan, as the forgotten people. When the world began to recognize their plight from the attention they had received because of the disaster, a latent nationalism became overt, and Mujib became a focal point for nationalism. But neither he nor anyone realized the depth of emotion for and against nationalism of East Pakistan. The worldwide recognition of the East Pakistan situation locked Mujib in a non-negotiable position. . . .

The Bengalis used the catastrophe to dramatize the dispute. That is why the number of dead from the disaster has grown so, from 12,000 to 28,000 to one and a half million. We figure that 300,000 people died. A staggering figure, but nowhere near the estimates from some of the Bengalis . . . But the predictions of cholera and smallpox never materialized. The tidal wave came. The people died—not by disease so much as by drowning.

Farland knew Mujib, and found him dynamic but overly fond of rhetoric. He knew Yahya better, though he denied the closeness of their friendship. "We had a normal diplomatic relationship," Farland said. "We have met twice socially . . . Normally, I met Yahya Khan on official business in the morning." With the pressure on, Yahya turned to his confidant. Farland cabled Washington: "I met with President Yahya at his residence at 1230 hours local Dec. 8. The conversation lasted for about 30 minutes and was strictly informal. The man just wanted to talk . . ." Such confidence in a foreign diplomat had few parallels.

Farland insisted he used his meetings with Yahya as a peacemaker. "When the history books are written on the war, it will be shown that U.S. policy, and our local efforts in Pakistan, kept Mujib alive," he said. "After Mujib's arrest, I talked frequently with Yahya and often mentioned Mujib. I told Yahya that we felt that Mujib was the key to future stability in Pakistan, east and west. I counseled Yahya not to kill this man. And finally, one night during the early summer, Yahya said to me, 'You have convinced me. He will not be executed.' "

Yahya was not so convinced that he intended to spare Mujib forever. When Yahya left office in disgrace at the end of the war, he left behind a death warrant for Mujib. The date was blank, so his successors could fill it in at their convenience, and blame the execution on Yahya. Yahya's successor wisely refused to use the document.

With a string of military reverses in Bengal, Yahya depended on Farland more than ever, and the two men developed a relationship that was unusual for a chief of state and a foreign ambassador. The Pakistani president needed a friend to confide in as his army fell back day after day. In some places the Pakistani troops stood and fought and were beaten, but at many others, they fled before the first Indian troops arrived. The Indians quickly established complete air superiority, and Indian ground troops cut off the route to Chittagong, East Pakistan's major port. Chittagong, on Bengal's southeastern panhandle, had been the Pakistani army's hope for supplies and, if necessary, escape.

Now it seemed inevitable that the Pakistan army would fall back to Dacca. But their strategy became clear. Dacca is surrounded by a network of waterways, and there are few bridges. A determined army could hold the city for months.

United Nations Assistant Secretary General Paul

Marc Henry, who headed the U.N. mission in Dacca throughout the war, told us about the plan. "We expected a tragedy of the same dimension as Stalingrad," he said. "They had prepared for a war of attrition. After a month or two, according to the strategy, the diplomatic situation would change. Pressure would increase for India to leave East Pakistan alone. The Americans and Chinese would send increasing amounts of supplies to the Pakistanis. The Russians would be forced to back down or enter into a major triangular conflict with the Americans and Chinese."

Not all of Yahya's officials had the courage such a stand demands. As Indian air force MIGs pounded Government House, Dr. A. M. Malik, the small, sad-eyed civilian governor of East Pakistan, cowered in a bunker as he and his entire cabinet handed their resignations to a U.N. representative and asked for asylum.

With the collapse of the civilian government, the last semblance of civilized behavior disappeared in Dacca. Squads of al Badar, armed Bihari irregulars, toured the city in buses and rounded up Bengali intellectuals. At gunpoint, doctors, lawyers, university professors, and writers were taken from their homes and driven to a swamp on the edge of the city. There they were tortured and killed. There was no trial and no appeal for those whose names appeared on the death lists. Most of the victims were not political activists. The fact that they were educated was crime enough against the state. It seemed that the Pakistani military was determined to destroy the future of Bengal.

The United States might have used its enormous influence with the Pakistanis at any time during the nine months of the horror to protect the Bengalis and their leaders. That was never done.

Policy of Deception

President Nixon and Henry Kissinger used the India-Pakistan war for cynical ends. While pretending to strive for peace, they actually extended the fighting and increased the risk of a wider war.

The President told Congress in his State of the World message: "If we had not taken a stand against the war, it would have been prolonged and the likelihood of an attack in the West greatly increased." True, the White House did take a public stand against the war. But in secret—in the President's offices, in the Situation Room, and at Yahya's Presidential Estate—the talk was quite different. The details make disturbing reading.

Late in the afternoon of December 10, Major General Rao Farman Ali Khan, the commander of the Pakistani forces in Dacca, delivered a note to U.N. Assistant Secretary General Paul Marc Henry asking the United Nations to arrange an immediate cease-fire and a transfer of power to the "elected representatives of East Pakistan." General Farman said the request was authorized by Yahya.

The proposal called for the "repatriation with honor" of the Pakistani troops to West Pakistan, the repatriation of other West Pakistanis who wanted to go back, safety for the marauding Biharis, and a "guarantee of no reprisals against any person in East Pakistan." The message said further: "The question of surrender of the armed forces will not be considered and does not arise, and if this proposal is not accepted, the armed forces will continue to fight to the last man."

Henry had sat with Farman earlier in the day while the Pakistani general drafted the text. "We met alone at first," Henry told us. "Half of the text was devoted to a peaceful transition to a civilian government. There were other conditions, but this was the heart of the message. I asked Farman if this had been authorized. He said it was."

Later that day, Henry and two of his assistants met with East Pakistan Governor A. M. Malik and a Pakistani officer to receive the final draft of the cease-fire offer from Farman. General Amir Abdulla Khan Niazi, the Pakistani commander for all East Pakistan and General Farman's superior, was not present.

"I again asked Farman, 'Has General Yahya authorized this?'" Henry recalled. "Farman said, 'I have just received a flash from Islamabad. Yahya approves. You have this on the word of a soldier.'"

Henry paid quick calls on the American, Russian, British, and French consuls, told them of Farman's offer, and then cabled it to U.N. headquarters in New York. When the report of Farman's offer reached Washington, the State Department instructed Ambassador Farland to ask Yahya whether he was also willing to seek a cease-fire in the west, "in which case we are ready to make a major effort to bring it about in order to preserve Pakistani territorial integrity and armed forces."

Having sent his message to the U.N., Henry returned to Government House, and found Governor Malik waiting in a corner of the building. "He again guaranteed that the offer had been approved," Henry said, "but he was a weak man, and there seemed to be some hedging about it. Later, two colonels visited me and said that the surrender was no longer approved. Yahya had changed his mind."

Other diplomats, stationed in Islamabad, had an explanation for Yahya's intransigence. They insisted that after Yahya had given his permission for the surrender, he was told of Nixon's decision to send part of the Seventh Fleet into the Bay of Bengal to aid the Pakistanis. It was only then, the diplomats assert, that Yahya changed his mind.

Throughout the war, and the incidents leading to it, President Nixon tried to wear the mask of a peacemaker while actually fanning the flames of war. He generally avoids press conferences and other open discussions of his policies, but on December 6, 1971, he allowed an NBC camera crew to film much of his day inside the White House for a TV special. Later that month TV viewers beheld the President putting through a call to Ambassador George Bush at the United Nations and giving instructions on the India-Pakistan crisis. "Some, all over the world, will try and make this basically a political issue," Nixon said. "You've got to do what you can. More important than anything else now is to get the facts out with regard to what we have done, that we have worked for a political settlement, what we have done for the refugees and so forth and so on. If you see that some here in the Senate and House, for whatever reason, get out and misrepresent our opinions, I want you to hit it frontally, strongly and toughly; is that clear? Just take the gloves off and crack it, because you know exactly what we have done, O.K.?"

The monologue was vintage Nixon, with the implication in the words "for whatever reason" that his critics might be unpatriotic and the image of a fighting President ready to "take the gloves off." Then, of course, there was the outright deception in the suggestion that he wanted "to get the facts out."

The White House did everything it could to keep the truth of its secret conspiracy from the American people, even to the point of staging a fake meeting of the Washington Special Action Group for the NBC cameras. In the television version, Nixon sat in his very private Executive Office Building suite with Secretary of State William Rogers, Secretary of the Treasury John Conally, CIA Director Richard Helms, and General William Westmoreland. The President spoke blandly about his communications with Yahya Khan and his November conversation at the White House with Mrs. Indira Gandhi. Rogers responded: "We can't be blamed for—there have been many, many areas of the world we just can't be responsible for."

The real WSAG sessions, of course, took place in the Situation Room in the White House basement and were presided over by Kissinger, who transmitted the President's wishes. At these meetings, Kissinger's orders to the other participants consistently reflected a definite sense of responsibility. "I am getting hell every half hour from the President that we are not being tough enough on India," Kissinger complained on December 3. "He just called me again. He does not believe we are carrying out his wishes. He wants to tilt in favor of Pakistan. He feels everything we do comes out otherwise."

On December 6, while the President spoke softly before the TV cameras, Kissinger ordered an increase in the pressure on India. The secret minutes of the meeting record this: "Dr. Kissinger also directed that henceforth we show a certain coolness to the Indians; the Indian ambassador is not to be treated at too high a level."

America's policy-makers had not uttered a public word about the slaughter of the Bengalis, which had precipitated the crisis in East Pakistan and had become more brutal in the ensuing nine months. Yet when the Indian army and the Mukti Bahini began rolling up military successes, there was a sudden fear in the WSAG for the safety of the million and a half Biharis who live in East Pakistan. The Biharis, like most of Yahya's soldiers, spoke Urdu rather than Bengali, and some assisted the army in its repression of the Bengalis.

At the December 6 meeting, Kissinger asked if there had already been a massacre of some Biharis. Maurice Williams, the deputy director of the Agency for International Development, said he expected one. To save the Biharis, he suggested an "international humanitarian effort." Kissinger said he thought the campaign should be launched immediately " to prevent a bloodbath."

At the same meeting, Under Secretary of State U. Alexis Johnson warned that after the fighting, Bangladesh would be an "international basket case." Kissinger grimly replied, "It will not necessarily be our basket case."

Williams corrected some earlier misinformation at the December 8 meeting. He said little money destined for refugee relief entered the Indian economy, and the Indians actually lost foreign exchange in the process of caring for refugees. Kissinger was not interested in helping India feed the reguees. He said the President "had made it clear" that no funds could be assigned to India without White House approval.

Then Kissinger asked what "the next turn of the screw" might be. He warned Williams that no money for India was to go into the federal budget. "It was not to be leaked that AID had put money in the budget for India, only to have the 'wicked' White House take it out," he added.

Kissinger complained about the Indian blockade of Pakistani ports. "Can we allow a U.S. ally to go down completely while we participate in a blockade?" he railed. "Can we allow the Indians to scare us off, believing that if U.S. supplies are needed they will not be provided?"

Johnson said America did not have a legal case to protest the blockade, since nations at war have the right to blockade their enemies. "We are not trying to be even-handed," Kissinger snapped at the career diplomat. "There can be no doubt what the President wants. The President does not want to be even-handed. The President believes that India is the attacker. We are trying to get across the idea that India has jeopardized relations with the United States. We cannot afford to ease India's state of mind. The lady [Mrs. Gandhi] is cold-blooded and tough and will not turn into a Soviet satellite merely because of pique."

Kissinger worked on India's fear that America would openly supply Pakistan. U.S. Ambassador Kenneth Keating reported from New Delhi that the new Iranian

envoy had told him Indian officials had asked whether
Iran was sending U.S. arms to Yahya. "He had denied
flatly that arms had gone from Iran to Pakistan," Keating cabled Washington. "I interjected that I had made
the same point on several occasions with respect to arms
transfers from Iran requiring U.S. approval."

Under Secretary of State John Irwin, following Kissinger's orders, admonished Keating in a return message: "In view intelligence reports spelling out Indian
military objectives in West Pakistan, we do not want in
any way to ease Government of India's concerns regarding help Pakistan might receive from outside sources.
Consequently, embassy should henceforth give GOI no
repeat no assurances regarding third country transfers."
Copies of the cable were also sent to U.S. embassies in
Saudi Arabia, Jordan, Iran, and Pakistan. The ambassadors in these countries were told "to report to department any indications third country transfers being contemplated by host government."

In another cable from Irwin, Keating was instructed
to talk to the Indian foreign secretary and intercede in
behalf of the Biharis, as well as war prisoners and foreign nations trapped in East Pakistan. The same message was sent to Farland in Islamabad, with the notation: "If you believe it is possible, we believe it would
also highly desirable if you could convey to Government
of Pakistan our humanitarian concerns with respect to
minorities and our hope that Pakistan army and administration will avoid actions which could intensify already
inflamed communal animosities. We realize this is extremely sensitive subject and leave it to your discretion
how and at what level such points might best be got
across."

Keating answered that he had been assured India
would observe international law "and to the best of its
ability prevent any possible excesses." We were not able
to locate any response from Farland.

Nixon himself was less than even-handed when he
greeted the new Pakistani ambassador, Nawabzada

Agha Mohammad Raza, at the White House with pomp and ceremony on December 6. The ambassador's statement was long, and it contained phrases that startled professional diplomats who were accustomed to hearing only bland generalities. He said, "Your unflinching support and understanding of our problems, Mr. President, which your countrymen can perhaps understand better than others, have been a source of immense strength to the government and to the people of Pakistan in meeting a grave threat to their existence as free people of an independent sovereign state." Nixon said in his answer, "In recent months, your nation has been buffeted by natural and other catastrophes. We are happy that the United States has been able significantly to assist in meeting the relief and reconstruction needs generated by these crises, and we have followed with sympathetic interest the efforts of the government and people of Pakistan to achieve an amicable political settlement in East Pakistan. We have also welcomed the efforts of President Yahya to move to reduce tensions in the subcontinent."

The real direction of American policy was recognized for what it was in other capitals. Top British officials told the American embassy in London they thought the United States had made a "tactical error" in its criticism of India. The British believed, the cable to the State Department said, "both sides are at fault and it is essentially sterile exercise at this juncture to attempt to apportion greater blame to one side or the other. British determination not to put themselves in this posture springs from this conclusion, and from their conviction that it is in British interest to be able to have reasonable relations with India and Bangladesh when conflict is over."

Nixon and Kissinger had no such foresight. The anti-India policy prevailed until the very end, with almost disastrous results.

Ominous Developments

In his call for a declaration of war against Germany on April 2, 1917, President Woodrow Wilson angrily described the German military-espionage operation. "Self-governed nations do not fill their neighbor states with spies or set the course of intrigue to bring about some critical posture of affairs which will give them an opportunity to strike and make conquest," Wilson said. "Such designs can be successfully worked out only under cover and where no one has the right to ask questions . . . They are happily impossible where public opinion commands and insists upon full information concerning all the nation's affairs."

Wilson was, of course, an idealist. He spoke long before there was a Central Intelligence Agency, before the military services also established the Defense Intelligence Agency, with its world-wide intelligence network to compete against the CIA. And before Richard Nixon sought to orchestrate public opinion from the White House.

On December 6 Nixon summarized for the benefit of the NBC cameras what he had discussed behind closed doors.

He said he had told the congressional leaders: "There really wasn't much more that we knew about it than they saw in the papers, because I said this is one area where we have no military advisers present . . . I told the leaders this morning there were no people with the troops . . . There are no Americans with any of the troops any place. I mean the attachés are at the embassies, and so basically what is happening, the Indian attaché will reflect the Indian reports and the Pakistan attaché will reflect the Pakistan reports."

"But we have a variety of independent sources, also," Kissinger interjected.

"Yeah, I know, I know," said the President brusquely as the cameras whirred. "None of them are reliable."

"None of them are totally reliable," Kissinger corrected, and he emphasized "totally."

The fact was that the CIA had penetrated the Indian government at every level and these "independent sources" sent a steady stream of reports back to Washington on troop movements, logistics, strategy, and even some of Prime Minister Indira Gandhi's secret conversations.

In modern espionage, adrenaline and muscle are supposed to be less valuable commodities than math degrees and photo analysis. The Directorate for Intelligence, which sifts the input from the CIA's arsenal of orbiting satellites and earthbound eavesdropping devices, is supposedly preeminent. Nevertheless, the bulk of the information on the India—Pakistan crisis was provided by the Directorate for Plans, CIA's old-fashioned "dirty tricks department."

This pervasive spying, however, could not be considered entirely partisan; the Directorate for Plans had agents stationed at key spots throughout India and Pakistan alike. It was also evident from the agents' reports that the infiltration had continued for some time; many informants were described as old and reliable sources.

Yet the CIA, or at least its director Richard Helms, was not infallible. There were times at the Washington Special Action Group meetings when he had to admit he did not know what was happening; there were other times when his assessments were wrong. On at least one occasion he told the group that he had forgotten to transmit an important piece of information. There were times when his failure to use all of CIA's resources irritated others at the table. "It would help," Joseph Sisco, an Assistant Secretary of State, suggested to him on December 3, "if you could provide a map with a shading of the areas occupied by India."

Helms was careful not to provoke the wrath of the two men who controlled his career, Nixon and Kissinger. When they told him to tilt, he leaned in the direction they suggested. The image of the detached, professional public servant, which he has carefully cultivated in Washington, was not apparent in the secret policy councils. Not once did he dispute Kissinger's distorted version of the facts, even when Helms's own agency had produced refutation.

Under pressure from Kissinger, on December 3, Helms allowed that the Indians were "definitely" occupying "small bits" of East Pakistan. He also told WSAG on December 5 that "the Indians have not yet broken through on the ground in East Pakistan."

The CIA operatives in the field went about their job of bribing officials and garnering information with professional dispassion. Many of their reports were similar to the news that reporters were sending back to American papers, but some of them were definitely exclusive. Almost all the raw reports were objective. The interpreting was done in Washington.

On December 8 the CIA uncovered reports from a source close to Mrs. Gandhi. It was whispered darkly that India might launch a major offensive against West Pakistan. The report was not considered the most important intelligence by CIA, which made it the fifth item in a situation report the next day: "The situation in the west may change radically should the fighting cease in the east. According to a source who has access to information on activities in Prime Minister Gandhi's office, as soon as the situation in East Pakistan is 'settled,' Indian forces will launch a major offensive against West Pakistan." However, the CIA report added: "The Indian Government hopes that all major fighting will be over by the end of December 1971."

A related intelligence item was rated even lower by the State Department, which mentioned it next to last in

Situation Report No. 30: "There have been reports that Mrs. Gandhi would accept a cease-fire and international mediation as soon as East Bengal had been liberated, and there have also been official hints that the GOI would accept a cease-fire now in return for an early surrender of Pak forces in East Bengal. On the other hand, we have had several recent reports that India now intends not only to liberate East Bengal but also to straighten its borders in Kashmir and to destroy West Pakistan's air and armored forces. To accomplish this, the Indian Army would transfer four to five divisions to the west as soon as it had gained full control in the east. There have been reports that initial movements of these forces have already begun."

It was from this thin gruel that the White House constructed an Indian plot against West Pakistan, even though military leaders had discounted India's ability to move its army across the country. The WSAG minutes for December 6 note: "General Westmoreland stated that Indian transportation capabilities were limited from west to east, and that it would probably take at least a week to move one infantry division. It might take as much as a month to move all or most of the Indian forces from the east to the west." And on December 13 the CIA reported that Nikolay M. Pegov, the Russian ambassador to India, "stated that India should try to occupy Bangladesh in the quickest possible time and that it should then accept a cease-fire . . . that India has achieved a marvelous military victory, Pakistan is no longer a military force, and it is therefore unnecessary for India to launch an offensive into West Pakistan to crush a military machine that no longer exists."

Nevertheless, President Nixon later told Congress: "During the week of December 6, we received convincing evidence that India was seriously contemplating the seizure of Pakistan-held portions of Kashmir and the destruction of Pakistan's military forces in the west. We could not ignore this evidence."

More accurate evidence was gathered by the U.S. defense attaché in Nepal, Colonel Melvin Holst, who informed Washington that as a result of discussions with Indian officials, he had uncovered the "Indian grand strategy" for the war. The Indian aim, he said, was to keep fighting in the east until the Bangladesh government was installed, and to fight to prevent a West Pakistani push into Kashmir. With victory in the east, India would then pull back to the previous borders, provided that West Pakistan did the same. He said the Indians planned to "weather world condemnation, U.S. termination of aid, etc., knowing U.S. public/leadership will 'forget' and reinstate aid within 6-12 months."

The probability of a greater conflict was being examined in the Pentagon. Senior officials carefully studied reports about the continuing dispute between Russia and China which had been heightened by Russia's support for India and China's encouragement to Pakistan. The Pentagon's estimates showed that in the event of a confrontation, Russia had overwhelming military superiority —more tanks, planes and ships, better transportation, a superior industrial base, and, of paramount importance, an arsenal of missiles with nuclear warheads.

The Chinese, however, were working furiously to overcome their nuclear disadvantage. Already they were at work on emplacements for new nuclear missiles, with range sufficient to hit key Russian targets. The first few had already been deployed when the India–Pakistan war erupted. Ultimately this would give China the deterrent it desired.

China's hydrogen-headed ballistic missiles are being developed mainly in Sinkiang Province, a bleak mountain-rimmed, sparsely settled area on China's western border. China has actively encouraged migration into Sinkiang since 1960, but the Turkic natives still comprise 61 percent of the population; they are descendants of nomadic Turkish tribes who once roamed central Asia. Their language is similar to that spoken in Turkey. They are also related in speech and in spirit to other Turkic groups on the Russian side of the mountain range that forms the border. Politics has not stopped the ancient custom of visiting over the passes.

The migration of Chinese into the province, and the demands from Peking for ideological conformity, have changed the life style for some of Sinkiang's rugged Turkic people. They have reacted by stirring up rebellions which the Chinese have suppressed harshly; some have escaped over the mountains and made their way to Turkey while others have crossed the border into Russia, where they wait for an opportunity to return.

There were more than a few parallels between Sinkiang's Turkic inhabitants and East Pakistan's Bengalis. Just as the Bengalis found sympathy across the border in India, China's Turkic people were welcomed by Russia. And just as the Bengalis established guerrilla bases in India, the Turkic people of Sinkiang were allowed to establish their own liberation front with their own general on the Soviet side of the border.

The men in the Pentagon examined another document, a secret intelligence report telling of a Soviet contingency plan for the invasion of Sinkiang. (Every military establishment keeps contingency plans for every possible military eventuality.) This one called for a preemptive Soviet strike into Sinkiang to liberate the Turkic element and, simultaneously, to destroy the Chinese nuclear and missile installations.

It was, of course, only a contingency plan.

Gilding the Truth

America's word, once as good as its gold, is no longer trusted around the world. Too many times, U.S. spokesmen have resorted to deception which, invariably, has produced more embarrassment than would have resulted from the incidents they tried to hide. They have been caught in one awkward lie after another until they are no longer believed even when they tell the truth. This has created a crisis in credibility which has reduced America's effectiveness in world affairs.

In matters big and small, it has become official habit to gild the truth when there is the possibility of some slight advantage by doing so. There were lies at almost every turn in the convoluted U.S. policy on the India–Pakistan war. Some of the most apparent involved White House efforts to convince the world that India was wrong and that the United States was neutral in the conflict.

On December 7, the thirtieth anniversary of Pearl Harbor, Henry Kissinger met with Washington newsmen for a "background briefing." This is a regular Washington ritual, which differs from a press conference in that no attribution is allowed—under the rules, the official is permitted to speak without pain of public identification.

Kissinger, accordingly, masqueraded as an anonymous "White House official" while he disputed press reports that the United States was pro-Pakistan. These reports, he said, were "inaccurate." But he insisted, sadly, that India was the aggressor, having attacked Pakistan without cause and without warning. He told of Pakistan's repeated offers to make concessions, of Washington's superhuman efforts to bring about peace. The nameless Kissinger was altogether urbane and persuasive, if not altogether truthful.

The fullest account of the Kissinger backgrounder was written by Alexander M. Sullivan for the International Press Service. This is the U.S. Information Service's official wire service, which distributes news free to foreign newspapers and radio stations. The Sullivan story was remarkable for its length, its detail, and its extraordinary succession of whoppers.

Sullivan wrote that the Administration "accepts the fact" with enormous pain that India was the military aggressor. It denied the anti-India charge, basing the disclaimer on long U.S. friendship and all the foreign aid given to India.

As the telegraph printer in the U.S. embassy in New Delhi chattered out the pious account, Kenneth Keating read the words and fumed. The story declared:

- Washington was surprised by the outbreak of war.
- At India's request, the United States gave $155 million to avert a famine in East Pakistan.
- Pakistan agreed that relief supplies should be distributed by international agencies so the central government in Islamabad would not appear to be taking credit.
- Pakistan agreed that it would "extend amnesty to all refugees."
- Pakistan authorized the United States to communicate with Mujib through his attorney (a man named Brohi who was appointed by the Pakistan government but rejected by Mujib).
- Kissinger in seven meetings and Secretary Rogers in another eighteen meetings with the Indian ambassador "made it clear that, in the U.S. judgment, autonomy for East Pakistan was the inevitable outcome of negotiations between Pakistan and Mujib's followers. They said additionally that Washington favored autonomy."
- "Washington and Islamabad were prepared to discuss a precise timetable for establishing political autonomy for East Pakistan."

When he had finished reading the story, Keating sent a cable to Washington, exposing its deceptions. The irate ambassador perceptively entitled his reply "U.S. Public Position on Road to War."

I was very interested to read byliner by IPS White House correspondent Sullivan in this morning's wireless file reporting White House officials' explanation of development of present conflict and U.S. role in seeking avert it. While I appreciate the tactical necessity of justifying our position publicly, I feel constrained to state elements of this particular story do not coincide with my knowledge of the events of the past eight months.

Specifically, Sullivan states that USG [U.S. government] $155 million relief program in East Pakistan was initated "at the specific request of the Indian Government." My recollection, and I refer Dept. to my conversation with Foreign Minister Swaran Singh, New Delhi 8053 of May 25, is that GOI (Government of India) was reluctant to see relief program started in East Pak prior to a political settlement on grounds such an effort might serve to "bail out Yahya."

In noting offer of amnesty for all refugees, story fails to mention qualification in Yahya's Sept. 5 proclamation that amnesty applied to those "not already charged with specific criminal acts," which I take to be more than a minor bureaucratic caveat in East Pak circumstances.

Story indicates that both the Secretary and Dr. Kissinger informed Ambassador Jha that Washington favored autonomy for East Pakistan. I am aware of our repeated statements that we had no formula for a solution, and our belief that the outcome of negotiations would probably be autonomy if not independence, but I regret I am uninformed of any specific statement favoring autonomy.

Also according to story Jha was informed by Department on Nov. 19 that "Washington and Islamabad were prepared to discuss a precise timetable for establishing political autonomy for East Pakistan." The only message I have on record of this conversation (State 211384) makes no reference to this critical fact.

With vast and voluminous efforts of intelligence community, reporting from both Delhi and Islamabad, and my own discussions in Washington, I do not understand statement that "Washington was not given the slightest inkling that any military operation was in any way imminent." See for example DIAIB, 219-71, of Nov. 12, stating specifically that war is "imminent."

Statement that Pakistan had authorized U.S. to contact Mujib through his attorney seems an overstatement, since according to Islamabad 11760 Yahya on Nov. 29 told Ambassador Farland nothing more than that a Farland Brohi meeting would be a good idea since Ambassador Farland "would be able to obtain from Brohi at least his general impressions as to the state of the trial and its conduct." I am unaware of any specific authorization from Yahya "to contact Mujibur" through Brohi. In any case as we are all only too unhappily aware, Yahya told Ambassador Farland on Dec. 2 (Islamabad 11955) that Brohi allegedly was not interested in seeing him.

The statement on GOP agreement distribution by UN of relief supplies in East Pakistan obscures the fact that the UN never had nor intended to have sufficient personnel in East Pak to handle actual distribution, which was always in Pak government hands. I have made the foregoing comments in the full knowledge that I may not have been privy to all the important facts of this tragedy. On the basis of what I do know, I do not believe those elements of the Sullivan story either add to our position or, perhaps more importantly, to our credibility.

Keating's disavowal of the White House attempt to distort the facts was intended only for the eyes of high-level State Department officials. He had been in politics all of his adult life, and had been eminently successful. While he opposed Kissinger's lies, he did not feel so strongly about them that he would take his case to the public. His complaints became known only after I obtained a copy of his secret cable. In any case, it would have been virtually impossible for Keating to correct all of the misinformation spread by the White House.

Another falsehood grew out of the status of Americans caught in the crossfire in East Pakistan. With commercial transportation halted, the Indian army hurrying toward Dacca, and the Pakistani army apparently ready for a street-by-street defense, U.S. Consul General Herbert Spivack raised the question of evacuation in a December 5 cable to Washington:

U.S. position emerging as result recent actions beginning to take on definite pro-Pakistan slant, and accordingly, bound to be increasingly resented by BD, MB, and overwhelming majority of East Bengali people.

Should India achieve its objective and independent (or ostensibly independent) BD come into being, situation this consulate general could become untenable . . . Assuming, as seems likely, territory of BD would include Dacca city, this consulate general would have no legal basis for operation and personnel remaining at post would undoubtedly be viewed with hostility by populace and government.

He recommended cutting the staff back to only a caretaker force and evacuating other Americans by "presumably special flights of U.S. aircraft under safe conduct negotiated with Indian and Pakistani governments."

On December 9 he also suggested that it might be time to initiate some contacts with the Bangladesh officials, which could lead to eventual diplomatic regonition. He and his "hard core" staff were willing to stay on, he said, to act in a "useful transitional role if permitted operate in whatever restricted fashion by Bangladesh government which now appears likely to assume *de facto* control over East Pakistan in near future."

There were about seventy-five Americans in Dacca, most of them members of the consulate staff. Their wives and children had been evacuated when the trouble first started in the spring. Counting other diplomats and United Nations personnel, the foreign population of beseiged Dacca amounted to approximately five hundred. In addition, there were reporters and relief workers who had little interest in evacuation. As the battle of Dacca appeared more imminent, plans were formulated for an international evacuation mission to haul out those who wanted to go. The British volunteered three transport planes, and the Canadians offered another.

There were some difficulties with the arrangements. The Indians, who promised to halt their bombing of Dacca during the evacuation, insisted that both the incoming and outgoing planes make an inspection stop in Calcutta. The Pakistanis at first balked at this condition but finally agreed to it. The British raised a bigger problem. They doubted that the Dacca runway, badly damaged by Indian bombing, could be repaired sufficiently to allow the planes to land. They asked about the availability of U.S. helicopters. None were stationed within flying range, but the request gave birth to the cover story for American naval intervention. A U.S. naval task force, it was announced later, had been dispatched to the Bay of Bengal to assist in the evacuation, but this version of the fleet's mission was a cover: the ships were already on their way—for strictly military purposes—before evacuation was ever mentioned in the exchange of top-secret messages with the fleet.

Perhaps it was only a coincidence that Admiral John S. McCain, the caustic commander in chief of the Pacific fleet who helped to mastermind the Bay of Bengal deployment, had commanded the amphibious task force which landed marines in the Dominican Republic in April 1965. On this occasion, too, the United States had used the pretense of evacuation to move against rebels fighting to restore a freely elected government.

It may also have been coincidental that on December 11, the day after the task force headed for the Bay of Bengal, the Pakistan military abruptly canceled evacuation flights that were supposed to leave that day. "General Farman said Yahya feared that the Indians would use the mercy flights as a cover to land paratroopers," the UN's Paul Marc Henry told us. It is not unlikely that Farman wanted civilians on hand to give the U.S. Navy the opportunity to save them and Farman's army.

The evacuation was finally carried out on December 12; only the "hard core" diplomats and reporters stayed behind. Those who wanted to leave were already gone when the Joint Chiefs sent Admiral McCain this warning: "If queried by press advise the Office of Assistant Secretary of Defense for Public Affairs of nature of query and request instructions. In general, it is planned to reply along the following lines: 'We do not discuss specific ship movements. We do have contingency plans to evacuate American citizens if necessary in emergency situations.'" Such an excuse was trotted out after I warned in the *Washington Merry-go-Round* that the task force was sailing toward a confrontation with the Russian navy. "They said they came for evacuation, but that was nonsense," commented Henry, speaking for those who stayed in Dacca.

Washington officialdom betrayed even greater hypocrisy over the lives of the citizens of East Pakistan. At 4 A.M. on December 9, the Islamic Orphanage, located about a mile from the Dacca airport, was hit by bombs which took the lives of hundreds of small boys asleep in their beds. The first press reports blamed the tragedy on the bad aim of the Indian pilots. The following night, a Dacca slum was hit, and again the Indians were blamed. These were the kinds of incidents that can spark international outrage.

There appeared to be no reaction inside the State Department. This curious silence followed a secret message from Herbert Spivack, the American consul general. He had been chosen to replace Archer Blood (who had lost his job after he protested about the Pakistan army's slaughter of the Bengalis) in Dacca because the State Department considered him an organization man, a career foreign service officer nearing retirement who would not make waves. But the bombing of Dacca's slums and the Islamic Orphanage, as he learned the details, wrought a change in his attitude. The "flash" cable he sent to Secretary William Rogers and Ambassador Joseph Farland was entitled "Villainy By Night." It reported:

United Nations Assistant Secretary General [Paul Marc Henry] and I are convinced on the basis of evidence we both regard as conclusive that bombing of non-military areas in Dacca last night (and inferentially bombing of orphanage on night of December 8-9) were carried out by a Pak government plane based at Dacca airport, and that the purpose of the attacks was to discredit the Indian air force.

Evidence which has brought us to this conclusion consists generally of following:

A. Sound of engines of plane carrying out bombing was markedly different from that of jets of IAF which have been observed in previous attacks; UN aircraft expert has given his opinion that the sound was compatible with that of small twin engine prop aircraft, almost certainly the Piaggio P-136-L, at least one of which was seen by army attache as recently as a week ago at Dacca airport. Consulate General employee on 10th floor of Intercontinental Hotel facing airport saw plane take off from airport and heard it circle immediately prior to bomb explosions. Another consular employee also heard aircraft and believes he saw bomb dropped, after which plane cut its engines and presumably landed at nearby Dacca airport. Senior local employee also saw plane, recognized it as twin-engine craft kept at airport for VIP use, and observed that cabin lights were on during flight.

B. In contrast to previous night bombings when Indian aircraft were involved, there was virtually no anti-aircraft fire, not at all except for two small tracer rounds fired at an angle away from site of bombing.

C. Recovered near scene of one of bombs and currently in possession UNEPRO (United Nations East Pakistan Relief Operations) is object which cannot have any other purpose than that of makeshift bomb rack. This object consists of boards nailed together to form rectangular base approximately size of space between cabin and float support of Piaggio aircraft. Fixed to this board are two semi-circular metal brackets facing downward. Dangling from the metal brackets is a web of white harness belting and various pieces strong twine. Obvious inference is that this makeshift bomb rack was fabricated for use with Piaggio aircraft in accomplishing last night's missions. Fact that it fell off and could be recovered is probably accident.

D. Basis for inference that bombing of orphanage on night 8-9 December was of same pattern is founded on similarity of aircraft sounds, absence of any anti-aircraft firing.

Henry is informing Secretary General urgently of his conclusions in this affair and is considering what other steps he can take. He is afraid that UNEPRO possession of incriminating bomb rack device might lead to subsequent attack by PAF to destroy evidence by bombing UN compound. He is also concerned for safety of Red Cross neutralized zones (Intercontinental Hotel where some 500 foreign nationals awaiting evacuation and Holy Family Hospital) since he conceives that PAF may engage in further stunts this nature in attempt solidify case against Indian Air Force. Members of UN staff have advised Paul Marc Henry against attempt confront any Dacca officials with evidence for fear that whoever does this might immediately be imprisoned or disappear. UN has photographed bomb rack and is considering disposing of it in obvious and disingenuous fashion by simply placing it in the street.

I strongly urge that Ambassador Farland and Ambassador Bush (possbly in consultation with Secretary General) make immediate demarche to President Yahya and Pak UN Rep Shahi to confront them with evidence and warn them that any future attempt of this kind will bring about full publicity. Already rumor circulating widely among Bengalis and foreigners in Intercontinental Hotel that bombings were work of Pakistanis. However, there is agreement between Henry and me that neither one will make any comment of any kind on these rumors.

I am fully conscious, as is Paul Marc Henry, of gravity of charges we are making. However, I believe that demarche I have outlined is only to put an end to this kind of unscrupulous barbarity which has already cost the lives of several hundred orphans in Dacca.

Spivack's story sent Farland scurrying. In conversations with Pakistanis, he referred cautiously to "circumstantial evidence"; in a telegram he sent Secretary of State Rogers, he reported that Foreign Secretary Sul Tan Khan told him "he would institute forthwith an investigation into the matter and would advise [him] the results thereof." In another hour, Farland was ready, from his vantage point fourteen hundred miles from Dacca, to plead the innocence of his Pakistani friends.

Both DRPN (Defense Representative to Pakistan) General Charles E. Yeager, and Defense Attache Colonel Robert A. Nolan, have serious reservations concerning the use of one Piaggio in described situation because of following facts:

(A) Crater 10 meters wide and 10 meters deep could only be caused by very large bomb (750-lb. range at least);

(B) Piaggio would require major structural modifications to enable it to carry and release even 100-lb. bombs;

(C) Fusing time required to arm a bomb after a drop normally requires 700 to 1,000 elevation;

(D) Minimum clearance above ground for dropping 750-lb. bombs is 1,000 feet to prevent frag and blast damage to dropping aircraft;

(E) Even with the best equipment, it would be very difficult for a pilot in any aircraft to hit a target within a city block level bombing at night from a thousand feet elevation.

Both Yeager and Nolan suggest:

(A) That the craters be measured, and the dud bomb, if available, be checked and identified for size, i.e., 500-lb., 750-lb., or 1,000-lb. bomb.

(B) The Piaggio, if possible, should be examined for structural modification.

Further, Yeager and Nolan suggest that the most logical conclusion as to what type aircraft would drop four bombs in an area the size of mentioned orphanage would be a Canberra, flying level at 8 or 10 thousand feet. This is above effective anti-aircraft fire. And, based on the information in the Dacca reftels, both believe it was most likely coincidental that the Piaggio was flying at that time.

General Yeager has in excess of 90 hours flying time in Piaggios.

The case was reduced to the credibility of a civilian on the scene in Dacca versus that of a general in Islamabad.

General Yeager is unquestionably a superb aviator. In 1947, as pilot of the X-1 rocket plane, he was the first man to fly faster than the speed of sound. But he did not see the bombing of the orphanage. And, we are told, the information quoted on the weight of the bombs and the width of the craters was supplied by Pakistani officials in Islamabad, not witnesses in Dacca.

But the explanation offered by Farland certainly did not impress Assistant Secretary General Henry. He talked to us after he returned to New York City. The bombings, he said, took place on three nights—December 9, 10, and 11. He described the wooden contraption he had examined as "obviously a crude bomb rack," and the orphanage as "an assembly of huts for poor, abandoned children."

"We felt sure that someone was bombing civilian areas in Dacca presumably to blame the Indians for killing civilians. This still seems likely to me," he said, "first, because of the strange lights that seemed to be accompanying the plane. The first night was well lit by the moon and there were no lights with the plane. But on the second and third nights, one could hear the chop-chop of a helicopter with a strong searchlight accompanying the droning sound of the slow propeller-driven craft. And no anti-aircraft fire was heard. It probably would have been ineffective anyway, but if it were an Indian aircraft, one would have suspected some response to the bombing."

There was no comment from Washington. The White House, so eager to exploit any propaganda that might justify the President and Kissinger for backing Yahya, was not interested in making an issue of the slaughter of Bengali children. The possibility that Pakistanis had bombed their own people was not an issue the White House wanted to raise.

Help for Yahya

While East Pakistan burned, Yahya Khan fiddled. "He liked to drink," his friend Ambassador Joseph Farland admitted to us. "And I am told he had many love affairs."

The United Nations' Paul Marc Henry was more blunt. "Yahya was half dead seven hours a day," Henry told us. "He was a very drunk, sick man most of the day. During the last days of the war, I am told, he sought younger and younger women."

Even in his cups, Yahya was enough of a soldier to know his troops in Bengal were doomed by his inability to supply and reinforce them. However, he thought he might work a miracle. He had a perverse faith that the fighting spirit of his troops might prevail, though they were outnumbered and outgunned. For the desperate Yahya, the capture of Kashmir, or even a sizable portion of it, would be a face-saver.

Unlike other observers, the Indian general staff detected a pattern in the December 3 raids on Indian airports. The bases that were hit were the logical staging areas for a war in Kashmir. Even by damaging the runways, Pakistan hurt India's military potential in the disputed territory.

There was little doubt in the Washington Special Action Group about Pakistan's war strategy. On December 7 General Westmoreland said he expected the "major Pak effort to be towards Kashmir and the Punjab." His prediction was not challenged.

AID Deputy Director Maurice Williams suggested at the December 8 meeting that the United States might focus its efforts on a cease-fire in West Pakistan. Under Secretary of State U. Alexis Johnson protested: "This might stop the Paks from moving in Kashmir." Kissinger was more interested in stopping the Indian offensive in East Pakistan than a Pakistani move against Kashmir. There was even hope for a Pakistani success. The minutes record that, "Dr. Kissinger asked for an assessment of the Pak capabilities and prospects in Kashmir."

Yet President Nixon told Congress afterward: "If we had not taken a stand against the war, it would have been prolonged and the likelihood of an attack in the West greatly increased." Clearly, our stand against the war did not keep Pakistan from scheming to take Indian territory in the west.

Yahya did not depend solely, of course, on the United States for assistance. Russia's support for India was mirrored, and possibly magnified, by China's aid to Pakistan. China and Pakistan shared many things, including a hunger for Kashmir and the friendship of Henry Kissinger.

The CIA was unusually restrained in its attitude toward the China-Pakistan relationship throughout the war. The agency discovered "the first hint of a Chinese threat to India" in the Peking *People's Daily* on December 8. The story said that if India's example in East Pakistan was followed, "a country neighboring India" could send troops to create a "West Bengal or Sikhistan." The CIA was almost apologetic: "This threat, however, is unaccompanied by any indication that Peking is departing from its current restrained policy of supplying political support and military equipment to Pakistan."

Yahya, however, spoke of no such restraints on December 11 when he confided to his newly anointed prime minister, Nural Amin, an aged and doddering politician, that help was on the way. The CIA intercepted their conversation. Yahya, according to the CIA, said he had been assured by the Chinese ambassador that the Chinese army would move toward India's NEFA border within seventy-two hours.

The CIA report, telling of Yahya's ominous conversation about Chinese intervention, caused considerable disquiet in Washington. The State Department's Bureau of Intelligence and Research, for example, had concluded that China seemed prepared to accept an Indian victory. "The Chinese appear unwilling to become too deeply involved in a situation where the risks, including a Soviet countermove, are real and the possible gains small," the State Department analysts predicted. "They are unlikely to go beyond political support and the provision of military supplies . . . If anything, China is more likely to be interested, in the longer term, in improved relations with India as a direct counterweight to Soviet influence in New Delhi . . . Since full-scale hostilities began, Peking has intensified its condemnation of India. It has, however, avoided implying that the hostilities threaten China's security. . . ."

These assurances paled as new intelligence reports arrived on Henry Kissinger's desk. The CIA reported that "President Yahya's claim cannot be confirmed," but added darkly that "recent indicators have been received which suggest that the PRC may be planning actions regarding the Indo-Pakistan conflict."

The China watchers in Hong Kong added that Peking was "offering virtually unconditional political and moral support for Pakistan," while charging India with seeking territory in East Pakistan and "putting primary responsibility for exacerbating tensions on the Soviets."

Outsiders watching America, and viewing the maneuvers in the White House, might have come to the same conclusion about this country.

The Great Plane Swtich

As India learned in December of 1971, the United States can move quickly to cut off aid to a nation in disfavor. For other more favored nations, cutoffs may be announced but the process never quite seems to be completed.

Under determined pressure from congressmen concerned about the use of American-made weapons against the people of Bangladesh, the Nixon Administration ordered a halt to new licenses for the export of military items to Pakistan in April 1971. But there was a loophole; items already licensed were allowed to be shipped to Yahya's forces.

In contravention of the order, the U.S. Air Force also solicited $10.6 million in new orders from Pakistan. Delivery was stopped when Senator Edward Kennedy confronted Administration officials with the Air Force documents. Still, $563,000 in spare airplane parts got through to Pakistan, which was already well equipped by the United States. Classified studies show that a total of $28.5 million in American military supplies were shipped to Pakistan in the fiscal year ending June 30, 1971.

When the war erupted and India's superior air force gained control of the skies over both Pakistans, Yahya pleaded for more American planes. At Yahya's urging, Jordan's King Hussein asked if he could send eight of the U.S. jets in his possession to Pakistan.

Kissinger wanted to do everything he could to help Pakistan, even if it meant violating the decree of Congress. He was vocal on the point at the December 6

WSAG meeting. He began by asking about the legalities of allowing Jordan or Saudi Arabia to transfer military equipment, provided by the United States, to Pakistan.

Christopher Van Hollen, speaking for the State Department, tried to discourage him. Van Hollen had been embarrassed in his appearances before Senator Kennedy's subcommittee. He had testified that the arms flow to Pakistan had stopped, only to be confronted with evidence the shipments were continuing. "The United States," Van Hollen told Kissinger, "cannot permit a third country to transfer arms which we have provided them when we, ourselves, do not authorize sale direct to the ultimate recipient, such as Pakistan. As of last January, we made a legislative decision not to sell to Pakistan."

Van Hollen's boss, Assistant Secretary Joseph Sisco, who has had some success negotiating with Israel and Egypt, tried to dissuade Kissinger with diplomatic reasoning. He pointed out that such a transfer would weaken Jordan, and "the Jordanians would probably be grateful if we could get them off the hook." He also cautioned that more such requests could be expected "as the Paks increasingly feel the heat."

"The President may want to honor those requests," Kissinger countered. "The matter has not been brought to presidential attention, but it is quite obvious that the President is not inclined to let the Paks be defeated."

Deputy Defense Secretary David Packard said the group should explore what could be done. Sisco agreed. "But it should be done very quietly," he cautioned.

The suggestion that the United States become a party to an illegal arms-smuggling deal upset most of the diplomats who were on a high enough level to learn of it. Some told us of their despair; others merely mumbled in the corridors. A few in foreign posts cabled Washington.

Kissinger, however, had not abandoned the idea at all. He asked the December 8 session of WSAG: "How do we get Jordan into a holding pattern to allow the President time to consider the issue?"

Packard, who had followed his own advice and had

explored the problem, came to the conclusion that the answer was nothing. "We cannot authorize the Jordanians to do anything that the U.S. government cannot do," he said. "If the U.S. government cannot give the 104's to Pakistan, we cannot allow Jordan to do so. If a third country had material that the U.S. government did not have, that would be one thing, but we could not allow Jordan to transfer the 104's unless we make a finding that the Paks, themselves, were eligible to purchase them from us directly."

Kissinger rejoined in his professional way: "If we had not cut the sale of arms to Pakistan, the current problem would not exist. Perhaps we never really analyzed what the real danger was when we were turning off the arms to Pakistan."

If Jordan delivered the F-104's to Pakistan, warned Packard, the United States would be expected to send replacements to Jordan.

"It could be," suggested Under Secretary of State U. Alexis Johnson, "that eight F-104's might not make any difference once the real war in the West starts. They could be considered only a token. If, in fact, we were to move in West Pakistan, we would be in a new ball game."

Packard, the practical businessman, said the overriding consideration was the practical problem of either doing something effective or doing nothing. "If you don't win, don't get involved," he advised. "If we were to attempt something it would have to be with a certainty that it would affect the outcome. Let's not get in if we know we are going to lose. Find some way to stay out."

Kissinger again said he wanted to keep Hussein in a "holding pattern" and did not want the King to be "turned off." Kissinger directed: "The United States government should indicate to Hussein that we do not consider trivial his feelings in this matter."

Kissinger's instructions were executed the following day, when a cable, bearing the signature of Under Secretary of State John Irwin, was sent to Ambassador Lewis D. Brown in Amman. "You should tell King Hussein," said the cable, "we fully appreciate heavy pressure he feels himself under by virtue of request from Pakistan, which we also recognize faces a serious situation. We are nevertheless not yet in a position to give him definite response. Whole subject remains under intensive review at very high level of United States government. We are fully alive to your delicate situation in not being able to give definite answer to King's urgent plea. But we ask you to bear with us and put situation to Hussein in best possible light."

Once again, the State Department was acting as Kissinger's messenger service. But unlike Ambassador Brown, we do not have to speculate about the identity of the "very high level" of government reviewing the request.

The reviewer was the only man who could make a final decision: Richard Nixon. Acting on Kissinger's recommendation, the President authorized Jordan to send 10 F-104's to Pakistan. But he did not totally disregard the advice of the WSAG members who thought the transfer was unwise. As Sisco had suggested, the transfer was accomplished "very quietly."

It was not until April 18, 1972, that the government admitted Jordan had given planes to Pakistan. The State Department piously insisted, nevertheless, that it was done without American permission; the transfer, said a spokesman, was a violation of the U.S. Foreign Assistance Act.

The admission came just after King Hussein had spent three weeks as a visitor in the United States, where he had met privately with Nixon. During his stay, the King was promised new American jets for his air force, just as David Packard had predicted.

The President told Congress that no American arms were sent to Pakistan during the war. "The pipeline dried up completely by the beginning of November," he said.

For some reason, he did not feel it necessary to mention the great Jordanian plane switch.

Policy and Propaganda

His official title is Assistant to the President for National Security Affairs. But the sign on his door would be more accurate if it said:

DR. HENRY A. KISSINGER
DIRECTOR OF U.S. FOREIGN POLICY
DIRECTOR OF U.S. FOREIGN PROPAGANDA

Kissinger reigns in the White House basement, and the focal point of his activity is the Situation Room. It contains elaborate electronic equipment that enables Kissinger, or the National Security Council which he directs, to speak to virtually anyone anywhere in the world. This is the end of the similarity to the Dr. Strangelove kind of war room that most people envisage. It is just a small conference room, with space for ten to sit comfortably around the table. For many of the Washington Special Action Group meetings, extra chairs had to be put around the table, and aides to the major participants were squeezed against the walls.

The corps of public relations men on the White House payroll insist that Kissinger was merely goading his minions when he told them, "I am getting hell every half hour from the President that we are not being tough enough on India." If so, it was a counter-productive goad. Many of Kissinger's underlings relished the idea of their boss getting hell. In any event, Kissinger was certainly invoking the President's name to push policy on unwilling officials.

At times, officials artfully sabotaged Kissinger's desire

to help Pakistan. That he was aware of this is shown by the order he gave as he closed the December WSAG meeting:

We need to think about our treaty obligations. I remember a letter or memo interpreting our existing treaty with a special India tilt. When I visited Pakistan in January, 1962, I was briefed on a secret document or oral understanding about contingencies arising in other than the SEATO context. Perhaps it was a presidential letter. This was a presidential letter. This was a special interpretation of the March, 1959, bilateral agreement.

In the State Department, diplomats sweated over interpretations of the SEATO treaty and the secret agreement with Pakistan. They agreed the wording was loose enough to mean anything, but they decided it meant the United States was bound to come to Pakistan's defense only if it was attacked by a Communist country. This interpretation became a caveat, which the State Department invoked in an attempt to maintain neutraility in the Indian-Pakistan conflict.

But the President did not want to be neutral. Whether Kissinger encouraged or reflected his bias has become the subject of speculation in the inner councils. Those who worked closely with Kissinger throughout the India-Pakistan crisis thought there was a personal animosity toward India in his attitude. But he was usually careful to attribute any anti-India actions directly to the President. For example, when he ordered harsh economic measures against India on December 3, he told WSAG: "The President wants no more irrevocable letters of credit issued under the $99 million credit. He wants the $72 million Public Law 480 credit also held." Public Law 480 is the program called Food for Peace. It allows the U.S. government to distribute surplus American crops to needy nations. Under the Nixon-Kissinger dictum, Food for Peace became a tool of war.

Kissinger was warned these strictures could generate bad publicity. "That is [the President's] order," responded Kissinger glibly, "but I will check with the

President again. If asked, we can say we are reviewing the whole economic program and that the granting of fresh aid is being suspended in view of conditions on the subcontinent."

At other times Kissinger betrayed his bias. After Helms told of the bizarre evening bombing of Indian airfields by Pakistani planes, Kissinger pressed him for details that could excuse the Pakinstani action and hang the blame on India. "Are the Indians seizing territory?" Kissinger demanded. "Is it possible that the Indians attacked first, and the Paks simply did what they could before dark?"

That same day, State Department spokesman Charles Bray appeared before newsmen to proclaim Kissinger's message. He spoke of "continuing Indian incursions into Pakistan" as he announced the cancellation of export licenses involving $11.3 million worth of spare airplane, electronic, and communications parts for India. Bray didn't say so, but the electronic and communications equipment was destined for Project Star Sapphire, a radar network designed to warn India of air attacks from China.

The close relationship between American policy and Yahya's wishes was lavishly illustrated by the U.S. moves at the United Nations. Despite the supposedly good intentions that gave birth to the U.N., it has been a propaganda forum almost since its inception. Kissinger set out to orchestrate the U.S. performance at the U.N., and he brought in the Pakistani ambassador as first violin.

Under Secretary of State Irwin informed WSAG that Secretary Rogers was planning to call the Pakistani ambassador, "and the Secretary leans toward making a U.S. move in the U.N. soon."

"The President is in favor of this as soon as we have some confirmation of this large scale new action," Kissinger said. "If the U.N. can't operate in this kind of situation effectively, its utility has come to an end and it is useless to think of guarantees in the Middle East."

"We will have a recommendation for you this afternoon, after the meeting with the ambassador," Sisco said. "In order to give the ambassador time to wire home, we could tentatively plan to convene the Security Council tomorrow."

"We have to take action," Kissinger insisted. "The President is blaming me, but you people are in the clear."

"That's ideal!" Sisco kidded.

Kissinger focused on the appeal U.S. Ambassador George Bush would make to the U.N. "The earlier draft statement for Bush is too even-handed," he complained.

"To recapitulate," said Sisco, "after we have seen the Pak ambassador, the Secretary will report to you. We will update the draft speech for Bush." In the newspeak of the Situation Room, "update" meant to rewrite, with an approved tilt and without "even-handedness."

"We can say we favor political accommodation, but the real job of the Security Council is to prevent military action," Kissinger said.

"We have never had a reply either from Kosygin or Mrs. Gandhi," said Sisco, referring to messages Nixon sent to Moscow and New Delhi calling for peace—a move designed to put the blame on the otherside.

"Are we to take economic steps with Pakistan also?" Williams wondered aloud.

"Wait until I talk with the President," Kissinger advised. "He hasn't addressed the problem in connection with Pakistan yet."

"If we act on the Indian side, we can say we are keeping the Pakistan situation under review," Sisco suggested helpfully.

There were many occasions in the WSAG sessions when Professor Kissinger spoke to the high-level diplomats and military brass as though he was addressing a primary school class for slow learners, and some of their comments recorded in the minutes indicate he may have been justified. But he was also harsh with men like Sisco, who thought the United States should maintain some diplomatic equilibrium.

"It's hard to tilt toward Pakistan if we have to match

every Indian step with a Pakistan step," Kissinger snapped. "If you wait until Monday, I can get a presidential decision."

Kissinger was in an equally waspish mood the next morning when WSAG met again, with Helms giving a report on the state of the war. He said India was driving into East Pakistan from all sides, and the Indians had bombed eight Pakistani airfields, though Mrs. Gandhi made it a point not to declare war. He said that Yahya, in a speech, "referred to the 'final' war with India and the need to drive back and destroy the enemy."

Kissinger sifted out what he wanted. "If the Indians announced a full scale invasion, this must be reflected in our U.N. statement this afternoon," he said.

Samuel DePalma, the Assistant Secretary of State for International Organizations, pointed out that both sides were talking tough. "Both Yahya and Mrs. Gandhi are making bellicose statements," he said. "If we refer to Mrs. Gandhi's in our statement, do we not also have to refer to Yahya's?"

Kissinger bristled with impatience at the men who tried to be fair, because they believed that to have success the United States must have some credibility. "The President says either the bureaucracy should put out the right statements on this, or the White House will do it," he stormed. "Can the U.N. object to Yahya's statements about defending his country?"

"We will have difficulty in the U.N." warned DePalma, "because countries who might go with us do not want to tilt toward Pakistan to the extent we do."

Kissinger was furious at DePalma and the State Department for what he considered their impertinence. He barked at DePalma, but his words were also aimed at the whole State Department. Deputy Assistant Secretary Christopher Van Hollen, in particular, was in Kissinger's bad graces for conducting a briefing that the professor considered altogether too even-handed. Van Hollen sat poker-faced and silent as Kissinger growled in his German accent: "Whoever is doing the backgrounding at State is invoking [sic] the President's wrath. Please try and follow the President's wishes. The President is under the illusion that he is giving instructions; not that he is merely being kept apprised of affairs as they progress."

Kissinger had more in mind than stopping the conflict when he gave his next instructions: "We have told the Paks we would make our statement. Let's go ahead and put in our own statement anyway regardless of what other countries want to do. We need now to make our stand clear even though it has taken us two weeks of fiddling. Everyone knows how all this will come out, and everyone knows that India will ultimately occupy East Pakistan. We want to insist on a cease-fire and withdrawal of forces *before* the details of a political settlement are considered."

The intimidated DePalma stated America's course at the U.N. "If the others are willing to go along with this resolution—fine," he said obediently. "Otherwise, we will go it alone."

Kissinger was still showing his contempt for the diplomatic process. "Nothing will happen at the Security Council because of the Soviet vetoes," he said. "The whole thing is a farce." He said the United States would go along in general terms with reference to political accommodation in East Pakistan, "but we will certainly not imply or suggest any specifics, such as the release of Mujib."

There was at least one occasion, however, when Kissinger's manipulations embarrassed even the President. As Nixon and his official party flew back to Washington from a meeting with French President Georges Pompidou in the Azores, Kissinger visited the five "pool" reporters on the plane, and conducted an off-the-record briefing. Under the ground rules, he was not supposed to be identified, and all stories were supposed to be attributed to "a high administration source."

After the plane landed, the *Washington Post* decided it would no longer honor the anonymous briefings and identified Kissinger as the source of its story. According to the *Post*, Kissinger said the President might reconsider his scheduled May 1972 trip to Moscow unless the Russians used their influence to halt the Indian army. This reconsideration, the *Post* reported Kissinger as saying, "could lead to a reassessment of the entire relationship between the United States and the Soviet Union."

When the planes landed at Andrews Air Force Base outside Washington, the pool reporters distributed copies of their interview to their colleagues aboard the press plane, and the shielded version was sent out over the press association wires. The *Post's* first edition, naming Kissinger, was still several hours away.

The reporters were summoned by White House Press Secretary Ronald Ziegler, who had not made the trip. He insisted that "no U.S. official was suggesting or intending to suggest that the United States was considering cancelling the United States-Soviet summit."

Henry Kissinger had gone too far.

The Brink of World War

For all the tough talk in the White House about the need to aid Pakistan, President Nixon behaved as he had in other crucial big-power situations. He was indecisive for an inordinately long time. When he finally made up his mind to flex America's great military muscle, he overcommitted.

His action brought America to the edge of a war that could have involved Russia and China. Indeed, the proximity to war and its probable scope were far greater than the press and the public could conceive. Despite the assurances of the State Department analysts that Russia and China would not enter the India–Pakistan conflict, both appeared quite ready to fight.

The military build-up for the confrontation began quietly. While Kissinger in his Situation Room was berating bureaucrats, Russia was readying its powerful Indian Ocean fleet. On December 3, three Soviet warships —a destroyer armed with surface-to-air missiles, a seagoing minesweeper and a naval oiler—passed from the Strait of Malacca into the Indian Ocean. Their movement was noticed, but American intelligence paid little attention. Russian ships were a familiar sight in the start, a 500-mile-long channel connecting the Indian Ocean and the China seas. No one paid much attention as the flotilla, following orders from Moscow, set a northwesterly course.

The Russian ship movements did not become a matter for consternation in Washington until December 8, when intelligence suddenly realized that the new vessels were in the Indian Ocean to augment, not replace, ships already there. Communications intercepts showed the three new ships were five hundred miles east of Ceylon, and heading north in the Bay of Bengal.

That put sixteen Soviet ships reasonably near the combat area. A minesweeper and a naval oiler were moving northward on oppsite sides of the Bay of Bengal. A guided missile destroyer, a naval oiler and a space-support ship were near the southern tip of India, moving westward toward the Arabian Sea. Another space-support ship was on station in the Arabian Sea, south of Karachi, and a third was cruising farther south. Russia maintains about a dozen space-support ships, presumably for tracking space vehicles. But their vast amount of sophisticated electronic equipment also makes them ideally suited to intercept radio communications.

Russia also had a tank-landing ship, a repair ship, a vessel believed to be a distilling ship, and an F Class submarine (a modern Diesel-powered attack sub) operating together northeast of the mouth of the Gulf of Aden, with a destroyer and a merchant tanker proceeding toward them. Another tanker was approaching the mouth of the Gulf of Aden. A minesweeper was south of the tip of India, and a second repair ship was in the Persian Gulf.

Not content with this seapower, the Russians were sending three more ships—a guided-missile light cruiser, a naval oiler and a J Class submarine (Diesel-powered and carrying four ship-to-ship missiles)—toward the Strait of Malacca. When they were observed on December 8, they were passing southward from the Sea of Japan into the East China Sea. Still another submarine followed in their wake.

The first signs of Chinese activity were detected in the Himalayas.

It was late at night on December 10 when Colonel Melvin Holst—the American defense attaché in Katmandu, capital of Nepal—was called at home by the Indian attaché, who asked Holst whether he had any information about Chinese military activity in Tibet. Holst reported afterward that the Indian attaché had been queried urgently by New Delhi. "The Indian high command had some sort of information that military action was increasing in Tibet," Holst said in his cable to Washington.

At a dinner party later that evening, Holst was asked about Chinese military activity by the Russian attaché, a man named Loginov. Holst reported Loginov had told him he "had either on 8 or 9 December called upon People's Republic of China military attaché Chao Kuangchih in Kathmandu advising Chao that PRC should not get too serious about intervention because U.S.S.R. would react, had many missiles, etc."

Holst added he was "confident that the above evidenced Indo/Pak concern is not merely an endeavor to pump information from DATT, and that both the U.S.S.R. and India embassies have a growing concern that PRC might intervene."

Not all of the top men in the Kremlin wanted to dissuade China from intervention against India. The intelligence reports from Moscow warned that hard-liners hoped the Chinese would move. This would give them an opportunity to activate a contingency plan long advocated by some top Russian military strategists but held in abeyance by Kremlin leaders Leonid Brezhnev and Alexei Kosygin. The plan called for a preemptive strike against Lop Nor.

Lake Lop Nor, in China's Sinkiang Province, is as strange as the land that surrounds it. The lake itself is said to wander, since its bed shifts on the sinking terrain. One end of Lop Nor is fresh water, the other salt. Until recently, its only visitors were Lopnik tribesmen, who made occasional forays to spear fish.

The latest military maps of the area show a road that moves from the south toward the lake but stops twenty miles short of its banks. Secret aerial photographs indicate there are other, unmapped roads. Chinese scientists and technicians now frequent the Lop Nor region. They detonated a nuclear explosion there on November 18, just before the India–Pakistan outbreak, and were preparing for another, their thirteenth, to be set off on January 7.

It is likely these activities were detected by Russian satellites just as other developments were observed and noted elsewhere on the desolate frontiers of China. The Chinese nuclear threat had been limited by the 600-1,000-mile range of its missiles, but new technology had produced a new weapon, a solid-fueled rocket that could carry a warhead up to 2,500 miles—bringing Moscow within the sights of Chinese missile men.

Inside the Kremlin, marshals talked about wiping out this new threat to Soviet security before it became a reality. It would be relatively simple, they argued, for ground forces to occupy Sinkiang while air strikes eliminated the relatively small atomic and rocket production facilities.

Without committing their forces to a preemptive strike, Russia's leaders moved ground and air forces into position along the Sinkiang border. Russia's missile men also received word to program their trajectories for Chinese targets.

Meanwhile, the Chinese continued their military preparations in the Himalayas. American spy satellites collected radio transmissions, several of which were particularly significant for the experts who sifted through them.

The CIA reported: "On 8 and 9 December, an air net terminal for Tibet and West China was noted passing hourly aviation surface reports to Peking for 11 Chinese civil weather stations along routes and areas adjacent to the border of India."

The CIA commented: "The continued passing of weather data for these locations is considered unusual and may indicate some form of alert posture." The sky was clear, with no snowfall since November 21. Temperatures were below zero at the 10,000–12,000-foot level along the China–India frontier. All of the passes on the main routes from Tibet to India were open.

More ominous, the CIA noted that a "war preparations" effort had been observed in Tibet over several months, that the 157th Infantry Regiment of China's 53rd Independent Infantry Division at Yatung, Tibet, had recalled its personnel to carry out an "urgent mission."

India's northeastern frontier is buffered by the three tiny states of Nepal, Sikkim, and Bhutan. The Chinese at Yatung were poised at the tip of a Tibetan finger jabbing southward between Sikkim and Bhutan.

Nikolay Pegov, the Russian ambassador to New Delhi, told Indian officials not to worry about a Chinese attack. If that should happen, he promised, the Russians would mount a "diversionary action in Sinkiang."

All of this information was, or soon would be, available to Richard Nixon as he deliberated on how best to help strengthen Yahya's feeble grip on East Pakistan. But these threats to world peace were kept secret from the American people as they prepared to celebrate the birth of the Prince of Peace.

The President also decided not to tell the public about a little Christmas party he was planning for the Indians and Russians in the Bay of Bengal. The U.S. Navy, with only a seaplane tender and two aging destroyers permanently stationed in the Indian Ocean, had been unhappy over Soviet eagerness to fill the vacuum left by the withdrawal of the British fleet. There was much muttering among American admirals about the Indian Ocean becoming a "Russian lake."

With the outbreak of hostilities between India and Pakistan the admirals saw their opportunity. After urgent discussions they gave Kissinger a plan. Their presentation was headed "Memorandum for the Assistant to the President for National Security Affairs" and was entitled "Outline Plan for Show of Force Operations in the Pakistan–India Area."

On December 9 Nixon's day was less cluttered than usual. He presented a report of the Presidential Commission on Federal Statistics, announced a few inconsequential appointments, and signed a proclamation naming December 17 "Wright Brothers Day." Most of the President's day was set aside for deep concentration, or —to use the 1950s word Nixon liked—"brainstorming."

Nixon disappeared into his hideaway office in the Executive Office Building, across a blockaded street from the White House, where he was inaccessible even to the few advisers who see him with any frequency. The suite was decorated with mementos of his past and, like its occupant, was orderly, political and Middle American.

There was nothing ordinary, however, about the Navy plan that had been submitted for his approval. As it had evolved in Kissinger's basement command post, a formidable naval task force would steam into the Bay of Bengal. The purpose was to draw the Indian air force away from Pakistani targets, to divert the Indian aircraft carrier *Vikrant* from its position off the East Pakistan coast and, possibly, to break the Indian blockade of East Pakistan ports.

It was part of the plan to ensure that the task force would be sighted at the Strait of Malacca and the Russians and the Indians would be alerted to its approach. Once in position, the task force was to launch reconnaissance flights by U-2 spy planes outside the 12-mile limit. These would be coordinated with overland flights by 2,000-mile-an-hour SR-71's, the nation's swiftest spy planes. More conventional planes would keep an eye on the Russian fleet and would act as bait for the Indian air force.

The plan also contemplated mobilization of part of the 82nd Airborne Division and the massing of transport planes at Pope Air Force Base in North Carolina. As a feint, the United States was to ask for permission to fly over Africa hoping the Russians would get word of this. The cover for the request was to be a humanitarian mission, possibly the evacuation of refugees from Pakistan.

The President pondered the plan and gave his consent. Only a few of the details were changed. Immediately, Task Force 74 was formed. It was spearheaded by the world's most powerful ship, the U.S.S. *Enterprise*, a nuclear-powered aircraft carrier with a crew of more than five thousand, plus seventy-five planes and five helicopters. Also in the task force were three guided-missile destroyers, the *King, Decatur*, and *Parsons*; four gun destroyers, the *Bausell, Orleck, McKean*, and *Anderson*; and the *Tripoli*, a helicopter carrier, with twenty-five marine assault helicopters and two companies of marines. Supply ships, including the three-year-old naval oiler *Wichita*, were added later.

They were ordered to assemble in the Strait of Malacca. The first ships were expected to arrive there at 7:45 P.M., Washington time, December 12. Three days later, at 8:45 P.M., they were to enter the Bay of Bengal.

In top-secret messages from the Joint Chiefs of Staff, the task force captains were warned: "Primary air threat to U.S. forces will be from Indian Air Force aircraft who will be covering seaward approaches to both parts of Pakistan and will be understandably nervous about SEATO nations moving forces into offshore positions. Anti-shipping weapons are conventional bombs, rockets, MG [machine guns], and cannon. No ASM [anti-ship missiles] are in IAF inventory."

The first element of Task Force 74—the *Enterprise* and four destroyers—sailed from Yankee Station off Vietnam. A second section—the *Tripoli* and three destroyers—put out from Subic Bay in the Philippines. Radio traffic was heavy between the ships, the Pacific command in Hawaii, and the top command in Washington.

Some of the messages reflected the seriousness and secrecy of the mission. The task force was instructed to alter part of its orders on communications and to send its situation reports "Specat Exclusive," the highest military secrecy classification. The distribution of these reports was limited to the commander-in-chief of the Pacific fleet at Pearl Harbor, the chief of naval operations the Joint Chiefs of Staff.

Admiral John S. McCain, the Pacific commander, had been a submariner and had spent a year as chief of information for the Navy. At Pearl Harbor, he continued to direct the Navy's part of the war in Vietnam even after his son, a Navy pilot, was captured by the North Vietnamese.

His experience as a Navy propagandist, as a key figure in the Vietnam war, and as the man in charge of the invasion of the Dominican Republic, would figure in the guidance of the task force.

In a December 11 message to the Joint Chiefs, McCain asked for permission to begin aerial searches for the Soviet ships in the Indian Ocean. Admiral Thomas Moorer, the Joint Chiefs chairman, told him to wait until the task force entered the Strait of Malacca. "At that time appropriate task force screening/surveillance flights are authorized, to include Soviet locator operations." (The Russian ships, of course, were already being watched by American satellites.)

In another message Admiral McCain told the Joint Chiefs the complete task group could be formed at the entrance of the Malacca Strait by 8 A.M. Greenwich time, December 13, and in the Bay of Bengal by 9 A.M., December 16.

The cover story that the task force was sailing to evacuate Americans from Dacca was still in gestation. Meanwhile the commander of Task Force 74, Rear Admiral D. W. Cooper, put his ships on wartime alert. But he said the chance of a "Soviet overflight . . . appears remote," since the only Russian reconnaissance planes capable of reaching the Indian Ocean without violating the air space of other countries were Badgers based in Cairo more than four thousand miles away.

Another message stated the mission of the task force, although the priorities were juggled: "To form a contingency evacuation force capable of helicopter evacuation of civilians, of self protection, and of conducting naval air and surface operations as directed by higher authority in order to support U.S. interests in the Indian Ocean area." The task force's nickname was more blunt. It was "Oh, Calcutta."

As the Navy's planners had anticipated, the word spread quickly that the task force was coming. The news had many repercussions. As noted earlier, it gave Yahya a reason to prolong the war. In India a rumor was circulated that the task force had sunk an Indian destroyer, and civilians were understandably outraged. The U.S. consul general in Bombay reported widespread anti-Americanism. "We do not have concern regarding Pak air raids," he said, "but rather are more wary of mob action."

On December 13, top Indian officials took up their fears of the fleet with Russian Ambassador Pegov. He told them not to worry. The CIA got a complete report of the Russian's secret conversations with the Indians.

"The movement of the U.S. Seventh Fleet is an effort to bully India, to discourage it from striking against West Pakistan, and at the same time to boost the morale of the Pakistani forces," the CIA quoted Pegov as saying. The CIA report added ominously: "Pegov noted that a Soviet fleet is now in the Indian Ocean and that the Soviet Union will not allow the Seventh Fleet to intervene."

Even allowing for some bravado, it cannot be said that Russia is in the habit of making empty pledges to its allies. And Pegov could back up his words with steel. Another Soviet naval force, headed by a Kresta-class guided missile cruiser, was not far behind the U.S. task force. Still another Russian submarine was sliding into the Sea of Japan. And in Vladivostok, yet another Russian guided missile cruiser began preparations for a voyage to the Bay of Bengal.

With the completion on December 12 of the evacuation of all foreigners who wanted to leave Dacca, the last plausible excuse for the mission of the task force was gone, but still the ships moved forward. Both the White House and the Pentagon knew of the imminent danger to world peace that was waiting in the Bay of

Bengal. It was also plain that the American people would not tolerate such a risk to save the remnants of a drunken dictator's regime. So rather than tell its citizens of the perils that lay only hours ahead, the U.S. government continued its policy of deception by talking of evacuation when that mission had already been accomplished. It is certain that neither the Russians nor the Indians were misled. Only the American people were fooled.

The crisis that had been building for so long became a reality on December 15. The Chinese renewed their ritual of saber rattling when an official of the foreign ministry in Peking delivered a note to the Indian embassy. The message asserted that two small groups of Indian troops on reconnaissance missions had crossed the China-Sikkim border on December 10. The Chinese called the supposed incursion "a grave encroachment," and insisted that India "immediately stop its activities of intrusion into Chinese territory."

China had made similar charges before attacking in 1962. We can only speculate about China's intentions in December 1971. But we do know that the place where China claimed its territorial rights had been violated was the same spot where Chinese troops had been put on alert for an "urgent mission" days earlier.

However, events in East Pakistan moved too fast for the Chinese. While Peking was involved in the diplomatic maneuvering that might precede an attack by a nation on its neighbors, the Pakistan army in the East was surrendering to the Indian forces.

At 6:30 P.M. on December 14, General Niazi, the Pakistani commander for East Pakistan, appeared at the American consulate general in Dacca seeking help. He wanted to ask the Indians for a cease-fire, but his own radio transmitter had been destroyed by Indian bombing. U.S. Consul General Herbert Spivack followed protocol to the letter, and sent Niazi's plea to Washington for rebroadcasting. It was received in the State Department at 7:45 P.M., Dacca time.

The State Department, despite its public pleas for

peace, did not expedite General Niazi's cease-fire message. The cable was forwarded to Ambassador Farland in Islamabad, to have him check with Yahya and make certain that he agreed to the move. Farland's first response, the State Department said later, was "ambiguous." It was 3:30 A.M. in Dacca before Washington received sufficient confirmation from Islamabad.

Although the U.S. government's radio transmitters can reach any spot on earth almost instantaneously, Washington chose to handle this life-and-death mission as though it were delivering invitations to a diplomatic reception. U.S. representatives at the United Nations were sent in search of Pakistani Ambassador Raza and Indian Foreign Minister Swaran Singh. Neither could be found. The message was finally sent to Ambassador Keating in New Delhi, where it was received at 12:56 P.M. It took another hour and a half to decode the message, locate Indian officials and deliver it to them. Still more minutes were lost while the message was retransmitted to the commander of the Indian forces in Bengal, General Jagit Singh Aurora.

From the time Niazi appeared at the consulate to the moment the guns fell silent, twenty-one hours passed, and more blood stained Bengal's soil. The State Department maintains the delays were all unavoidable, and that there was no intention to prolong the war or subvert Niazi's decision.

Meanwhile the White House had a twenty-one hour headstart in its efforts to disguise the efforts it had been making to assist Pakistan. For China, however, this was not time enough—despite its poised forces—to invade. The Russians therefore had no excuse to open any diversionary action in Sinkiang. And Task Force 74 was still far from the fray when the fighting stopped.

The world was spared, but none of the big powers can take credit. The war was ended not by the menacing moves of the Russians, Americans, and Chinese, but by application, apparently, of an ancient Oriental cure. "There is something fishy about this war," U.N. Assistant Secretary General Paul Marc Henry told us. "In retrospect, it all seems pre-staged, pre-arranged. General Niazi [the Pakistani commander] is the key to it all. My own personal feeling is that they were paid to give up."

The Indians, for their part, wasted no time in stopping the shooting once the surrender was received. With an eye perhaps on the Chinese border, they declared an immediate, unilateral cease-fire without waiting for Pakistan to concur. The reeling Pakistani dictator agreed— grudgingly it seemed, hours later—to end the fighting on both fronts.

The actions of the United States were reprehensible throughout the death agony of East Pakistan and the birth pangs of Bangladesh. The evidence that both the Soviet Union and Communist China were equally callous in their disregard for human life and their devotion to big-power politics is hardly mitigating. America has a 200-year tradition of morality and honor. The catalog of deception and duplicity at the highest levels, which is recorded here, can only bring shame to America's government and its people.

The United States blundered its way into a situation that could have developed into a war of incredible magnitude. The President recklessly played the Metternich game of balancing world power. While doing so, he demonstrated that the power of great nations is never so apparent as when it is misused.

EPILOGUE

Epilogue

Our government was not working. The FBI was chasing the wrong people. The Justice Department, instead of prosecuting white-collar crooks, was helping them. Men who answered to neither Congress nor the electorate had seized the power of life and death over all of us. Knowledge affecting our destiny was kept secret under the guise of national security. Presidents and their agents, fearing the truth, deliberately lied to us. I hundreds of ways, government was enslaving a supposedly free people.

American government must be reformed and redefined—not by revolution, but by restoration. The Founding Fathers believed that the people of this country had both the strength of purpose and the nobility of spirit to work with their elected leaders and make government both responsive and responsible. They envisioned a nation where the President would execute the will of Congress and at the polls every two years the people would indicate their approval or disapproval of the decisions made and actions taken in their name.

Very consciously, Congress has let the real power slip from its hands. Old, tired, and often corrupt men, from areas so geographically remote or politically regimented that they need not hear or reflect the desires of the people, hold their seats for a lifetime and rise to positions of great authority through the patently undemocratic process known as the seniority system. The beneficiaries of this patriarchal dictatorship prosper as they grow older, using their committee chairmanships to carefully protect their special interests. The new and vibrant voices, elected by citizens eager for change, are relegated to the bottom of the congressional heap and are politically impotent. Decades can pass before they gain sufficient longevity to make an impact on national policy.

By abdicating its role as the most direct link between the citizens and government, Congress has made it easy for ambitious Presidents to enlarge their own roles and become makers, rather than the executors, of the nation's will. The opportunities are abundant to abuse power so closely held. As we have detailed, the opportunities are exercised. The ability and the obligation to correct the abuses rest with Congress, which must reform itself before it can clean up the executive branch. The areas for congressional action are clear.

If government is to regain the trust of the nation, the administration of justice must be even-handed and freed from the pressures of political favoritism. The recent custom of appointing election campaign managers as attorneys general must cease. It is transparent that the men who raise the money to elect a President cannot be expected to deal honestly with major contributors. The Justice Department, if its name is to have meaning, should be led by the nation's best lawyers, not its political hacks. Its proceedings should be open, its prosecutions just.

The FBI, Justice's investigative arm, must be allowed to free itself from the web of politics now entangling it and regain its reputation as an unbiased, straightforward servant of the people. The responsibilities for internal security were thrust upon the bureau as America hurriedly geared itself for World War II. The emergency is long past; it is time for a new approach. No agency is as well-equipped to fight crime as the FBI. That should be its job. The responsibility for evaluating political thought and activity should be turned over to a new branch of government closely supervised by Congress. America cannot afford a political police force.

Perhaps most important of all, Congress must rip aside the veil of censorship that prevents the American people from knowing what their government is doing.

The United States now possesses more than twenty million documents that are hidden from public scrutiny by the censor's stamp. Men familiar with this hoard insist that only ten to thirty percent of the papers have any genuine bearing on national security. The rest are classified to keep Americans from learning of malfeasance, or bungling, or simply because the censor lacked the wit to make the papers public.

We are willing to agree, albeit grudgingly, that the President cannot make many of the cold, hard decisions he faces in the bright light of publicity. There are maneuvers of extreme delicacy that must be executed, and unpublicized deals that must be negotiated, if he is to meet his responsibilities. Let him keep these documents secret, for up to two years if necessary. Documents dealing with national security, of course, should remain secret as long as they remain sensitive. But the President and his underlings cannot be allowed to decide arbitrarily what will remain secret.

We call for the establishment of a national commission on security, comprised of intelligent, trustworthy individuals from outside the government, who would periodically review those documents the government feels must remain classified. The burden of establishing the need for secrecy would be on the government, rather than the present rule, which compels scholars and researchers to show why certain papers—some dealing with World War II—should be made public.

No other nation has been as successful as the United States in maintaining a free society. Yet the invasion of this freedom—secrecy, the politicization of justice, the hoarding of authority, official deception—are abuses of power that threaten our freedom.

Power corrupts not only those who abuse it, but whole nations as well, when they tolerate this abuse.

About the Authors

Born in Long Beach, California, but brought up in Salt Lake City, Utah, JACK ANDERSON served two years as a Mormon missionary and briefly as a cadet officer in the Merchant Marine during World War II and then as a civilian war correspondent. When he was drafted he was with a band of Chinese guerrillas behind Japanese lines—and was inducted in China and assigned to the Shanghai edition of *Stars and Stripes*. He joined Drew Pearson's staff in 1947 and took over the Washington Merry-Go-Round when Pearson died in 1969. He is also Washington editor of *Parade* magazine and does syndicated TV commentary. He lives in Maryland with his wife and nine children.

GEORGE CLIFFORD, an associate of Jack Anderson, has reported on the revolutions in Hungary, Cuba and Lebanon, and done investigative reporting for the Washington *Daily News*. In 1971 Mr. Clifford was an assistant national editor for the Washington *Star*.

He is married and has three sons.

INVESTIGATING THE FBI

edited by
Pat Watters
and
Stephen Gillers

The *only* current comprehensive examination of the FBI in paperback. The articles stem from the historic Conference on the FBI sponsored by the Committee for Public Justice and Princeton University's Woodrow Wilson School of Public Affairs.

Scholars, lawyers, journalists, former Justice Department officials, former FBI agents, and other participants examined a wide range of issues, such as the Bureau's history, responsibilities and public image; its relations with other police forces; its performance in the areas of civil rights and organized crime; the collection and dissemination of personal and political information; and the use of electronic surveillance and informers. Also included in the conference papers is a letter from Hoover, explaining why he refused to send an official representative to the conference and defending the Bureau's record at length.

$1.95

To order by mail, send $1.95 per book plus 25¢ per order for handling to Ballantine Cash Sales, P.O. Box 505, Westminster, Maryland 21157. Please allow three weeks for delivery.

FICTION
from

BALLANTINE BOOKS

THE BEST AMERICAN SHORT STORIES OF 1973
Edited by Martha Foley $1.65

A GAME FOR CHILDREN,
William Bloom $1.75

THE RESURRECTION,
John Gardner $1.50

LUANA,
Alan Dean Foster $1.25

DR. SYN RETURNS,
Russell Thorndike $ .95

SADHU ON THE MOUNTAIN PEAK,
Duncan MacNeil $1.25

LONG SUMMER DAY,
R. F. Delderfield $1.50

POST OF HONOR,
R. F. Delderfield $1.50

Available at your local bookstore, or

To order by mail, send price of book(s)
plus 25¢ per order for handling to Ballantine Cash Sales, P.O. Box 505, Westminster, Maryland 21157. Please allow three
weeks for delivery.

BESTSELLERS
from

BALLANTINE BOOKS

◆

RABBIT BOSS, Thomas Sanchez	$1.95
THE SENSUOUS COUPLE, Robert Chartham	$1.25
WHAT TURNS WOMEN ON, Robert Chartham	$1.50
THE SECRET TEAM: THE CIA AND ITS ALLIES, L. Fletcher Prouty	$1.95
THE ANDERSON PAPERS, Jack Anderson	$1.75
SWEET STREET, Jack Olsen	$1.50
THE TEACHINGS OF DON JUAN, Carlos Castenada	$1.25
ENEMY AT THE GATES, William Craig	$1.95
SUPER MARRIAGE-SUPER SEX, H. Freedman	$1.50
REVOLUTIONARY SUICIDE, Huey Newton	$1.95
LONG SUMMER DAY, R. F. Delderfield	$1.50
BACK TO THE TOP OF THE WORLD, Hans Ruesch	$1.50
THE IPCRESS FILE, Len Deighton	$1.25
CITY POLICE, Jonathan Rubinstein	$1.95
POST OF HONOR, R. F. Delderfield	$1.50
THE UFO EXPERIENCE, J. Allen Hynek	$1.50
MAUDE, Harold Flender	$1.25

At your local bookstore, or

To order by mail, send price of book(s) plus 25¢ per order for handling to Ballantine Cash Sales, P.O. Box 505, Westminster, Maryland 21157. Please allow three weeks for delivery.

WATERGATE

by Lewis Chester,
Cal McCrystal,
Stephen Aris,
and William Shawcross

A clear and readable account of The Full Inside Story by the London Sunday Times Team.

The roots of what we call "Watergate" lie in Vietnam, say the authors of this clear overview of the scandal.

Secrecy, "national security," came to justify almost anything—wiretaps, bugging, and the construction of an extralegal "domestic intelligence" apparatus, the existence of which guaranteed its use. Its operations slid ever deeper into illegality, finally demanding the composition of lists of "enemies" against whom it could operate.

Here, then, is the full story to date. Of bizarre events and disputed facts. Of the progressive isolation of the Nixon administration. Of participants such as Gordon Liddy, pistol-packing romantic, and Howard Hunt, the spy who came in from the cold and didn't like it.

$1.50

also available in hardcover at $6.95